Satellite Realms

# Satellite Realms

## Transnational Television, Globalization and the Middle East

Naomi Sakr

I.B.Tauris Publishers

LONDON ● NEW YORK

Published in 2001 by I.B.Tauris & Co. Ltd
6 Salem Road, London W2 4BU
175 Fifth Avenue, New York, NY 10010
www.ibtauris.com

In the United States of America and Canada distributed by
St Martin's Press, 175 Fifth Avenue, New York, NY 10010

ISBN: Hardback 1-86064-688-3
Paperback 1-86064-689-1

A full CIP record for this book is available from the British Library
A full CIP record for this book is available from the Library of Congress

Library of Congress catalog card: available

Typeset in Goudy Old Style by A. & D. Worthington, Newmarket
Printed and bound in Great Britain by MPG Books Ltd, Bodmin

# Contents

# Tables

# Acknowledgements

This book represents a milestone on a personal research journey that began long before the book was conceived. The longer the journey, in both distance and time, the more impossible it becomes to thank everyone whose insightful comment, however brief, worked like a signpost along the way. One special example is a chance piece of advice from Annabelle Sreberny in 1993, which redirected me from a well-trodden path to one far less worn. I thank her for that, and for reading and reacting to parts of the research that resulted.

The book grew out of a study I wrote on the Palestinian media at the time of the Israeli withdrawal from Gaza and Jericho in 1994. That was a busy time for Middle East satellite broadcasting, with the launching of channels in full swing and the banning of satellite dishes in Saudi Arabia, Tunisia and Iran. While talking to Palestinians, I was struck by the hopes of independent programme-makers that the new satellite channels would soon start to commission innovative and challenging documentaries, dramas and feature films, freed from the narrow political controls restricting terrestrial television. But it was also apparent that the move from national to transnational broadcasting risked marginalizing still further the voices of local communities which, in the Palestinian case in particular, had been denied access to the media for so long. Two alternative approaches suggested themselves for exploring cost-benefit tensions like these. Either I could trace the emergence and trajectory of one of the new satellite television companies. Or I could examine the permeability of a single state. In choosing the latter option for my doctoral thesis, and familiarizing myself more closely with Egyptian broadcasting prowess, I also set out to comprehend the dynamics at work in the regional and international context. Those are the dynamics discussed in this book.

It will be obvious from this background that I could have made little headway without the help of dozens of interviewees and providers of information, in Amman, Beirut, Cairo, Dubai, Jerusalem, London, Paris, Tunis and Washington. Many are gratefully named in person in the notes accompanying each chapter. Some, who spoke off the record, have not been named. They all have my very sincere thanks. So do others whose friendly personal contributions are not formally acknowledged elsewhere in these pages. Among them are Hussein Amin, Muhammad Ayish, Sonia Dabous, Nabil Dajani, Jihad Fakhreddine, Carol Forrester, Abdullah Hasanat, Mustafa Karkouti, Hisham Kassem, Mona Khalaf, Daoud Kuttab, Trevor Mostyn, Steve Negus, Sundus al-Qaissi and Mohammed El-Sayed Said. I wish also to record my debt to people in the NGO sector who have been instrumental in widening my contacts, knowledge and understanding. Special mention goes to Saïd Essoulami, Peter Frankental, Bahey El Din Hassan, Brenda de Jager, Tudor Lomas, Toby Mendel and Mahmoud Mohamedou.

On the academic front I am pleased to have an opportunity to express my thanks to Phillip Drummond, Bob Ferguson, Peter Goodwin, Dov Shinar, Colin Sparks and Bruce Stanley. My deepest and everlasting gratitude goes to my former supervisor and now friend and mentor, Jill Hills. Without the benefit of her scholarship, skill and encouragement the business of writing this book would have been so different it might never have been finished.

Finally, my mainstay in this project, as always, was my husband Ahmad, to whom this book is dedicated.

# Note on Sources, Citations and Transliteration

Two methods have been adopted for citing sources, depending on their type. Primary sources, such as interviews, internal reports, newspaper or magazine articles, press releases, speeches and talks, are treated as archival material and cited in full in the endnotes but not the bibliography. Books, monographs, conference papers, journal articles, academic theses and published reports are cited in both the footnotes and the bibliography.

Arabic names and sources are transliterated following an informal method that omits diacritical marks, representing only the hamza by an apostrophe. Where the letter 'jeem' appears in Egyptian names it is represented with a hard 'g', as in Gamal, in accordance with Egyptian pronunciation.

# Glossary

| | |
|---|---|
| AI | Amnesty International |
| ANN | Arab News Network |
| Arabsat | Arab Satellite Communications Organization |
| ART | Arab Radio and Television |
| ASBU | Arab States Broadcasting Union |
| AUC | American University in Cairo |
| AUSACE | Arab–US Association of Communication Educators |
| bandwidth | the capacity of a communications path, affecting the quantity of information transmitted and speed of transmission |
| BSS | Broadcast Satellite Services |
| CAPMAS | Central Agency for Public Mobilization and Statistics |
| CBS | Columbia Broadcasting System |
| CFI | Canal France International |
| CNE | Cable Network Egypt |
| CNN | Cable News Network |
| COPUOS | Committee on the Peaceful Uses of Outer Space |
| CSA | Conseil supérieur de l'audiovisuel |
| DBS | Direct broadcast satellite |
| digital compression | transmission of signals in binary code, allowing greater concentration of channels |
| downlink | transmission of signals from a satellite to earth |
| EDTV | Emirates Dubai Television |
| ENTV | Entreprise National de Télévision |
| EOHR | Egyptian Organization for Human Rights |
| ERTU | Egyptian Radio and Television Union |
| ESC | Egyptian Space Channel |
| EU | European Union |

| FNF | Friedrich Naumann Foundation |
| FSS | Fixed Satellite Services |
| GATS | General Agreement on Trade in Services |
| GATT | General Agreement on Tariffs and Trade |
| GCC | Gulf Co-operation Council |
| HRC | Human Rights Committee |
| ICCPR | International Covenant on Civil and Political Rights |
| IMF | International Monetary Fund |
| *intifada* | uprising |
| ITC | Independent Television Commission |
| ITN | Independent Television News |
| ITU | International Telecommunication Union |
| LBC | Lebanese Broadcasting Corporation |
| LCHR | Lawyers' Committee for Human Rights |
| MAI | Multilateral Agreement on Investment |
| MBC | Middle East Broadcasting Centre |
| MMDS | Multichannel multipoint distribution system |
| MPAA | Motion Picture Association of America |
| MTV | Music Television |
| NAFTA | North American Free Trade Agreement |
| NBC | National Broadcasting Company |
| NBN | National Broadcasting Network |
| NDP | National Democratic Party |
| NGO | non-governmental organization |
| PA | Palestinian Authority |
| PARC | Pan-Arab Research Centre |
| PBC | Palestinian Broadcasting Corporation |
| PAS | PanAmSat |
| PTT | Posts, Telephones and Telegraphs |
| RMC-MO | Radio Monte Carlo-Moyen Orient |
| SIS | State Information Service |
| transponder | pick-up point of a satellite that receives and transmits a signal |
| TRIPS | Trade-Related aspects of Intellectual Property Rights |
| UAE | United Arab Emirates |
| UNDP | United Nations Development Programme |
| UNESCO | United Nations Educational, Scientific and Cultural Organization |

| UNICEF | United Nations Children's Fund |
| UNISPACE | United Nations Conference on the Peaceful Uses of Outer Space |
| uplink | transmission of signals from earth to a satellite |
| USAID | United States Agency for International Development |
| WARC | World Administrative Radiocommunication Conference |
| WRC | World Radiocommunication Conference |
| WTO | World Trade Organization |

# CHAPTER ONE

# The Potential of Satellite Television in the Middle East

Satellite television, by transcending territorial and jurisdictional boundaries, raises a host of questions in which political, economic, social and cultural issues are linked and matters of domestic and foreign policy are intertwined. International shortwave radio demonstrated long ago the potential for cross-border broadcasting to serve imperialistic or propagandistic ends. It also underlined the potential for conflict between the principle of national sovereignty on the one hand and that of freedom of expression across frontiers on the other. The transmission of television programmes by satellite direct to homes in other countries intensified and increased such contradictions. Publicly financed and nationally regulated terrestrial broadcasters began to face competition from private satellite companies operating offshore. As more channels became available, audiences fragmented, undermining established assumptions about the organization and financing of content. In parts of the world where state censorship prevailed, such threats to the status quo seemed to offer advantages to viewers. In the Middle East and North Africa, satellite broadcasting held out the promise of liberation from government-controlled media monopolies and tight censorship of terrestrial television.

The emergence of transnational television to, from and within the Middle East was a phenomenon of the turbulent 1990s, a decade that started traumatically with the Iraqi invasion of Kuwait and the deeply divisive 1991 Gulf war. Political divisions within and among countries were then exacerbated by economic upheaval, as governments confronted Western prescriptions for economic reform and liberalization, involving the sale of state assets and opening of markets to private entrepreneurship, both domestic and foreign. Multiparty legislative elections became a more regular and prominent - if not altogether convincing – feature of the political landscape, even in countries still retaining elements of martial law. Meanwhile funding and encouragement from various sources contributed to a proliferation of civil society groups struggling to secure long-denied civil and political rights. New diasporic links were forged with emigrant Middle Eastern communities in Europe and the USA. Indeed, the rise of satellite television in the region not only coincided with a profusion of structural adjustments and superficial changes but seems to have been implicated in them. This book sets out to formulate and answer some of the questions raised by the proliferation of satellite channels within this environment of real and cosmetic change.

While the book's immediate focus is the Middle East, transnational television, by definition, requires that developments related to the region should be seen in a wider context. To that end, the exploration is conducted on two levels. One level of analysis considers why and how certain interest groups invested in satellite channels during the 1990s and traces the cross-border interconnections of people, money and programming created or consolidated in the process. It delves into relationships among channel owners and executives, content providers, regulators, advertisers, audiences and others, in an effort to discover the obstacles yet to be overcome if the developmental potential of cross-border broadcasting in the Middle East is to be fulfilled. Later chapters investigate the effectiveness of relevant regional and international regulatory frameworks, track down the input of national and transnational non-governmental groups and review the role that demographic, technological and other changes could play in the future orientation of satellite broadcasting for the region.

The second, more general, level of analysis attempts to assess how far notions and theories of globalization can illuminate or explain the specific forces and processes described. Here the aim is to test the serviceability of concepts such as deterritorialization, interdependence and global civil society by taking them as starting points from which to evaluate whether globalization, as a catch-all term, can appropriately be applied to the transactions and relationships that lie behind satellite broadcasting in the Middle East and North Africa, or whether it misrepresents them. The significance of this exercise is determined by the high expectations that the launch of so many satellite channels generated among people inside and outside the region. The book's first task, therefore, is to consider those expectations, the reasoning behind them and the environment in which they arose.

### 'Offshore democracy'

It is not often that programme-makers from different Arab satellite television channels meet together in private to discuss the programmes they have made. So when such a meeting took place in the year 2000, at Columbia University in New York, it reminded participants just how profoundly the content of programmes watched across the region had changed since the first Arab satellite channel arrived on the scene in 1990. Interviewers putting tough questions to heads of state; live phone-ins and studio audience participation; programmes dealing with subjects like divorce and homosexuality; adversarial talkshows featuring Islamist guests who would be jailed if they set foot in their own countries: these examples of gritty current affairs programming marked a major advance on what passed for current affairs on Arab television stations ten years earlier.

Participants in the New York gathering, like many other observers, were led to ponder whether satellite television could bring democracy to the Arab world.[1] The organizers, by inviting Israeli broadcasters along too, also demonstrated their interest in whether Arab satellite channels could open up new avenues of Arab–Israeli understanding.[2] It was clear to most people, after a decade of rapidly expanding satellite broadcasting activity to and from the Middle East, that styles and structures of public communication in the region were undergoing significant change. These shifts might be said to amount to what John Keane has called the 'restructuring of communicative space'.[3] But while much attention focused on their political implications, less was said about the political, economic and social causes of these shifts. This is despite the fact that causes and outcomes need to be seen together for either to be fully understood. Harold Innis, half a century ago, explored the relationship between forms of communication and forms of political organization across space and time. That relationship is as central to the case of satellite television and globalization as it was to the ancient civilizations Innis studied.[4] In any situation where a restructuring of communicative space appears to be under way, it is necessary first to investigate and uncover the dynamics at work behind the restructuring before assessing how far optimism about eventual outcomes is justified.

Rising expectations about the implications of satellite channels may have been partly due to frustration over a dearth of other evidence of political liberalization in the Middle East. While state controls over broadcasting were being removed in other parts of the world during the

1990s, state broadcasting monopolies and strict government censorship remained the norm in most Arab states and Iran. In the face of these controls on both ownership and content, transnational broadcasting offered a means not only of bypassing national restrictions but of influencing the output of state monopoly broadcasters, by forcing them to face unwonted competition. As their countries' chief censors, Middle Eastern information ministers had to face the possibility that foreign broadcasters would regale local viewers with news of, and commentaries on, local affairs that information ministries were responsible for hushing up. During his tenure as Jordan's information minister, Nasser Judeh captured the potential of satellite transmission in the phrase 'offshore democracy'.[5] While state officials fumed, intellectuals basked in the limelight state television had denied them. The satellite channels appeared to provide people outside government with a unique platform from which to communicate with policy-makers and the wider public. For the first time, commentators felt they could have their say 'without governments breathing over their shoulders'.[6]

Underlying this censorship tussle was the widespread conviction that television has the power to affect political events as well as broadcast them. Such touching faith in the propaganda potential of transnational media is by no means exclusive to the Middle East. The British and US governments were sufficiently convinced of the role played by shortwave radio during the Second World War that they continued to finance external broadcasts after it was over. Indeed the medium had to be financed by government because even US advertisers failed to provide the backing needed for commercial shortwave radio operations attempted by NBC and CBS.[7] The extent to which Western radio broadcasts were jammed by countries at which they were directed provided ample testimony to their assumed effectiveness. External broadcasting in the language of listeners rather than senders was considered so worthwhile that, by the end of the war in 1945, 55 countries had formal foreign-language shortwave broadcasting services.[8]

It has become part of media folklore to suggest that television images brought down the Berlin Wall. Detailed evidence does suggest that some cross-border television broadcasts made a critical contribution to the sequence of events in the collapse of regimes in eastern and central Europe in 1989–90. Television pictures of East German police brutality were received by East Germans via West German television, while scenes of the Timisoara uprising in Romania were seen by Romanians thanks to Hungarian television. The latter was accessible outside Hungary to some

3 million Hungarians over the border in Romania, who translated for Romanian speakers.[9] Since then, the use of mobile satellite equipment to send instant pictures of war, famine and genocide all around the world has evoked a public response in many receiving countries, which has sometimes fed into policy-making processes.[10] David Harvey's late-1980s suggestion that 'power in the realms of representation may end up being as important as power over the materiality of spatial organization itself'[11] appeared quite uncontentious in the context of NATO's calculated bombing of the Serbian government-controlled television station RTS in 1999. It would seem that the wider the realm, as determined by the size of satellite footprints, the higher the stakes in the struggle for power over the technologies of representation.

If Arab regimes were particularly exercised by the emergence of certain Arabic-language satellite channels in the mid-1990s, it was not only because of their geographical reach but their ability to reach the literate and illiterate alike. At a time when some governments were still only reluctantly allowing the publication of non-government newspapers, they refused outright to relinquish control over television broadcasting. Implicit in their refusal was the knowledge that images on television screens reach a much larger public than the written word. Illiteracy is rife in many Middle East and North African countries, as indicated by the literacy rates recorded in Table 1. Aggregate illiteracy across the Arab countries was 38.7 per cent in 2000, according to figures revealed at a regional education conference in Cairo in March that year.[12] Even in Saudi Arabia, where ample oil revenue funded the expansion of education from the mid-1970s, official Saudi data released in 2000 put the rate of illiteracy among Saudi nationals at 20.4 per cent.[13] In less well-off countries, such as Morocco and Yemen, the rate was over 50 per cent. Outside the Arab world, Iran had a rate of over 25 per cent. Across the region, illiteracy is particularly prevalent among women, who, throughout most of the region, have the closest access to television as they work principally in their homes.

High rates of illiteracy among people thirsty for uncensored information account for much of the perceived potency of satellite television in the Middle East. A third factor is a regional predisposition towards home-based entertainment, especially in rural areas and searing heat. In these circumstances popular television programmes, whether transmitted terrestrially or by satellite, can count on millions of viewers. Lila Abu Lughod, describing the huge nightly audiences for serialized television dramas in Egypt, has said these dramas seem to 'set the very rhythms of national life'.[14] In Gulf countries too, although the presence of large expatriate populations makes viewing patterns more fragmented, long hours are spent in front of the television. Surveys conducted in Saudi Arabia and the UAE have shown a high proportion of respondents watching television for more than three hours a day, with those on lower incomes spending most time in front of the screen.[15]

## Table 1: Literacy in the Middle East and North Africa

(*Percentage literacy rate in 1998 among those aged 15 and over; youth rate is for those aged 15 to 24 years*)

|              | Total | Female | Male | Youth |
|--------------|-------|--------|------|-------|
| Algeria      | 65.5  | 54.3   | 76.5 | 87.3  |
| Bahrain      | 86.5  | 81.2   | 90.2 | 98.0  |
| Egypt        | 53.7  | 41.8   | 65.5 | 68.3  |
| Iran         | 74.6  | 67.4   | 81.7 | 93.2  |
| Iraq         | 53.7  | 43.2   | 63.9 | 70.7  |
| Israel       | 95.7  | 93.7   | 97.7 | 99.6  |
| Jordan       | 88.6  | 82.6   | 94.2 | 99.3  |
| Kuwait       | 80.9  | 78.5   | 83.2 | 91.6  |
| Lebanon      | 85.1  | 79.1   | 91.5 | 94.6  |
| Libya        | 78.1  | 65.4   | 89.6 | 95.8  |
| Morocco      | 47.1  | 34.0   | 60.3 | 65.5  |
| Oman         | 68.8  | 57.5   | 78.0 | 96.6  |
| Qatar        | 80.4  | 81.7   | 79.8 | 94.1  |
| Saudi Arabia | 75.2  | 64.4   | 82.8 | 92.0  |
| Sudan        | 55.7  | 43.4   | 68.0 | 75.1  |
| Syria        | 72.7  | 58.1   | 87.2 | 85.9  |
| Tunisia      | 68.7  | 57.9   | 79.4 | 92.0  |
| UAE          | 74.6  | 77.1   | 73.5 | 89.2  |
| Yemen        | 44.1  | 22.7   | 65.7 | 62.6  |

Source: UNDP, *Human Development Report 2000*

A fourth factor contributing to the feeling that Middle East satellite television is both 'offshore' and potentially 'democratic' is its ability to reunite communities scattered by war, exile and labour migration. Arab media corporations based in Europe could tap into the pool of talent among generations of Middle Eastern expatriates who have grown accustomed to asserting their right to freedom of expression. The region's two dispersed and stateless peoples, the Palestinians and Kurds, have long struggled to communicate across geographical divides. The

1975–90 civil war in Lebanon, persistent civil war in Sudan, the 1979 Iranian revolution, the Iraq–Iran war of 1980–88, the Gulf war of 1991 and sanctions on Iraq, the civil strife which erupted in Algeria in 1992, the Yemeni civil war of 1994: all these have contributed to exodus after exodus of people escaping violence and hardship in their home countries. Over the same period the oil price explosions of the mid- and late 1970s fuelled massive labour migration to the rich Gulf Arab oil-exporting states.

The widespread displacement of people and re-creation of communities with shared ethnicity or language in other settings has blurred social and national identities. It has opened up possibilities for 'multiple affiliations and associations' outside and beyond the nation state, giving rise to something Robin Cohen has described as 'a diasporic allegiance' – a proliferation of 'transnational identities that cannot easily be contained in the nation-state system'.[16] Such multiple identities are fostered by and reflected in a multiplicity of media from local, national, regional and intercontinental sources, including satellite television. Benedict Anderson argued that print capitalism created the possibility of an 'imagined community', in which individuals came to feel intimately connected to millions of people they had never met.[17] By the same token it is fair to suggest that migrant communities may be encouraged by the availability of different satellite channels to feel they belong to two or more imagined communities at the same time. John Sinclair and his co-authors, tracing 'new patterns' in global media, noted the emergence of 'diasporic communities' and the 'restratification of audiences into imagined communities beyond national boundaries'.[18] Indeed, these are the very ethnoscapes and mediascapes which Arjun Appadurai so famously envisaged.[19]

In the Middle East, the most pronounced cases of outward and inward migration are those of Egypt and Saudi Arabia respectively, while the best-trodden route for migrants leaving the region is the one to Europe. Results of Egypt's 1996 census, released in mid-1997, showed that 2.18 million Egyptians lived abroad temporarily and that another 720,000 had set up permanent homes abroad. The approximate total of 2.9 million migrants represented 4.7 per cent of the total number of Egyptians, both at home and abroad, recorded by the census.[20] Of the 2.9 million, around 1.2 million were to be found in Saudi Arabia, which alone, some sources estimate, may host as many as 3.5 million non-Saudi Arabs.[21] As for migration out of the region, the number of migrants from Morocco, Tunisia and Algeria living legally and illegally in Europe reached an estimated 2.6 million in 1993, of whom more than 1 million were Moroccan and 1.4 million were legally resident in France.[22] An estimated 2 million Kurds live in Germany, France, the Netherlands, Switzerland and Scandinavia.[23] The number of Iranians living outside Iran has been put at over 2 million.[24]

**Table 2: Expatriate Arabs in Saudi Arabia**

(*Based on 1992 census*)

| Country of origin | Number[1] |
|---|---|
| Egypt | 1,195.189 |
| Yemen | 424,398 |
| Sudan | 242,508 |
| Syria | 168,354 |
| Jordan | 155,410 |
| Kuwait | 122,519 |
| Palestine | 110,611 |
| Lebanon | 52,560 |
| Morocco | 21,243 |
| Tunisia | 13,511 |

[1] Total adds to less than the 3.5 million quoted elsewhere.

Source: *Asharq al-Awsat*, 12 December 1995, reprinted in Anders Jerichow, *The Saudi File: People, Power, Politics* (Richmond, 1998), p 6

Satellite television broadcasts in Middle Eastern languages have the capacity to respond to these population movements, linking communities in different parts of the globe on the basis not of their nationality or location but of their linguistic and cultural affinities. Meanwhile governments in the countries of origin have strong economic reasons for wanting to keep channels of communication open with expatriate groups, whose collective remittances and investments can give the national balance of payments a healthy boost. The coming together of government objectives, technological developments, intra-regional relations, and popular responses constitutes the next phenomenon to be explored.

## Catalysts and competition

When considering the 'where, who, how and why?' of decisions that led to the creation of Middle Eastern satellite channels, there are strong analytical advantages in recognizing that the four interrogatives are interlinked. This approach, in keeping with the 'new' or 'critical' school of international political economy, rejects the idea that states and markets are separate phenomena, acknowledging instead that markets are constructed and maintained by the exercise of power.[25] It sees structure and agency as fused, in the same way that the sociologist Anthony Giddens fused them in his theory of structuration, thereby overcoming the analytical pitfall of privileging agency over structure or vice versa. Structuration recognizes that social structures are constituted by human agency and yet are simultaneously the medium by which human actions are constituted. Structures can be tangible, like the girders of a building, or intangible, like systems of rules and resources. Either way they are the result of human agency. Yet, at the same time, human actors are constrained by structures; they are not self-contained entities able to pursue any course of action they choose.[26]

The aim of tracking structures and actors together, to grasp the interaction between them, problematizes the choice of a starting point for the story of satellite television in the Middle East. The most accurate point in time is probably the mid-1970s, in the aftermath of the first oil price explosion. The most accurate place is arguably Saudi Arabia, which was helped by the sudden influx of oil revenue to use television to assert a regional leadership role. The Saudi government had introduced television in the 1960s, countering deep-seated religious opposition to the medium with various political imperatives, including the need to divert Saudi listeners away from the Nasserist propaganda broadcast by Egyptian radio stations from Cairo.[27] But entertainment was not to take precedence over religious programming, especially given Saudi responsibility for guardianship of Mecca and Medina, the holy places visited by Muslims on pilgrimage from all over the world. Saudi television began live coverage of Ramadan prayers and pilgrimage rituals in 1975 and, in 1980, after the siege of the Grand Mosque of Mecca by religious extremists and the revolution that created the Islamic Republic of Iran, the proportion of religious programming in Saudi TV was dramatically increased.

While this was happening, the Arab League plan to create the Arab Satellite Communications Organization (Arabsat) was conceived, with Saudi Arabia playing a prominent part. The first Arabsat agreement was signed in 1976 and the project evolved with Saudi Arabia alone holding 29.9 per cent of the shares. At that stage the next biggest shareholder was Kuwait, with 11.9 per cent, followed by Libya with 9.2, Iraq with 8.3, Qatar with 8.0 and Egypt with just 5.2 per cent.[28] In 1979, however,

Egypt was suspended from Arabsat, and from the Arab League in general, because of its peace treaty with Israel. Thus Arabsat temporarily lost the country which had most to offer in terms of the volume of its television output and level of expertise. Egypt was finally readmitted to the Arab League at the end of the 1980s. In the meantime, however, the first Arabsat satellite was launched. Saudi Arabia used it to transmit live coverage of the pilgrimage far and wide. But for the first five years, after its launch in 1985, the facility was heavily underused, whether for telecommunications, regional programme exchange or the domestic networks of member countries.

This situation changed dramatically at the end of 1990, after Iraq invaded Kuwait. Although the invasion split the Arab world into two camps and led, among other things, to a freeze on plans for a second generation of Arabsat craft, the advantages offered by the first generation suddenly became overwhelmingly clear. They were made obvious by the arrival in Baghdad of teams from Ted Turner's 24-hour-a-day television news service, Cable News Network (CNN). Before the Iraqi invasion a great deal of scepticism still surrounded the idea of 24-hour news. CNN's live international broadcasts from Baghdad dispelled much of that scepticism and helped to build CNN into one of the world's most recognizable brands.[29] At the same time they demonstrated the stark contrast between instant, live television with minimum commentary and the stale, turgid and censored coverage available on local Arab stations. The news sense of the latter was exemplified by the fact that Saudi state broadcasters not only refrained from reporting on the Iraqi invasion when it happened but avoided mentioning it for the next three days. Members of the Saudi elite who had satellite dishes learned of the invasion from CNN or US Armed Forces Television beamed to US troops already stationed in the Gulf.[30] The power of satellite television had been proved.

In the wake of the invasion, the Egyptian government sided with Syria, Saudi Arabia and the other Gulf emirates and shaikhdoms that joined the US-led coalition created to expel Iraqi forces from Kuwait. Egyptian troops were duly dispatched to the Gulf, where they came within earshot of Iraqi propaganda designed to justify the occupation and fuel doubts among Arab ranks about US double standards in coming to the aid of rich and unpopular Kuwaitis while leaving the stateless Palestinians to their fate.[31] The Iraqi authorities had stepped up their external radio services for this purpose, partly by exploiting facilities seized in Kuwait, while also jamming incoming radio signals. In December 1990, in the final build-up to the war that began on 15 January 1991, the state-owned Egyptian Radio and Television Union (ERTU) arranged to lease an Arabsat transponder to broadcast television programmes across the Arab world all day, every day, for the next three years. The previously unused transponder had originally been designated for a pan-Arab community television service.[32] Within days the ERTU was using the facility to send news and entertainment programmes to the Gulf, for the benefit of Egyptian soldiers and local viewers with the necessary receiving equipment. The service became known as the Egyptian Space Channel (ESC).

In this way, the war provided a major catalyst for the spread of satellite broadcasting to the Gulf. On the other side of the Arab world, in Algeria, satellite television had by that time already started to make its mark. A small number of Algerians started to receive satellite television from France in the late 1980s, via a France Télécom satellite.[33] As part of a shake-up in the French media at that time, including some partial privatizations, the French government had taken pains to ensure that French television programmes were easily obtainable in francophone Africa, including the Maghreb countries of Morocco, Algeria and Tunisia.[34] The arrival of French satellite channels coincided with a process of political liberalization that began in Algeria in 1989 and lasted until the army intervened in 1992. That intervention deposed the president and banned the Islamist party, the Front Islamique du Salut, just as it was poised to win a second round of parliamentary elections. During the short-lived period of liberalization, Algerians seized the initiative in gaining access to satellite programmes through improvised neighbourhood cable networks, or *mini-réseaux cablés*, that allowed large-scale sharing of a single satellite dish. After the 1992 coup, the government tried to regulate the spread of satellite access but by then it was too late. As the violent conflict between Islamist extremists and government forces escalated and censorship was tightened, French-speaking Algerians turned en masse to the news and analysis available by satellite. Islamist militants, initially opposed to satellite programmes, became less hostile on discovering that they had some chance of airing their views on foreign stations, as compared to no chance at all on Algeria's single government-owned national television channel, the Entreprise National de Télévision (ENTV).[35]

Following the 1991 Gulf war, transformation of the Middle East media landscape gathered pace, involving physical expansion of satellite capacity serving the area, a rapid increase in the number of channels and

matching growth in the size of the satellite audience. Two satellites
belonging to the European consortium, Eutelsat, were launched in
August 1990 and January 1991, doubling the Eutelsat fleet and serving
the Mediterranean basin as well as Europe. Star TV from Hong Kong
started up on Asiasat in October 1991. Its target audiences included the
large number of expatriates from the Indian subcontinent and South-
East Asia working in Gulf countries, especially the UAE. In time, Iranian
viewers were also to discover Star TV, provoking direct action against
satellite dishes by local vigilante groups. While all this was under way,
September 1991 saw the launch in London of the Middle East Broadcasting Centre (MBC), founded by two rich and well-connected Saudi
entrepreneurs, Shaikh Saleh Kamel and Shaikh Walid bin Ibrahim al-
Ibrahim. MBC started up just in time to cover the October start to the
ground-breaking multilateral Arab–Israeli peace talks in Madrid. Emirates Dubai Television (EDTV) began its satellite channel a year later, in
October 1992. It started out on Arabsat but soon arranged for the signal
to be carried by Eutelsat, Galaxy and Intelsat satellites, so that, by 1995,
its programmes even reached South America. At that point EDTV was
able to boast to potential advertisers that it was the world's second
biggest satellite broadcaster in terms of area covered.

In 1993, Saleh Kamel was encouraged to withdraw from his partnership in MBC. He left to start his own satellite channel, Arab Radio and
Television (ART), which was to be developed into a pay-TV venture.
Orbit, another Arabic pay-TV service, owned by the Al-Mawarid group of
Saudi Arabia, came on the market in May 1994. Meanwhile an increasing number of television channels directly owned by Middle East
governments were starting to follow the Egyptian example, packaging
general terrestrial programmes for satellite delivery to their nationals
abroad. In part, having a satellite channel seemed to be seen as an
obligation on countries with large numbers of migrant workers abroad,
especially since failure to provide national satellite programming might
mean that expatriates from one country would watch the satellite
channel (and government propaganda) of another. Thus the Jordanian
state broadcaster launched the Jordan Satellite Channel in 1993,
Morocco's RTM went onto satellite in 1994, and Syria and Yemen
followed in 1995. Yemen, which did not side with the Western coalition
in the 1991 Gulf war, did not use Arabsat initially; it started test transmissions via Intelsat in December 1995.[36] Even Libya, despite the effects
of UN sanctions, inaugurated a space channel in 1996.[37] By the time the
stalled second generation of Arabsat craft, Arabsat 2A and 2B, was finally

launched in 1996, demand for satellite transponders had changed out of all comparison with the situation five years earlier. Just five years after the Gulf war, Iraq and Lebanon were the only Arab countries to have no state-owned satellite television service.

Lebanon may have had no state-owned satellite service in 1996, but this did not signify that Lebanese broadcasters were absent from the scene. In fact, satellite television in the Middle East entered a new phase in 1996, marked by the arrival of two new players from Lebanon and one from the small Gulf emirate of Qatar. All three broke the mould, but in different ways. Despite traditional Lebanese renown in media affairs, the early 1990s found Lebanese broadcasters recovering from their country's 1975–90 civil war. In October 1994, the Lebanese parliament passed the Audiovisual Media Law, to close most of the myriad stations that had mushroomed during the war and regulate the rest. This law, put into effect in September 1996, officially revoked the state's broadcasting monopoly, making Lebanon the first Arab state to authorize private radio and television stations to operate within its borders. Another law of 1996 specifically catered for satellite channels. Armed with a licence under these laws, the private Lebanese Broadcasting Corporation (LBC, founded as a Christian militia station in the 1980s) launched its own satellite station. So did Future TV, a private station part-owned by the Lebanese prime minister, Rafiq Hariri.

The Lebanese entrance instantly challenged the dominance enjoyed until then by Egyptian and Saudi satellite channels. Flamboyant gameshows, general informality and attractive female presenters were noted as hallmarks of the two Lebanese channels. Their presence on Arabsat C-band made it easy for viewers to switch between MBC, ESC, EDTV and the two new arrivals. The other newcomer of 1996, Al-Jazeera Satellite Channel from Doha in Qatar, did not enjoy a similar advantage, being obliged to start out on Arabsat Ku-band, which was less widely received. It was not until a C-band transponder became available on Arabsat on 1 November 1997 that Al-Jazeera began to be seen by large numbers of people throughout the Arab world.[38] As a channel devoted to news and current affairs, it soon made up for lost time by astonishing viewers with uncensored political coverage quite different from any Arabic-language television programming previously seen. It was encouraged to do so by the new Qatari emir, and was equipped to do so because of the unusual background of its founding staff. These were journalists fresh from the BBC Arabic television news service. The BBC service had been set up in 1994 to supply the Saudi-owned pay-TV operator Orbit, but had its contract cut short by disagreements over editorial content in 1996. With the contract terminated, and many Arab journalists redundant, Al-Jazeera did not have to look far for a ready-made team of professionals representing many different nationalities.

Because of the technical limitation on Al-Jazeera's availability in 1997, the first full year of real open competition among the major Middle East channels was 1998. In 1998, the pioneer channels faced competition from Al-Jazeera at a time when the satellite stations of LBC and Future TV were banned by their own government from broadcasting political news.[39] Meanwhile Al-Jazeera itself was challenged by another all-news upstart, the London-based Arab News Network (ANN). This venture arrived on the scene in May 1997, under the private ownership of a semi-exiled branch of the Asad family of Syria. Behind the scenes, the new rush of competition was served by the rapidly increasing availability of satellite platforms other than the Saudi-dominated Arabsat. As Al-Jazeera's wait for a C-band transponder suggested, capacity on Arabsat's main broadcasting satellite, the 22-transponder Arabsat 2A at 26°E, could no longer meet demand. In contrast, the Eutelsat consortium, jointly owned by 46 European states, increased its ability to serve the whole Mediterranean basin and northern Gulf by steadily building up its fleet of Hot Bird satellites, all in the same geostationary orbital location at 13°E. The fourth and fifth Hot Birds, their capacity boosted by digital technology, went into position in February and October 1998 respectively. This expansion was part of a programme that took Eutelsat capacity from four satellites at the start of 1990, broadcasting a total of 18 channels, to 13 spacecraft carrying nearly 200 transponders by the end of 1998.[40]

Eutelsat capacity was crucial to broadcasters who, for political reasons, could not hope to transmit from Arabsat. Med TV, a UK-based Kurdish television operator, was set up to provide Kurdish programming that was banned in Turkey and most Middle Eastern countries where Kurds also live, namely Syria, Iraq and Iran. It started transmissions in 1995 from Intelsat 705 but decided to take transponder space on Eutelsat in 1997 because viewers in Turkey found it inconvenient to point their dishes at the Intelsat beam.[41] ANN, linked with Rifaat al-Asad, the estranged brother of the then Syrian president, Hafez al-Asad, likewise relied on a Eutelsat platform in its first year. Iran joined the throng of state satellite broadcasters in December 1997, also using Eutelsat. It inaugurated its international satellite service, Jam-e Jam, to coincide with the holding of a summit meeting of the Organization of the Islamic Conference in Tehran. Some observers were surprised to see Jam-e Jam carrying scenes of women, with their faces fully shown, playing music.[42] Such scenes seemed to reflect official acknowledgement that television is made to be watched.

From 1995 there was also the option of choosing PanAmSat 4 (PAS-4), owned by the world's first private global satellite service provider. PanAmSat was founded by Rene Anselmo, a US associate of the head of Mexico's major broadcaster, Televisa.[43] The first PAS satellites, launched between 1988 and 1994, served the Atlantic and Asia Pacific regions and it was not until August 1995 that PAS-4, with a total of 40 transponders, went into position at 68.5°E over the Indian Ocean. After Anselmo died in 1995, the satellite manufacturer Hughes Communications, part of General Motors, became the dominant shareholder in PanAmSat.[44] When Showtime, a joint pay-TV venture between a Kuwaiti company and the multinational media conglomerate Viacom, started up in June 1996, it chose PAS-4.

**Table 3:  Selected satellite channel start-ups, 1990–98**

| Start-up | Name | Country link | Ownership |
|---|---|---|---|
| 1990 | ESC | Egypt | State |
| 1991 | MBC | Saudi Arabia | Private |
| 1992 | EDTV | Dubai, UAE | State |
| 1993 | JSC | Jordan | State |
| 1994 | ART | Saudi Arabia | Private |
| | Orbit | Saudi Arabia | Private |
| | RTM | Morocco | State |
| 1995 | STV | Syria | State |
| 1996 | LBC-Sat | Lebanon | Private |
| | Future International | Lebanon | Private |
| | Al-Jazeera | Qatar | Independent |
| 1997 | ANN | Syria | Private |
| 1998 | Nile Thematic Channels | Egypt | State |

Sources: Press reports; company promotional material

In April 1998, with the launch of Arabsat 3A still nearly a year away, came the successful launch of Egypt's own satellite, Nilesat, at 7°W. This much-fanfared event was yet another milestone on a path that was to continue in 1999 with the arrival of yet more satellite channels, including the privately owned London-based Al-Mustakillah (The Independent) and Abu Dhabi Satellite TV. But, for Egypt, it was also the culmination of plans made during the country's decade-long suspension from the Arab League and Arabsat. Having a footprint very similar to that of Arabsat but equipped to accommodate scores of television channels through digital compression, Nilesat arrived at a time when the long-anticipated political ramifications of satellite broadcasting activity were at last beginning to be felt. Nilesat's management immediately demonstrated their independent leasing policy by renting out a transponder to Iraq, which was still viewed with intense suspicion by Arabsat's main shareholders, Saudi Arabia and Kuwait, eight years after the invasion. This leasing decision was made despite Nilesat rhetoric about co-operation with Arabsat rather than competition. It provided one of the clearest signs up to that point of the intensity of the struggle for supremacy among interest groups involved in satellite broadcasting to, from and within the Middle East.

## Quirks of access

The story so far has tried to strike a balance between broadcasters' initiatives and the structures through which they acted. The preceding section swept through a quarter of a century, sacrificing a mass of detail about actions and their context for the sake of illuminating just how entangled structures and actors are. It touched on structures such as those arising from economic resources (oil earnings), legal controls (including laws affecting ownership possibilities and levels of censorship) and technology (satellite platforms and digital compression). It touched on actors in the shape of satellite operators and broadcasters. Yet it paid only marginal attention to a group of actors whose role increased dramatically as the 1990s progressed: the audience. The corollary of satellite transmission is reception. The mushrooming of stations and the spread of dishes went hand in hand. In the year following the arrival of LBC, Future TV and Al-Jazeera on the satellite scene, satellite access boomed. Eutelsat monitoring of cable and satellite penetration among households in Algeria, Egypt, Israel, Jordan, Lebanon, Morocco, Saudi Arabia, Syria, Tunisia and Turkey showed an increase of 61 per cent in 1997 alone. Further increases of 35 and 38 per cent were recorded in 1998 and 1999. To quote the words of an advertising executive who surveyed Saudi viewing habits in 1997, the arrival of LBC, Future TV and Al-Jazeera encouraged audiences to 'vote with their remotes'.[45] The combination of increased access and more discriminating use of remote controls was a potentially powerful one.

Table 4:  Increase in cable and satellite penetration in ten countries,[1]
          1994–99[2]

|       | Million homes | Percentage increase |
|-------|---------------|---------------------|
| 1994  | 3.6           | n/a                 |
| 1995  | 3.8           | 5.6                 |
| 1996  | 4.1           | 7.9                 |
| 1997  | 6.6           | 61.0                |
| 1998  | 8.5           | 34.8                |
| 1999  | 11.7          | 38.0                |

[1]  Algeria, Egypt, Israel, Jordan, Lebanon, Morocco, Saudi Arabia, Syria, Tunisia and
     Turkey.
[2]  Increases are approximate, being affected by changes in the availability of data
     from year to year.

Source: Eutelsat, *Penetration Results for Hot Bird Satellites*, 1997, 1998 and 1999

This power was by no means equally spread across the region, however. On the contrary, the advent of satellite television revealed striking
differences from country to country in terms of both government and
popular reactions. This was despite consistently high rates of television
ownership throughout the Middle East, with data from a variety of
reliable sources indicating that, in most countries, an average of 90 per
cent or more of urban and rural households owned at least one television set.[46] In spite of this similarity, clear contrasts emerged within and
among subregional groups of states. Examples can be cited from opposite
ends of the Mediterranean and the Gulf.

Differences in satellite reception were obvious in the case of the three
Maghreb states, Morocco, Algeria and Tunisia. The Tunisian government took a much more obstructive stance towards satellite access than
the governments of either Algeria or Morocco, while Algerian and
Moroccan households took different approaches to ownership of satellite
dishes. In 1994, Tunisia attempted to ban the import and installation of
satellite dishes, replacing the outright ban in 1995 with a licensing
regime.[47] This required that dishes be reserved solely for individual use,
be registered with the Ministry of Interior and installed by an approved
technician. An annual tax on dishes was introduced, payable to the local
authority, with fines imposed for non-compliance. Not all applications
for dish installation would be approved, with the result that clandestine
dish ownership became widespread.[48] In consequence, the proportion of
Tunisian households enjoying satellite access may well have been higher
in 1997 than the 3.4 per cent reported by Eutelsat for that year.

The Algerian government tried to clamp down on all forms of media activity under the State of Emergency it declared in 1992. A decree issued in April 1992, dealing specifically with broadcasting frequencies and the distribution of television by cable, attempted to impose some order on the proliferation of small, localized cable networks which most Algerians relied on to receive satellite transmission. Despite this, 1992 saw a major increase in satellite connections around the country, as people sought out alternative sources of information about Algeria's internal conflict. As the violence escalated, satellite television came to be used not only for information about the crisis but also as a means of escaping from it, through films, drama and music provided by the Egyptian Space Channel and MBC. By the mid-1990s, an estimated 9 million Algerians, or nearly one-third of the population, had access to satellite broadcasts, in rural as well as urban areas. Around 90 per cent of these people were organized into groups of 100–300, subscribing to an informal cable system based on one or two shared dishes, one used mainly for Arabic-language programming and the other for French channels.[49]

Moroccan expatriates working in Europe familiarized their families back home with satellite technology during the 1980s. Those gaining satellite access at that time tuned into the range of French channels from the France Télécom satellite network. Households situated near the king's palace found they were able to receive terrestrial spillover from the television signals relayed to satellite equipment at the palace; in 1986 King Hassan acknowledged this by explicitly granting Moroccans the right to watch TV5.[50] In 1992, the Office National de Postes et Télécommunications attempted to regulate access to satellite television by imposing an annual tax on individuals for the use of a satellite dish. The tax, payable in a single instalment, was fixed at Dh 5000 ($515), approximately three times the minimum monthly wage in Morocco at that time. Two years later, however, the tax was abolished, after the Constitutional Court ruled in August 1994 that the 1992 decree imposing the tax was unconstitutional because parliament had not been consulted. In the intervening period many Moroccans had dismantled their dishes, disgruntled at being taxed for a service freely available over the airwaves and not provided by the Moroccan government. A few months before the Constitutional Court ruling, opposition parties in parliament had pushed for an amendment to the 1958 Press Law that would authorize the Ministry of Information to jam satellite television programmes deemed immoral. This effort proved no more successful than the short-lived tax. It evoked an outcry from the local freedom of information lobby and was dropped when the impossibility of mounting the necessary jamming operation was realized. By the late 1990s, around one-quarter of households in Morocco had access to satellite channels. It was reported in the mid-1990s that roughly three-quarters of urban households with satellite access owned their own dish.[51]

Patterns of access and prohibition that developed in the Arab countries of the East Mediterranean were as varied as those in the Maghreb. Paradoxically, Egypt's role as creator of the first Arab satellite channel in 1990 reflected an abundance of domestic television output that in turn dampened enthusiasm for foreign satellite offerings. Access to satellite, whether via individual dishes or the shared systems common in cities and urban areas, remained substantially lower in Egypt than in any other Arab country, despite the absence of any official ban on dish ownership. There being no formal survey, estimates of satellite penetration remained varied and inconsistent throughout the decade. The only consensus seemed to be that the level of access in Egypt by 1998 (the year after Eutelsat recorded a 61 per cent climb in access region-wide) was still below 10 per cent of households with television sets. Audience research conducted for the BBC in late 1996 indicated that 93 per cent of households in the country as a whole had television sets, but that only 1 per cent of those questioned had seen satellite television during the previous week.[52]

In Syria, in contrast, satellite access spread quickly, despite initial government disapproval. Under Syria's State of Emergency Law, still in force at the end of the century after nearly 40 years, and a raft of other repressive legislation, the government in Damascus had the means to keep a tight grip on all media activity. In 1994, in the same year that Saudi Arabia and Iran officially banned satellite dishes, there were signs Syria might also put the squeeze on satellite television. Mahmoud al-Zoubi, prime minister from 1987 until 2000 (when he was removed, charged with corruption and then committed suicide), announced in November 1994 that the authorities planned to retransmit suitable foreign satellite programming by cable to viewers in Syria. This would have allowed the screening and censorship of all incoming material. He warned Syrians that there would be 'no future' for those installing satellite receiving equipment without a licence.[53]

In the event, however, the cable network failed to materialize and those members of the elite with interests in the lucrative import business were able to profit from the boom in sales of satellite dishes. By early

1998, before government permission was granted to a Beirut-based agency to survey Syrian viewing habits, some estimates suggested that 30 per cent of Syrian homes with television had satellite access.[54] Meanwhile the government considered the option of taxing dishes but discarded it.[55] As a result, the price of dishes, while high in comparison to the average wage of a Syrian public sector employee, remained within the reach of the large number of people prepared to invest in an important and long-lasting source of information and entertainment. Individual households showed a strong preference for owning their own dish.

Unlike their Syrian counterparts, Lebanese viewers took their time before turning to satellite television. Under the terms of the Audiovisual Media Law that went into effect in September 1996, Lebanese households had a choice of domestic terrestrial stations operating alongside the state broadcaster, Télé-Liban. With six officially licensed television broadcasters operating in a market generally considered big enough for no more than two or three, competition for audiences and advertising revenue was keen. Programming reflected this, with a large number of foreign films, soap operas and Western sources of news, including retransmission by LBC of news bulletins from CNN International, ABC and Antenne 2 from France. By mid-1997, satellite access in Lebanon was estimated at less than 8 per cent. From that point on, however, the situation started to change dramatically. By March 1998 the proportion of households receiving satellite television is believed to have increased around fivefold, to over 40 per cent. The sudden increase was achieved through a boom in the informal, unregulated cabling of neighbourhoods, bringing groups of up to 300 households together to share a dish or dishes, along with pirated subscriptions to pay-TV channels. Anecdotal evidence suggests that news of Al-Jazeera's arrival spread rapidly by word of mouth. This factor, together with entrepreneurship that facilitated cheap and easy access, provided a major incentive for families to join the neighbourhood networks. These offered to supply a large number of pay-TV and free-to-air channels for just $10–12 per month, whereas the daily purchase of a single newspaper in Lebanon would cost around $30 per month.

On the Arab side of the Gulf, contrasts in government responses to satellite television were belied by uniformly high rates of popular access. In yet another quirk, Saudi Arabia's satellite ban, intended primarily to appease local religious conservatives, was scarcely enforced. Satellite dishes and receivers were banned in the kingdom in March 1994, when would-be viewers of channels such as MBC were promised that they would have access via the SARAvision MMDS (wireless cable) network. In the event, the MMDS system, designed to enable the authorities to preview incoming material for objectionable content, was delayed. Its name was changed to Al-Rawwad (The Pioneers) and trial runs took place in Jeddah and Riyadh in late 1998. Thereafter, however, the whole project was scrapped. Cable subscriptions that might have looked like an attractive option in 1995–96 looked much less tempting just two years later. By that time dish ownership had spread to over 58 per cent of households with television, or (since 99 per cent of homes in Saudi Arabia own one or more televisions) nearly 58 per cent of all households in the kingdom.[56]

The UAE government, meanwhile, far from considering a ban, made much of its 'open-skies' approach. The information minister (and president's son), Shaikh Abdullah bin Zayed al-Nahayan, told the Gulf Newspapers Conference in Abu Dhabi in March 1998: 'Here in the UAE, we have adopted an open skies policy because we believe in the free flow of information. We believe also that any attempt to place constraints on the free flow of information is futile.' He went on to stress the importance of information for development and to argue that the best way to deal with incoming material conflicting with traditional Gulf values and beliefs was to ensure that 'our own domestic media are of such quality that they can provide an attractive alternative view'.[57] With the UAE emirate of Dubai renowned as a regional entrepot for trade in consumer electronic equipment, and with the UAE's foreign workers eager for television programming in their own languages, satellite penetration soon reached predictably high levels. An academic survey published in 1995, based on questionnaires circulated to students at the Emirates University in Al-Ain, found that 81 per cent of respondents or their families in this group had access to satellite channels.[58]

Iran, Dubai's major trading partner, took yet another policy route regarding authorization of satellite access – one that was different from either of the two alternatives adopted by Saudi Arabia and the UAE. The Iranian Majlis (parliament) voted for a dish ban in September 1994, but the workings of the Iranian constitution ensured that the ban was not total. The Council of Guardians, which vets legislation passed by the Majlis for compliance with Islamic law, left some loopholes for the country's existing dish owners, by ruling that Articles 2 and 3 of the law prohibiting dishes should be sent back to the Majlis to be amended. These were the articles requiring removal of equipment already installed and outlawing the import and distribution of dishes.[59] Thus the prohibition succeeded only in slowing the spread of satellite access, not in halting or reversing it.[60] Already, in the spring of 1994, a few months before the ban was passed, the number of dishes in Tehran alone was unofficially estimated at 200,000–300,000. Local companies had also started producing dishes and receivers.[61] When it came to legislating for a ban, many Iranians drew analogies with an earlier attempt to ban video cassette recorders, which had collapsed when the Majlis speaker himself admitted owning one.[62]

Mohammed Khatemi's election as president in 1997 could have only an indirect impact on official attitudes towards satellite television, despite his mandate to pursue political reform. For one thing the state-owned Voice and Vision of the Islamic Republic remained under the influence of the conservative camp. For another, as Khatemi's new culture minister pointed out, only the Majlis could repeal the dish ban.[63] Nevertheless, the Iranian state broadcaster launched its own international satellite channel in late 1997 and, in March 2000, expanded its reach to include the large Iranian communities in the USA and Canada. Iranian expatriates in the USA set up transmissions of pre-revolutionary entertainment in the opposite direction through a channel named National Iranian Television, NITV.[64] In the meantime, an evolution of Voice and Vision policy, in favour of greater diversity and fresh input from the private sector, reflected a widespread recognition that satellite programming necessitated improvements in the quality and quantity of local programmes. This was a lesson observed throughout the Middle East.

### New borders for old?

This chapter has briefly outlined the contours of the satellite media landscape that took shape in the Middle East during the 1990s. By collating the responses of governments, broadcasters, satellite operators and audiences it has indicated some of the ways in which satellite television seemed to disturb the traditional alignment between audiovisual broadcasting flows and spatially integrated nation states.[65] It remains now to take the first step towards one of the main tasks of this book. That is to consider whether and, if so how, the processes of dislocation and potential realignment accord with any of the phenomena collectively recognized as globalization. Satellite television is routinely cited as a vehicle of cultural globalization, favouring concentration of media ownership, enlargement of audiences and homogenization of cultural production.[66] The starting point of the present study is that these and other routine assumptions call for careful examination, at least in the context of satellite television to and from the Middle East. To round off this introductory overview and set the scene for what follows, three region-wide developments associated with the growth of satellite television are identified and queries raised about ways of interpreting them.

Globalization is a slippery concept, not least because, as Marjorie Ferguson pointed out, it exists as both a means and an end.[67] Later chapters will engage more closely with various ways in which it has been understood. For now, and for the sake of argument, ideas centred on one-ness will suffice. For example, globalization sometimes refers to a set of policies designed to turn the world into a single place.[68] Related to this is a sense that an ever-increasing portion of the globe is becoming enmeshed into a single system.[69] These processes are said to be paralleled by a developing consciousness of the world as a single society.[70]

Perceptions of the world as a single place have obvious resonance in the context of Middle East satellite broadcasters' migration between bases in the Middle East and Europe. If MBC, ANN and Med TV were able to establish bases in London, and Orbit in Rome, this was due to deregulation in Europe and the efficiency of communications technology in shrinking the distance between Europe and the Middle East. Global-ization discourse in business in the 1990s was mostly highly prescriptive, urging governments to remove barriers to foreign trade and private investment so that companies could treat different parts of the world as though they were the same. The emigrant media corporations benefited from an environment in which regulatory barriers had crumbled suffi-ciently for them to pick and choose from a mixture of local and foreign sources of labour, finance and technology. Representing interests based in the south but established in capitals in the north, these broadcasters undermined received wisdom about the direction of media flows: their output combined production values and techniques from north and south and was directed at viewers in three continents. But what about editorial or other constraints on their business, unconnected with decisions about location, labour, finance and technology? What about Egyptian and Lebanese satellite broadcasters, still based at home? Their broadcasting may have become multidirectional, flowing north, south, east and west, but they remained subject to national regulation. As this study will show, despite the transnational business interests of some Middle East media moguls, there are many obvious and less obvious ways in which the world is not yet a single place for the Middle East satellite broadcasting business.

If globalization is taken to mean the expansion of a single system of transnational political and cultural-ideological practices across the globe, here again the evidence to be drawn from Middle Eastern satellite television seems inconclusive. True, it helped to stimulate contacts among linguistic and cultural communities, grouped not according to the geopolitical borders of nation states but according to the extent and direction of satellite beams. Middle East geography is such that terrestrial broadcasting has long spilled across certain borders, especially those in the eastern Mediterranean. With the advent of satellite broadcasting, however, spillover moved onto a different scale and so did the scale of jamming operations required to block incoming signals. Whereas shortwave radio and terrestrial television can be jammed by competing signals, albeit with great difficulty and at considerable expense, the effort involved in jamming direct broadcast satellite (DBS) signals deters most states from trying. Turkey managed to jam Med TV signals from Eutelsat during 1997 but kept it up for only ten days.[71] In line with these new realities, mounting evidence in the late 1990s pointed to forms of interconnectedness corresponding more closely to multiple satellite footprints than to the borders of nation states. A policy paper written for decision-makers in Washington suggested that, by linking members of the Arab diasporas in Europe and the USA with their countries of origin, the pan-Arab satellite channels such as MBC, LBC-Sat and Al-Jazeera were contributing to a 'new Arabism'. Yet the paper saw this as signalling a potential backlash. It predicted that this new Arabism would be vocal in its objection to unilateral American action, whether in backing Israel or continuing to insist on sanctions against Iraq.[72]

While the misalignment between satellite footprints and nation states gave viewers a window onto unfamiliar political practices, it may have helped to close windows as well as open them. Jordanian, Egyptian and other viewers within the footprint of the Israeli satellite Amos could tune into, and understand, Israeli programmes with Arabic subtitles. Like this they could follow probing and non-deferential interviews with Israeli ministers of a kind that Jordanian, Egyptian or other Arab ministers had hitherto rarely faced. In Algeria and Morocco, where around half the population speaks French, viewers learned to orient themselves towards the Arab world for music and drama on Arabsat channels and towards the European world for French-language news and documentaries via the France Télécom satellite system. From the latter they could see that rights denied to many people in the Maghreb, such as the right to strike, or demonstrate, or criticize the head of state, were enjoyed by citizens of France. Yet some European governments worried that cross-border connections could work both ways and prove unsettling to immigrant groups. When Arabic-speaking households in France started to install very large satellite dishes, the French authorities were alarmed, interpreting this as an affront to the country's policy of cultural assimilation. Similar concerns about integration in host communities were expressed in Denmark and Sweden, where researchers charged with assessing the impact of Arab satellite channels on Arab immigrant households likened satellite dishes on rooftops to ears listening out for news of 'home'. In these circumstances, any link between satellite viewing and homogenization must be questioned. Words like resistance and reorientation seem more to the point.

Finally, if talk of globalization refers to an emerging consciousness of the world as a single society, this shifts the focus to viewers' perception of themselves and their place in the world. Satellite beams do not only cross state borders; they also cross divides within societies. By the end of the 1990s the sprouting of dishes in rural as well as urban areas had led to a situation where satellite channels reached a quarter of homes in countries such as Syria and Morocco, over a third in Algeria and Lebanon, and as many as two-thirds in Saudi Arabia and the UAE. The new satellite viewing communities were configured more broadly than the readerships of national or even pan-Arab newspapers. They incorporated people who, whether for reasons of sex, illiteracy, remoteness from newspaper distribution circuits, or disinterest in overt government propaganda, were previously left out of the media loop. More and more people therefore, would appear to have become enmeshed in a process where 'images, values and ideas flow ever more swiftly and smoothly across national boundaries'.[73] The question here is whether values and ideas really flow as swiftly and smoothly as images.[74] Old divides corresponding to the use of terrestrial and print media may simply have been replaced by new ones reflecting affinities for certain satellite channels based on age, sex and priorities. Sophisticated ratings data are lacking, but academic studies of satellite viewing habits in the region and among expatriates in Europe pointed to the crystallization of different preferences between men and women, between generations and between new and settled migrants.[75]

Even superficially, therefore, the transnational television phenomenon in the Middle East exhibits no straightforward correlation with globalizing processes as these are sometimes understood. The following chapters delve deeper into the relationship, uncovering the local, regional and transnational forces at play and the degree to which they interact.

# CHAPTER TWO

# Whys and Wherefores of Satellite Channel Ownership

Arjun Appadurai used the term 'deterritorialization' to signify disjunctures between state borders and cultural communities like those identified in Chapter 1. He used the word to describe, among other things, the displacement of people, the creation of 'invented homelands' and the conduct of homeland politics among emigrant groups, in ways that certain media interests may reinforce or magnify.[1] In Appadurai's 1990 model of global cultural flow, people, machinery, money, images and ideas follow dissimilar paths around the globe, which makes the cultural flows associated with deterritorialization disjunctive and unpredictable.[2] The model is a generalized one. Appadurai identifies the actors in terms of their nationality or ethnicity, but otherwise they remain anonymous.

It is easy to see why, in some accounts of cultural globalization, individuals remain backstage. The task of isolating precisely who plays what role would seem to serve little purpose if globalization is perceived to be an unstoppable and irreversible process. Even if the purpose is clear, the task of identification is complicated by the rise of a multitude of non-state actors, from transnational corporations to international bureaucracies, from powerful families to non-governmental organizations. Non-state actors' expanding influence invalidates a state-centred analysis of events but provides no obvious alternative focus. Indeed, non-state actors' influence is sometimes so pervasive that lines between the state and private sectors are blurred, while both sectors may be permeable to outside forces of both the state and non-state kind.[3] When the focus of enquiry is satellite television, where both public and private broadcasters deliberately cross state borders, the aim of tracking all significant transnational interventions is especially hard to meet.

Susan Strange acknowledged the analytical difficulties that follow from recognizing that politics involves not just states but all sources of authority.[4] She recognized the problem of where to draw sectoral boundaries and understood the risk of losing sight of market-authority dynamics. Her solution was to start out with the questions: 'who is exercising authority ... with what purpose, by what means and with what consequences'.[5] This, she wrote, would mean untangling a complex web of overlapping and conflicting authority, which in turn would probably reveal a pattern of 'interlocking, interacting bargains'.[6] Strange's self-styled 'new realist' approach thus entails more than simply looking elsewhere than the state for sources of authority. It also necessitates deconstructing the notion of state control. For one thing, statehood may mean different things at different points in history.[7] For another, the state itself is not a unitary phenomenon but a cluster of institutions or 'institutionalized nexus of central power'.[8] As Philip Abrams insisted, what is to be grasped in studying a state is the state-system or state-idea, the idea that attributes 'unity, morality and independence' to the workings of government that are in practice 'disunited, amoral and dependent'. It is the concrete practice of government going on behind the state mask that has to be uncovered by research.[9] To this end the state, instead of being seen as a unit or entity, may be viewed as an arena where forces compete.[10] An arena is a sphere of action which is not encompassed by rigid barriers and where several interactions may be going on at the same time.

Appadurai's generalized insights about deterritorialization, combined with Strange's and Abrams' advice about the specifics of power structures, make it possible to chart a course for closer scrutiny of the 1990s proliferation of Middle East satellite channels. This chapter examines who exactly was making satellite television policy at this stage. It locates the sources of finance they relied on and posits some unofficial reasons as to why the new broadcasting ventures were set up. Nine separate broadcasting operations are analysed in five groups. The first is Egyptian. It consists of the Egyptian Space Channel and Nile TV as well as the digital Nile Thematic Channels that came into being later on the Egyptian satellite, Nilesat. The second group comprises the three Saudi-owned companies (MBC, ART and Orbit). In the third and fourth are the two Lebanese operators, Future TV and LBC-Sat, and the two news and current affairs channels, Al-Jazeera and ANN. The survey ends by recalling the rise, fall and reincarnation of the expatriate Kurdish station,

MED TV, and considering what has been revealed by a 'who, why, how?' account of channel ownership and control.

## Packaging Egypt

An Egyptian video producer once said of government control over the Egyptian Radio and Television Union (ERTU) that, clearly, someone in government thinks whoever runs the ERTU runs Egypt.[11] Using the same analogy, there seems to have been a school of thought claiming that whoever runs the ERTU's satellite channels has a say in the running of Arab politics. The ERTU is, officially, owned by the Egyptian public through the state. In practice, because of the way it is regulated, its policies are determined by the head of state through the minister of information. Law No 13 of 1979 and Law No 223 of 1989 gave the ERTU a monopoly over broadcasting in Egypt, and challenges to this monopoly during the 1990s were brushed aside.[12] The ERTU executive director reports to the minister of information, who is not an elected member of parliament but a presidential appointee.

Egyptian presidents have traditionally played a pivotal and prolonged role in national policy-making, including media policy. When Hosni Mubarak took power in 1981, he was only the fourth president to hold office since the monarchy was overthrown in 1952. The first, Mohammed Neguib, was replaced in 1954 by Gamal Abdel-Nasser, who nationalized the press as well as the Suez Canal. Nasser promoted a populist brand of Arab nationalism, opened Egypt to the Soviet Union and died of illness in 1970 after presiding over the country's defeat and loss of territory in the 1967 'Six-Day War' with Israel. He was succeeded by his vice-president, Anwar al-Sadat, who terminated the Soviet role in Egypt as abruptly as Nasser had started it. Sadat was assassinated by Islamist militants in 1981 after signing a peace treaty with Israel in 1979. Mubarak became president, having been vice-president to Sadat. Under Egypt's constitution, the president is nominated by the People's Assembly and the nomination then goes to a plebiscite. Although aged 71 at the time, Mubarak stood unopposed for a fourth six-year term of office in September 1999 and was returned with 94 per cent of the vote.[13] The People's Assembly is overwhelmingly dominated by the president's own political organization, the National Democratic Party, which increased its share of seats during the 1990s, obtaining 94 per cent in 1995.[14] Throughout the decade Mubarak chose to leave the post of vice-president empty, apparently to avoid cultivating any potential competitor to himself.

The constitution empowers the president to initiate and veto legislation and to rule by decree. Additional powers are conferred by the State of Emergency Law, which has been in force for most of the past three decades and was renewed by parliament yet again in February 2000. Key appointments are also a presidential preserve. The president selects the prime minister and the rest of the cabinet as well as the 26 provincial governors, all of whom have ministerial rank. He appoints the heads of the armed forces and security and the main national religious institutions, top university personnel and editors-in-chief of government-owned newspapers.[15] The information minister behind the ERTU's expansion, first domestically and then into satellite broadcasting, was Safwat al-Sharif. While Sharif's speeches dutifully credited the president with these initiatives, people involved in them further down the hierarchy were equally punctilious in giving the credit to Sharif.[16] A former intelligence officer and head of the State Information Service (SIS), Safwat al-Sharif joined the cabinet as minister of state for information when Mubarak became president in 1981, playing his part in building up the new president's media image. The bond between the two men became evident as Safwat al-Sharif remained in office throughout the 1980s and 1990s, while prime ministers came and went.

The Ministry of Information has control over the government-owned press as well as the monopoly broadcaster, the ERTU. The minister is, ex officio, chair of the ERTU Board of Trustees (Majlis al-Umana), issuing political 'guidance' on an annual basis.[17] As of 2000, no ERTU director had ever enjoyed the same long and entrenched tenure as Sharif, since the post had changed hands on average around every five years. Meanwhile many of the 36 trustees on the ERTU board owe their own appointments to the presidential chain of command, since they represent ministries, universities and departments within the ERTU. The Board of Trustees is advised by 18 special committees each consisting of 17-20 members chosen personally by the ERTU director.[18] The process of co-opting so many people lends an aura of consensus-building to a structure in which policy initiatives may have their roots somewhere below the ministerial level but can only see daylight if approved by the key players at or above it.

As recounted in Chapter 1, the trigger for the launch of the Egyptian Space Channel on 12 December 1990, was the Iraqi invasion of Kuwait on 2 August of that year. The channel that later came to be known as

ESC 1 was started primarily as a means of feeding Egyptian soldiers an alternative media diet to the one offered by Iraq. Its launch involved an agreement between the ERTU and the secretariat of the Saudi-based and Saudi-dominated Arab Satellite Communications Organization (Arabsat) for the three-year lease, at a cost of $2 million per year, of an unused transponder on Arabsat.[19] It also involved the installation of downlinks and cable connections in Saudi Arabia and the emirate of Sharjah in the UAE.[20] With these arrangements, Egypt became the first Arab country to use Arabsat for a dedicated television channel carrying varied programmes, including news and current affairs, films and entertainment, sports, and educational and religious material.

Importantly, however, the ERTU was able to respond so swiftly because the idea of creating an Egyptian satellite channel predated the Iraqi invasion of Kuwait. The idea was aimed at reaching remote areas of Egypt that were being settled but were beyond the reach of a wireless cable network being developed at the end of the 1980s.[21] For a country like Egypt, with a film industry that had been developing since the 1930s and internal and external broadcasting services developed assiduously since the 1950s, the initiation of satellite broadcasts fitted an established pattern. It required no major innovation in terms of media production or new departure in terms of government policy, since Egyptian radio and television had long been used as an arm of government, and funds had always been made available for expansion. Ever since Egypt joined the ranks of overseas broadcasters in 1953, the External Services of Egyptian Radio had continued to expand; 40 years later, they were broadcasting in 32 languages for a total of nearly 57 hours per day.[22] Moreover, every phase of expansion had reflected foreign policy. The original choice of languages and target audiences stemmed from Nasser's ranking of Egypt's foreign policy priorities, enshrined in the concentric circles (Arab, African, Islamic and, later, non-aligned) which he described in *The Philosophy of the Revolution*, published in 1954. Nasser's pan-Arab ambitions ensured that, as demand for television programming increased during the 1960s, fuelled by the creation of television channels in other Arab states, Egypt was ready to meet the demand with little concern for payment. When, after Nasser's death, the oil price explosion of 1973-74 funded further expansion of Gulf television capacity, Egyptian programme exports came to be seen as a source of revenue, but also as a means of enhancing Egypt's image as a worthy recipient of Gulf investment.[23]

During the 1980s, while Egypt was boycotted by other Arab states because of its 1979 peace treaty with Israel, attention focused on domestic television. Between 1985 and 1990 the ERTU increased its terrestrial channels from two to five, adding a further three channels later, in 1994.[24] It was during the boycott, with Egypt excluded from Arabsat, that the idea of launching a separate Egyptian broadcasting satellite was conceived, though not carried out. When the boycott ended, the ERTU's political managers were poised to expand again into Arab markets. Safwat al-Sharif told the press in 1989 that Egypt now had a good opportunity to consolidate its position as a pioneer of television programming in the region. In order to benefit from this opportunity, he said, Egyptian output had to deal with Arab problems; it should not be 'limited to the restricted national context'.[25]

In this way it seems that the ending of the boycott, followed so soon by Iraq's invasion of Kuwait, caused a pan-Arab approach to take precedence over the early objective of broadcasting by satellite to remote parts of Egypt. Arab governments' receptiveness reinforced this shift. The governments of Kuwait and Bahrain liked the Egyptian Space Channel well enough to arrange for it to be distributed terrestrially through their national television networks.[26] Thereafter the process of spreading the signal proceeded through a symbiotic combination of the Egyptian state authorities making arrangements with foreign satellite and cable operators and viewers on the ground taking the necessary steps to gain access. For about nine months after its launch ESC remained the only regular Arabic-language satellite service available to Saudis seeking alternatives to monotonous and uninformative local programming. It was also regarded as an attractive alternative to French satellite channels and lacklustre local channels by viewers in Algeria and Morocco who hankered after the Arabic music and drama presented on ESC. Less than eight years after the channel's creation, its head, Sana Mansour, felt able to declare that '200 million people in the Middle East and North Africa' look on ESC as 'their own channel'.[27]

The size and nature of this audience influenced programming decisions. In 1992, as armed extremists reacted to the cancellation of elections in Algeria with violence perpetrated in the name of militant Islam, and Islamist militants launched a wave of attacks in Egypt, Sharif charged Egyptian satellite television with the task of 'safeguard[ing] Arab and Egyptian national security'.[28] After surviving an assassination attempt in 1993, he became even more convinced of the need for 'anti-terrorist' television. The next few years saw Egyptian television dramatists dragooned into scripting heavily didactic serials about brainwashed fanatics discovering the error of their ways.[29] When the Islamist militant groups were left split and weakened by local public outrage at their attacks, Sharif's emphasis shifted from television-for-security to television geared to preserving what he called an 'Arab-Islamic' identity. The idea that the ERTU broadcasts not only to the Arab world but also on behalf of the Arab world was repeated regularly in official speeches and interviews.[30] Addressing an international conference in Cairo in 1998, the minister rationalized the ERTU's satellite broadcasting activities in terms of a 'need to keep a balance between the national and international'. It was Egypt's duty, he said, to 'honour its long role in the media' and its role as 'an effective country' in the region.[31]

The launch of Saudi-backed satellite channels, notably MBC and ART, in the early 1990s, added a new dimension to the rationale for Egyptian satellite broadcasting and provided another incentive for its expansion. Satellite rivalry allowed the government in Cairo to respond to the anomalous mixture of complementarity and mistrust characterizing the multidimensional Egyptian–Saudi relationship. Given Egypt's ten-year exclusion from Arab organizations during the 1980s, its subsequent major contribution to the US-led coalition to protect Kuwait and Saudi Arabia against Iraq evoked mixed responses within Egypt itself. Egyptian soldiers in the Gulf in 1991 found themselves fighting to defend people who had gained an unenviable reputation for their oppressive treatment of expatriate Egyptian workers,[32] their often ostentatious and arrogant conduct in Cairo[33] and their inability to defend themselves. The Gulf war split the Arab world more deeply than any previous event, with the governments of Egypt, Syria, Saudi Arabia and Kuwait on one side, opposed by Iraq on the other, flanked by the Palestinians, Jordanians, Yemenis and Tunisians, who either supported Saddam Hussein's defiance or declined to condemn it. This rift fatally undermined the Arab nationalist cause, leaving the Egyptian government and its regional counterparts in need of some additional, or alternative, legitimizing and unifying ideology.

While some policy considerations pulled the Egyptian and Saudi governments in similar directions, others pushed them apart. For example, as major Arab allies of the USA, the two countries found themselves joined in a strategic regional alliance. For helping to defend Saudi Arabia against the threat of invasion by Iraqi forces, Egypt's $4.5 billion debt to the Saudis was cancelled and, unlike the Yemenis and others who suffered from their governments' stance, the 1.2 million

Egyptians working in the kingdom kept their jobs. Rich Saudis contin-ued to spend leisure time in Cairo, making up nearly a quarter of tourist arrivals in some years and spending more freely than other tourists. Saudi investment also resumed, with Prince Alwaleed bin Talal bin Abdel-Aziz, a nephew of the Saudi monarch, investing millions in hotels and real estate in addition to $1 billion in the Toshka land reclamation scheme.[34] However, at the same time as these economic and security ties were being reinforced between Cairo and Riyadh, Egyptian commenta-tors were warning against Saudi efforts to use the satellite media to stamp their own 'tribal Saudi version of Islamic values' on Egypt's socio-political life.[35] They pointed to recruitment of Egyptian film-makers and television presenters by the Saudi media entrepreneur, Shaikh Saleh Kamel of ART, whose censorship guidelines to producers closely matched the internal censorship guidelines of official terrestrial Saudi TV. The latter, issued in the early 1980s, outlawed criticism of religion, political systems or those in authority and forbade scenes showing smoking, dancing, consumption of alcohol, gambling, crime, non-Muslim religious symbols or places of worship, female singers or sports-women, unmarried couples alone together or people of the opposite sex showing affection for each other.[36]

With elements of the Saudi satellite media enforcing suffocating con-straints like these, ERTU department heads with a say in the spread of Egyptian television by satellite could take credit, tacitly, for resisting a Saudi cultural invasion as well as cultural invasion from the West. But the twin aims of countering Saudi influence and boosting Egyptian influence across the Arab world were not the only reasons for the expansion and development of the project that started with the launch of ESC. Egypt's renewed economic opening to the West after the 1991 Gulf war appeared to create a perception among government officials that the country had to be packaged and 'showcased' for the benefit of potential foreign investors, trade partners and tourists. Since investment was also forthcoming from Egyptian and Arab expatriates in Europe and the USA, interest in maintaining ties with emigrants and their families was also reinforced. The aim of fostering links with these communities had long provided justification for Egypt's extensive external radio services, which were intended, among other things, to keep expatriates up to date with developments in their country of origin and give them a clear picture of its future and 'their future in it'.[37] Since satellite televi-sion met the same objectives, its expansion went hand in hand with the promotion of tourism and investment. ESC became a marketing tool. It was presented as the 'mirror which reflects the Egyptian civilization to the world' and the 'cultural bridge' between the homeland and Egyptian and Arab communities abroad.[38] Care was taken to ensure that the ESC signal reached Europe as well as the Middle East. In 1992, as Arabsat 1A became less efficient, ESC was moved to Arabsat 1C and, in December that year, was also beamed from Eutelsat II-F3 to Europe.[39]

The investment stakes in the tourism industry in Egypt are high. Despite periodic scares caused by attacks on tourists, the country's popularity as a holiday destination had increased to the point where, in the year to end-June 1997, before the Luxor massacre of November 1997 caused temporary mass cancellations of tour bookings, a record 4 million tourists visited Egypt, spending some $3.7 billion. Of this total an estimated 56 per cent came from Western Europe, encouraging the government to talk of quadrupling the annual number of tourists over the next 20 years.[40] Given the need to play up Egypt's attractions as a tourist destination to the widest possible audience, ministers felt a corresponding need to play down internal divisions. With the president and information minister refusing to countenance the possibility of diversifying broadcasting capacity through even partial privatization of government broadcasting assets, the ERTU took the initiative of setting up Nile TV, the Arab world's first satellite channel to be broadcast in English and French. Launched from within the same department responsible for ESC, Nile TV started experimentally in October 1993, got under way officially for four hours daily in May 1994 and raised its output to 12 hours daily by 1997. Its official purpose was to 'embody Egypt's image' to foreigners and 'develop relations with the people of countries it addresses in their own tongues'.[41]

Nearly every satellite that carried ESC carried Nile TV too. In 1994 Egypt's satellite programming reached the USA via the AlphaStar digital satellite system.[42] In 1995, with the first generation of Arabsat craft failing and the second generation not yet launched, Intelsat 702 was chosen as an interim means of sending a stronger signal to the Middle East.[43] The lease of a C-band transponder on AsiaSat 2 followed in 1996, making the ERTU Asiasat's first Middle East customer[44] and taking ESC to East and South-East Asia and Australia. In July 1997 ESC joined several other publicly owned channels to become part of a digital package broadcast via Astra to France, Germany, Belgium, Luxembourg and Spain.[45] Meanwhile arrangements were made for ESC and Nile TV to be broadcast by various means, including satellite feeds and retransmission, to Azerbaijan,[46] Uganda and Zambia.[47] These agreements involved the supply by Egypt of equipment and technical help. In 1997, 15 African states were said to have agreed to receive ESC and Nile TV and retransmit these channels on their national networks.[48]

The difficulty of sending a good signal from Arabsat in the mid-1990s gave Egypt another good reason to think about launching its own telecommunications satellite. According to Amin Bassiouny, chairman and chief executive officer of the Egyptian Satellite Company (Nilesat), the Egyptian government first dreamed up this project when Egypt was expelled from the Arab League in 1979. Excluded from Arabsat and believing that a time might come when Egypt would need a satellite of its own, the government in Cairo notified the International Telecommunication Union (ITU) of its intention to use the geostationary orbital slot it had been allocated at 7°W.[49] The idea was raised again in 1985, when the first Arabsat craft was launched, but no further steps had been taken by the time Egypt's membership of Arabsat and other pan-Arab bodies was resumed at the end of the 1980s. However, once the Egyptian Space Channel had started on Arabsat in December 1990, reasons began to accumulate for seeking an alternative satellite. The signal from both Arabsat 1A and 1B deteriorated during the early 1990s, prompting the ERTU to transfer its satellite channel to Arabsat 1C. In February 1992, MBC gained an important advantage over ESC by leasing the powerful S-band transponder on Arabsat 1C, making it possible for viewers in the centre of the Arabsat footprint to pick up the MBC signal with small dishes of 60–80 cm and even with Yargi aerials similar in size to standard television aerials.[50] ESC made do with a lower-power C-band transponder, but the ERTU remained concerned about the lifespan of the first generation of Arabsat craft.[51] When the $158 million contract for building and launching the Nilesat system was signed with Matra Marconi Space[52] on 15 October 1995, Arabsat 2A and 2B had not yet been launched. At that point Nilesat 101 was expected to go into orbit in September 1997.[53]

By 1995 the government also wanted more satellite capacity to extend the national television network to developing areas in remote parts of Egypt, including new oil and gas discoveries and land reclamation projects; some 25 places had been identified that were beyond the reach of terrestrial broadcasting.[54] That Nilesat was to be used solely for broadcasting purposes was evident when the contract with Matra Marconi was signed for Egypt by Amin Bassiouny, who was then director of the ERTU Board of Trustees.[55] It was Safwat al-Sharif, not the transport and communications minister, Suleiman Metwalli, who attended the signing ceremony, leaving no doubt that this was a Ministry of Information project. Sharif presented Nilesat as a money-spinner, predicting that it would provide annual revenue of $50 million over its 15-year lifespan.[56] This was despite the fact that the ERTU was intending to keep two of the first satellite's 12 transponders. Two years later, Hamdi Abdel-Halim, head of transmission projects at the ERTU, confirmed the financial calculations. He described Nilesat as 'an economic project' which would bring in enough money to repay the initial $200 million government investment to the Treasury in 'about four years'.[57] By then, 1997, the plan to increase Egypt's satellite television output still further, by broadcasting eight digital thematic channels from Nilesat, had been conceived.[58]

As happens with satellites, however, not everything went according to plan. October 1997, the date originally set for Nilesat to go into operation, came and went, as did the second target date of January 1998, until the satellite was successfully launched at the end of April 1998. Matra Marconi reportedly compensated Egypt for the delay by adding enough fuel to extend the satellite's lifespan from 12 to 14 years.[59] But, as the launch date approached, the number of transponders set aside for the ERTU doubled from two to four and the early emphasis on revenue receded, reflecting changes in the balance between supply and demand in satellite capacity serving the Middle East. In contrast to earlier expectations that transponder leases would bring in $50 million a year, the market in 1998 was such that each of Nilesat's 12 transponders were offered for lease at $3 million per year, while the annual rate for a single slot on a shared transponder was $0.5 million.[60] Addressing a press conference soon after the Nilesat 101 launch, Sharif confirmed that the project had cost $158 million and told reporters that the allocation of such a sum was 'not a luxury but a necessity'. He said that Egypt faced 'fierce competition in the fields of information and communication' and that Nilesat was needed to keep up with media technology.[61]

The information minister's commitment to Nilesat, despite the expense, re-emerged in May 1998 when he confidently predicted that Nilesat 102, costing an additional $140 million, would be launched to join Nilesat 101 within a year.[62] He repeated the announcement six months later.[63] In fact, Nilesat 102 was originally intended as a back-up satellite. The contract for Nilesat 101 included 10 per cent of the cost of manufacturing Nilesat 102, which was to be kept on the ground pending clearer indications as to future market trends.[64] In theory, decisions about its deployment were up to the Egyptian Satellite Company

(Nilesat), formed in July 1996. In theory also, the ERTU was not the sole owner of Nilesat, holding only 40 per cent of the company alongside the Egyptian Company for Investment Projects, the Arab Organization for Industrialization and two state-owned banks. In practice, however, because of the state's overall majority share in the project and the ERTU-government chain of command, it seems decisions about Nilesat did ultimately rest with the Ministry of Information. In early 1999, a senior ERTU official was unsure who would be using space on Nilesat 102. He continued to regard it as a back-up facility and could think of possible uses for only a third of its capacity.[65]

Suspicions about whether television content would be sufficient to fill the new capacity led some people to infer that the Nile Thematic Channels, launched exclusively on Nilesat 101, were dreamed up to justify the large amount of Nilesat capacity reserved for the ERTU. Together the six Thematic Channels (Nile News, Nile Sport, Nile Drama, Nile Culture, Nile Family & Children and Nile Variety) occupied one of the four Nilesat 101 transponders reserved by the ERTU and were not broadcast from any other satellite. They were launched when Nilesat became fully operational during June 1998, starting out with four hours of programming each, repeated twice daily. This was less than a year after the plan for them had been announced,[66] during which time there was discussion over whether they would be separate from, or incorporated into, the ERTU.[67] Some indecision was also evident as to whether they should be freely available to anyone with a set-top box able to receive digital transmissions, or whether they should be encrypted and available on subscription only. In the event they were made free to air.

The fact that the Nile Thematic Channels have their own department in the ERTU, separate from the Satellite Department that runs ESC and Nile TV, gives some indication that their profitability is not a primary consideration. The same assumption can be drawn from the overall organization of the nine departments of the vast ERTU, which occupies a 27-storey building in central Cairo and employs a staff of around 18,000 people full-time and possibly 33,000 in total. While the Engineering Sector deals with satellite operators, the General Secretariat takes responsibility for ratings research, which it conducts only inside Egypt. The Financial and Economic Sector handles advertising sales and income. In this way the satellite channel managers are not directly accountable for their channels' financial and ratings performance, while it seems the costs of any particular department and its financial benefits are rarely directly compared. The benefits are viewed collectively by the government and ERTU staff more in terms of intangibles, such as Egyptian prestige and influence in regional affairs, than in the measurable income that comes from advertising or sponsorship of programmes. The costs are meanwhile subsumed in the ERTU's overall operating deficit. This was put at $200 million in 1994.[68]

The limited information available for advertising sales suggests that, despite the wide reach of the ESC and Nile TV signals, their advertising income is low compared to other satellite channels. Comparative figures for advertising revenue produced by the Pan-Arab Research Centre (PARC), which is virtually the only organization to collate this data on behalf of advertising agencies, show that in 1998 the Egyptian satellite channels gained less than $27 million, or less than 8 per cent of the combined advertising income of the nine leading Arab satellite channels. Despite an absolute increase to an estimated $36 million in 1999, the relative position vis-à-vis other channels remained the same.[69] Moreover, since that figure is calculated on the basis of so-called 'rate card' rather than the final discounted prices, it is likely to have been an overestimate. It can also been assumed that earnings in 1998 were higher than any previous year, since the number of advertising slots on ESC rose steadily from nine per day when ESC first started to 150–200 per day by 1998.[70] The number of hours broadcast by the channel each day also increased over the same period, from 13 at the start to 24. Private advertising agencies suggested to anyone who would listen that they could have boosted ERTU revenues had they not faced daunting competition from the advertising agency attached to the government-owned Al-Ahram publishing house. Al-Ahram was reportedly able to bulk-buy daily advertising slots of 20 minutes at a time on ERTU television and offer its clients additional discounts of 20–25 per cent, while escaping the 36 per cent tax levied on private agencies' sales.[71]

In other words, the approach to advertising on Egypt's numerous satellite channels in the late 1990s provided yet more evidence that income from the channels themselves was not the chief motive behind them. They were linked instead to the ruling elite's determination to present an image of Egypt as a 'cohesive community'[72] to viewers at home and abroad. The many components of the satellite project conceived and implemented in Cairo – from Nilesat itself to various television programmes – were geared to a particular official view of Egypt's role in the region and internationally, its ability to provide a counterweight to Saudi Arabia and its future economic development. As Safwat al-Sharif told Arab information ministers at their 33rd meeting in June 2000:

We shall open on the world from a position of confidence ... Our sea is our Arab culture. Our ship is the ship of values and ethics of our nation. Our shore is the one where the customs, traditions, aspirations and ambitions of our peoples grew, from the ocean to the Gulf.[73]

## Saudi space

The daily *Al-Riyadh* contained an article in November 1997 which began: 'When talk in Arab media circles turns to Arab television news, the sentence "space is Saudi" is often heard'. The author of the article went on to attribute the expression to the satellite media activities of a select and experienced 'elite' of Saudi businessmen. In doing so, he not only highlighted the remarkable concentration of satellite media in Saudi hands, but also touched on two apparently basic distinctions between the predominant Saudi approach to satellite television and that of other Arab states, especially Egypt. Unlike the Egyptian channels, all run by the state-owned ERTU and emanating from the Egyptian capital, Cairo, the three Saudi ventures referred to in *Al-Riyadh*, namely MBC, ART and Orbit, were established in capitals outside Saudi Arabia by private entrepreneurs. Yet, despite these contrasts, the article also picked up on a nationalistic thread common to both the Saudi and Egyptian efforts. 'As Saudi nationals', the author wrote, 'we are proud of the phrase "Saudi space".'[74]

It is an important facet of the Saudi nation state that it bears the name of its ruling family, the Al Saud. Abdel-Aziz al-Saud (or Ibn Saud), who unified the Nejd and Hejaz to become the first king of Saudi Arabia in 1932, fathered 45 recorded sons by at least 22 different mothers between 1900 and 1953.[75] At the end of the century, up to three generations later, 25 of those sons were still living and the total number of princes was widely estimated at 3000, scores of whom held posts at all levels of government. Even after the appointment of a new Council of Ministers in 1995, the first serious shake-up of the cabinet for 20 years, the key senior ministries of defence, foreign affairs and the interior were reserved for members of the Al Saud – a situation unchanged by the reshuffle of 1999. Whether as ministers and deputy ministers, provincial governors and deputy governors, head and deputy head of the Department of General Intelligence, head of the Youth Welfare Organization or other official institution, princes occupied the majority of influential positions. King Fahd's youngest and favourite son, Prince Abdel-Aziz,[76] took up his first post as minister of state without portfolio in May 1998 and was made head of the Office of the Council of Ministers in January 2000, at the age of just 28. His brother, Mohammed bin Fahd, was meanwhile governor of the Eastern Province. Prince Bandar, son of the defence minister, Prince Sultan, was Saudi ambassador to the USA. These royal appointments are just a few examples from a very long list.

Under the 1992 Basic Law, which is effectively Saudi Arabia's written constitution, there is nothing to prevent members of the ruling family from playing as prominent a role in the media as they do in government. On the contrary, the media are viewed more or less as a tool of government and, internally, Saudi radio and television are run by the Ministry of Information. Article 39 of the Basic Law states:

> Information, publication and all other media shall employ courteous language and the state's regulations, and they shall contribute to the education of the nation and the bolstering of its unity. All acts that foster sedition or division or harm the state's security and its public relations or detract from man's dignity and rights shall be prohibited. The statutes shall define all that.[77]

In this situation, whether or not the ownership of a Saudi newspaper or externally based broadcasting station could be traced to King Fahd or one of the Saudi princes, the ruling family's control over the Saudi media in the 1990s was something many Saudi nationals took for granted. If a certain columnist in the widely read Al-Riyadh used his column to take the authorities to task over censorship issues, it would be equally widely supposed that he had been given the green light by the minister of the interior, Prince Nayef, to achieve some objective of the Al Saud vis-à-vis the kingdom's conservative religious establishment. If another widely read daily, Okaz, appeared to have the inside track on the border agreement with Yemen, it would be assumed their story had princely blessing. But what of the satellite media? If the media were being used internally in pursuit of the interests of specific members or branches of the royal family, would the same people or groups have a political or economic interest in exerting control through satellite television, and what constituency would these satellite channels be addressing? As the Saudi private sector expanded throughout the 1990s many companies complained, privately and anonymously, that the unwritten requirement on them to share their profits with one or more princes was tantamount to a tax. Could royal involvement in satellite television be explained as a form of tax, or were princes themselves prime movers in the creation of Saudi satellite channels?

MBC, founded in London in 1991, followed a path already established by the two Saudi-owned pan-Arab daily newspapers, *Asharq al-Awsat* and *Al-Hayat*, in being based in London and closely linked to the Al Saud. However, links to the Al Saud did not mean these ventures were based on similar objectives. Grudges exist and score-settling occurs not only among the sons of Abdel-Aziz's different wives but even among the so-called Sudairi Seven. The seven sons of Abdel-Aziz by Hassa bint Ahmad al-Sudairi include King Fahd, the defence minister Prince Sultan, and the governor of Riyadh, Prince Salman. Ahmad bin Salman, the prince behind the daily *Asharq al-Awsat*, launched in London in 1979, is a son of Prince Salman. As someone who is said to have avoided taking commissions on foreign contracts, Prince Salman earned himself a reputation for integrity and a willingness to listen. When another prince, Khaled bin Sultan, son of the defence minister, nurtured a competitor to *Asharq al-Awsat* in 1990 by putting his money into a Beirut-registered title, *Al-Hayat*, his target was not *Asharq al-Awsat* but King Fahd. As head of the Arab forces in the US-led coalition that repulsed the Iraqi invasion of Kuwait, Prince Khaled attracted too much attention for King Fahd's liking and lost his post. In contrast to both *Asharq al-Awsat* and *Al-Hayat*, MBC was directly linked to King Fahd himself. It was set up by two private entrepreneurs, one of whom, Shaikh Walid al-Ibrahim, is the brother of King Fahd's third wife and uncle of the king's youngest son, Abdel-Aziz, whose favoured position in the royal family was noted above. Shaikh Walid was still in his twenties when he founded MBC.

While the financial support MBC received from King Fahd in its early years will remain a matter of conjecture, the extent of the king's logistical support is a matter of record. Despite the official ban on satellite dishes in Saudi Arabia, there was no attempt to hide MBC's large Saudi following, while the MBC-FM radio station, launched in 1994, became the only commercial radio station allowed to cover the kingdom terrestrially. Saudi Arabia's majority shareholding in Arabsat was deployed to MBC's advantage when the company was allowed to lease the powerful S-band transponder on Arabsat 1C, thereby boosting its signal and increasing its audience in the kingdom. Shaikh Walid al-Ibrahim's company SARAvision, registered in Riyadh in 1995, was granted an exclusive licence to deliver a wireless cable service to major population centres in Saudi Arabia, enabling satellite channels to be screened for objectionable content before being retransmitted to Saudi screens. MBC was to supply four thematic channels to the cable network, later renamed Al-Rawwad. Despite long delays and the eventual cancellation of the Al-Rawwad system, no alternative took its place. The evidence of MBC's support from King Fahd was so strong it gave rise to the joke that Fahd himself had chosen the initials MBC to stand for 'My Broadcasting Company'.[78] Given the focus of other Saudi satellite companies set up afterwards, it should be noted here that MBC, launched just in time to cover the October 1991 start of the Arab–Israeli peace talks in Madrid, was promoted on the strength of its international news coverage and for most of its early period considered itself 'news-led'.[79] The emphasis was on international and regional news, however, not on news of politically sensitive developments in Saudi Arabia or other Arab countries of the Gulf.[80]

The second investor in MBC was Shaikh Saleh Kamel, a billionaire banker who started out as a contractor in Saudi Arabia in the 1970s and established the Dallah Albaraka holding company in Jeddah in 1982. During the 1980s Shaikh Saleh was linked with Prince Alwaleed bin Talal bin Abdel-Aziz when the two businessmen took a controlling stake in the kingdom's National Industrialization Company. Their partnership was renewed in 1994 when policy differences led MBC's principal backers to buy out Shaikh Saleh's 37.5 per cent stake and he set up his own company, Arab Radio and Television (ART) together with Prince Alwaleed, the latter holding a 30 per cent share to Kamel's 70 per cent. Prince Alwaleed was at that time rising to international prominence by making timely investments in US and European companies (several of which are discussed as part of the review of Middle Eastern media magnates' international connections contained in Chapter 3).

ART's first offering, in 1994, consisted of four free-to-air channels: one general, one exclusively for sport, one for children and another showing only films. The company had acquired the rights to a sizeable library of old Egyptian films from the Egyptian Ministry of Culture, allegedly for a knockdown price of $1200 per film.[81] Television programmes produced by Egyptian and Jordanian companies backed by Shaikh Saleh had also reportedly built up around 6000 hours of programming.[82] In autumn 1995 ART, uplinking from near Rome, began the switch to digital transmission via PanAmSat 4 and then moved to becoming subscriber-only in the spring of 1996. Ample supplies of receiving equipment were reportedly made available on a complimentary basis to promote the ART service to potential subscribers.

Significantly, as a bouquet of encrypted digital channels carrying no news, ART avoided presenting itself as a competitor to MBC. Instead the company found itself in competition with the third Saudi-owned satellite operator to be established in the early 1990s, namely Orbit. The competition was all the more intriguing since Orbit, like both MBC and ART, was started by members of the Al Saud. The prince behind Orbit was Khaled bin Abdullah bin Abdel-Rahman Al Saud, a cousin of King Fahd.[83] Prince Khaled's Mawarid Group had built up interests ranging from gas stations and fast-food chains to banking and construction and medical supply organizations. Prince Khaled's son Fahd was also involved in Orbit, which chose Rome as its base. Its multiple encoded television and radio channels went on air in May 1994, from Arabsat, and its decoders went on sale for $10,000 each. Subscriptions, priced at $20–60 per channel per month, were handled from an office in Limassol in Cyprus. Orbit's early sales pitch included an emphasis on news coverage that it said would be 'live and uncensored'.[84] It certainly seemed, from the high price of the Orbit package and the large audience targeted in the company's business plan, that the investors behind it were aiming primarily for profit. They based their calculations on a target market of 250,000 affluent households in the Middle East and North Africa, a further 5 million speakers of Arabic in Western Europe and 1.5 million potential viewers in the USA.[85] Orbit soon discovered, however, that this audience needed more persuasion. Within a year of starting up, the company had slashed the price of its decoders to around a quarter of the original amount.

This chapter began by framing three questions to be asked about each satellite venture: who was behind it, why did they get involved and by what means. So far, the investigation into the Saudi channels has confirmed the commonly held view of a ubiquitous Al Saud presence and extensive Al Saud control. But the question of motivation seems to elicit a less uniform response. Acknowledging the unprecedented concentration of media ownership in the hands of members of the Saudi ruling family is not the same as saying the king and princes acted in concert. It is clearly important that each of the three groups of investors was able to draw on existing political and economic power to establish a major media operation. In pursuit of their objectives, all three groups left the confines of the kingdom, bearing testimony to the fact that harsh censorship laws and the self-appointed but government-financed religious police (the feared *mutawwaeen*) had created an environment intolerant of public entertainment or media debate. They did so using the billions of dollars at the disposal of ruling family members and their business partners. Thirdly, they did so in spite of the official ban on satellite dishes in Saudi Arabia. When it comes to asking why the Al Saud got involved in satellite broadcasting, the answers for each of the different ventures bear similarities but are not quite the same. Moreover, the answers appear to have changed over time.

Media censorship inside Saudi Arabia has long imposed a straitjacket crafted by the joint efforts of senior, and now elderly, princes and their highly conservative allies in the religious establishment. The tighter the constraints, the greater the turmoil likely to result from relaxing them. Yet the pressure for relaxation is intensified by the weight of the kingdom's population of young people and is recognized at various levels of government. Today, more than two-thirds of Saudis are aged under 40, and a large number of them question the extent and purpose of censorship.[86] The authorities' censorship dilemma was thrown into sharp relief when Iraq invaded Kuwait and the official Saudi broadcast media remained silent on the event for the next three days. CNN not only filled the breach in terms of coverage but soon gained a reputation for its style, based not on wooden editorializing but on what had all the appearance of instant, live news with minimum editing. The presentation of what one specialist describes as 'pure, untainted, spontaneous' news[87] marked a turning point for Gulf viewers. The message was not lost on MBC. 'We want CNN in Arabic' was the phrase one staff member remembers hearing when he was recruited.[88]

Hundreds of millions of dollars went into the project to emulate CNN. MBC started with $300 million in working capital and an annual budget of $60 million.[89] It spent at least $12 million on new headquarters in the London district of Battersea, which were opened by John Major, then British prime minister, in a ceremony attended by the Saudi information minister, Ali al-Shaer, in March 1995. Its staff expanded to well over 300. By 1997 the favoured 'guesstimate' for its annual outgoings was in the region of $100 million. The severe financial cuts that followed in 1998 were widely interpreted to reflect Shaikh Walid's understanding that, given King Fahd's advanced age and failing health, his subventions to MBC would not continue indefinitely. These cuts, including around 120 redundancies, were accompanied by a change in management and editorial direction that shifted the emphasis from news to entertainment. The appointment of Ian Ritchie to the post of managing director in April 1998, replacing Hala Omran of Bahrain, set in train a process of putting control over running the station increasingly in the hands of men with experience of commercial media in Britain. Ritchie, whose background was in the UK's national Channel 5 and in regional television, soon acquired the title of MBC chief executive officer. He was joined in January 1999 by Philip O'Hara of Mirror Group Newspapers, who took over as sales and marketing director of MBC and was appointed six weeks later as chief executive officer of ARA Media Services.[90] October 1999 saw Ritchie taking the major step of combining MBC's news and production departments under the newly appointed Steve Clark, who was formerly head of Regional Programmes at Central TV in the UK.[91]

MBC's new evening schedules for autumn 1998 demonstrated a clear decision to compete head-on with the Lebanese satellite channels. This was evident in an upgrading of entertainment, in the form of films, quizzes and gameshows, and a downgrading of news, reflected in a move to shorten the late evening news and screen it at a later time. A year later Ritchie intimated in a press interview that Walid al-Ibrahim would have no objection to benefiting from the 'synergy' that might be derived from investment by a Western multinational media corporation.[92] Saudi Research and Marketing, the group behind *Asharq al-Awsat*, was seen by some as a natural partner for MBC but declined to become involved.

Like MBC, ART was an expensive operation from the outset, especially given Saleh Kamel's heavy investment in a brand new high-tech production and transmission complex at Avezzano, south of Rome. But Kamel and his partner in ART, Prince Alwaleed, had ample financial resources. Kamel's Dallah Albaraka business group, with interests ranging from Islamic banking and manufacturing to trade, shipping, farming and tourism, had assets estimated at $7 billion by 1998.[93] Prince Alwaleed's fortune by that time was in the region of $13 billion, amassed from land deals and construction work in Saudi Arabia and timely investments in companies such as Citicorp and Saks Fifth Avenue. The prince seemed ready to subsidize the Arab Media Corporation, owner of ART, from the profits of his other businesses. From ART's staggered launch, between 1994 and 1996, to the end of the 1990s, there was no evidence that it had made any money. On the contrary, some industry estimates suggested it was losing $168 million per year.[94] In 1998, the same year that the two shareholders ploughed in another $250 million to cover the cost of adding four more channels, advertising revenue was probably less than $26.5 million.

Prince Alwaleed's motives in absorbing such losses could only be gleaned from his wider preoccupation with the media business as a 'powerful investment tool'. Describing himself as 'proud to be a member of the ruling family of Saudi Arabia', he told one interviewer that he was deeply involved in media not only as an investor but as an enthusiast. 'Media', he said, 'helps me pave the way for new investments and strengthens existing ones.' The prince linked ART's wide reach with his own personal feeling of being at home in 'Riyadh, Paris, Cape Town, New York, Tokyo or any other city on earth'. He continued:

> I also believe that this feeling stems from the fact that the telecommunications revolution has put the world at one's fingertips. I, for instance, adore the fact that ART is present wherever I go, given that I travel extensively and my work has necessitated that I travel to every continent. And since ART channels cover the earth, I always feel a little closer to home.[95]

Shaikh Saleh regularly hinted in speeches and media interviews that ART's content mattered more to him than the money it cost to produce. It was aimed, he told his associates, at a conservative but silent majority of Muslims who were neither secularists nor so-called 'Islamic fundamentalists'.[96] The emphasis in programming was on what Shaikh Saleh described as Islamic values and presenting Islam 'as it should be presented to the rest of the world'. 'Someone like me', he told an interviewer in 1997, '[who is] not completely to the left or the right – and there are millions like me – wanted to present a more tolerant, middle-of-the-road message to the Arab and other peoples of the world.'[97] This focus on Islam was enshrined in a new ART channel launched in 1998 under the name *Iqra* (Read), to teach the Quran. In all ART channels, however, editorial staff freely admitted to a high degree of self-censorship.[98] As already noted in reference to Egypt, producers commissioned by ART were required to conform to guidelines very similar to those issued by Saudi Arabia's domestic terrestrial television in 1982. Shaikh Saleh's associates say he made a deliberate business decision to reject the idea of producing news bulletins or a news channel, calculating that it would either damage his relations with Arab governments in the many countries where Dallah Albaraka has interests or create a means by which the same governments would ask him for favours.

Being based on concern for content over profit, it appears that some of Shaikh Saleh's decisions actually created obstacles to reception of ART channels rather than facilitating it. In 1997 he suddenly abandoned his shared satellite and decoder arrangements with another pay-TV operator, Showtime, jointly owned by a Kuwaiti company and Viacom. This move was later attributed to ART's wish to dissociate itself from Showtime's more relaxed and Westernized content.[99] Kamel himself declared that advertising revenues could never cover the cost of television production of the kind he wanted to see. Addressing a seminar on the sidelines of the Cairo Radio and Television Festival in 1998, he argued that pay TV offered the best means of financing alternatives to the 'dazzling shows that are offered by the West, which do not suit our religion and our traditions'.[100] It is said that the least unprofitable ART channel was the non-commercial one, *Iqra* (Read). Instead of advertising revenue, this brought in donations from pious Saudis.[101]

The sums spent on creating Orbit were even larger than those lavished on ART. One well-informed account of the investment involved in establishing Orbit gives a figure of at least $1 billion, suggesting it may well have been the most costly direct satellite broadcast effort in the world.[102] Costs were driven up by a series of setbacks, including a weak signal on one of the ageing Arabsat craft and strong resistance to expensively priced decoders. But the company started out with big ambitions and kept going. Its backers were originally interested in buying Star TV, based in Hong Kong, from its first owner, Richard Li. It was when this sale failed to materialize that they headhunted Alexander Zilo, an American who had worked in US television before helping to found Star. Zilo, quoted in *Newsweek*, said Orbit's aim was to provide a niche market of well-travelled and affluent Middle Eastern professionals with programming that would not otherwise be available to them in their home countries. 'These people travel a lot and watch Western television when they're away. When they come home, there's nothing,' he said.[103] Yet Orbit was to be a 'self-regulating, conscientious broadcaster, espousing family values'.[104] Rather than flouting local traditions, the company's managers professed themselves committed to socially responsible programming that would reflect the interests, tastes and 'political and religious sensibilities of the region's distinctive cultures'.

By linking political and religious sensibilities in this way, Orbit affirmed its closeness to the thinking that drives government-owned media inside Saudi Arabia, where religious reference points are used to legitimize political structures. Under King Khaled the *mutawwaeen* or religious police, grouped in the Committee for the Prevention of Vice and Propagation of Virtue, were made state employees, while King Fahd adopted the title of Custodian of the Two Holy Mosques. A Saudi-born researcher has argued convincingly that the *mutawwaeen*, by preserving a moral order where outward appearances are deemed to matter most, have played a crucial role in enforcing a political discipline that benefits the Al Saud.[105] Orbit's own role in shielding the ruling family from political questioning was made plain in 1996, less than two years after its start. One of its early initiatives was to sign a ten-year £100 million contract with the BBC in 1994 to provide an Arabic television news service. Although the contract ruled out editorial interference in the BBC's output, friction between the two sides mounted as BBC journalists reported on the activities of an exiled Saudi dissident, Mohammed Masari. Orbit's refusal to screen such items led to breaks in transmission in January 1996.[106] When a BBC Panorama programme, called *Death of a Principle* and highly critical of Saudi Arabia's human rights record, was aired in April, the contract was brought to an untimely end. Orbit's chief executive, Alexander Zilo, denounced the programme as a 'sneering and racist attack on Islamic law and culture'.[107] His reaction, while ostensibly defensive of Saudi Arabia's political status quo, may also have reflected the determination of Orbit's management to safeguard business viability by ensuring unbroken transmission to viewers inside Saudi Arabia. Orbit had already encountered distribution difficulties in its early days. Its service had been launched in May 1994, just weeks after Decree No 128 of 10 March banning the use, manufacture or import of satellite dishes and outlawing the delivery of television satellite feeds to subscribers in the kingdom. The Ministry of Interior was charged with enforcing the ban, which it did selectively. In fact the main result of the so-called ban on dishes was not their removal from the market but a steep rise in their price. Nevertheless, the Orbit–BBC news service provided enough coverage of Saudi dissident activities for the authorities in the kingdom to make a special point of confiscating Orbit decoders.

This and other evidence presented here shows the limited explanatory value of saying simply that the three major Saudi-owned satellite ventures were set up under the auspices of members of the Al Saud. The power relations underlying these satellite ventures were complex from the outset because they reflected the shifting alliances known collectively, at any given moment, as the Saudi state. Different branches of the extended Saudi ruling family may have diverging interests vis-à-vis each other, even if they have a shared overall interest in safeguarding the supremacy of the ruling family as a whole. Satellite technology provided a new arena in which state and non-state actors in Saudi Arabia could collaborate and compete. It is in the tension between the interests of individuals, the monarchy and the state that the story of 'Saudi space' is played out.

## Lebanese fractures

Fragmentation and disorientation are the two words chosen by Nabil Dajani to capture the processes whereby the Lebanese media reflect and reinforce the contradictions of Lebanon's confessional society, in which religious affiliation assumes deeply entrenched social and political significance.[108] The fragmentation of society into sects is mirrored by the media. The broadcast media, in turn, instead of enabling Lebanese citizens to engage with their society as a whole, have further distanced them from it.[109] Dajani's insight provides a helpful starting point from which to locate and identify the main players behind Lebanon's satellite television channels. It is precisely the same starting point signalled by Lebanon's political structure, based on power-sharing among Maronite Christians and Sunni and Shia Muslims, with Lebanon's bigger and more powerful neighbour, Syria, acting as ultimate arbiter and main power broker. It is likewise the same starting point arrived at via Lebanon's Audiovisual Media Law (Law No 382 of 1994), devised to prune the chaotic proliferation of broadcasting stations that mushroomed during the 1975–90 civil war but to prune it in such a way as to ensure that the country's *zuama* (political-sectarian leaders) would end up with channels of their own. The provisions and the application of the law set the scene for LBC and Future TV to create their satellite channels in 1996.

By revoking the broadcasting monopoly granted in 1977 to the state broadcaster, Télé-Liban, Law 382/94 made Lebanon the first Arab state to authorize private radio and television stations to operate within its borders.[110] This decision deprived the country's only non-confessional station of a monopoly it had been promised would last until 2012. By licensing a total of six terrestrial stations, the law obliged Télé-Liban to face five competitors in a country of just 4 million people with a television advertising market that most people thought could support two or three stations at most. The magic number of six licences, whittled down from 63 applications, had nothing to do with spectrum shortage or any other technicality.[111] It was determined by confessional thinking and the minimum number of constituencies that the government of Prime Minister Rafiq Hariri felt it needed to satisfy. Thus, besides Télé-Liban, Maronite Christians were supposed to content themselves with LBC, Sunni Muslims with Future TV, Christian Orthodox with Murr TV and Shia Muslims with NBN. The sixth licence was eventually awarded to Al-Manar TV, run by Hizbollah, the Lebanese Shia political group dedicated to resisting Israel's occupation of the south. It was only ceded after a political struggle in which Télé-Lumière, an unlicensed Christian religious station, was allowed to continue broadcasting openly, supposedly to restore the delicate sectarian balance by providing a counterweight to Al-Manar. Yet while a blind eye was turned to Télé-Lumière, and NBN's licence was granted when NBN did not even exist, two other established and reportedly profitable television broadcasters, New TV and ICN, were denied licences and closed down. Both New TV and ICN had criticized the Hariri government.[112] With the 1996 licensing round leaving some disappointed broadcasters determined to re-apply, post-war Lebanon's crowded television stakes had a built-in incentive for lucky licensees to build quickly on their advantage. They could do this by extending their horizons beyond home ground and broadcasting by satellite.

Although satellite broadcasting was envisaged under the Audiovisual Media Law, it was to be controlled by a separate piece of legislation, Law 531. Whereas, nominally at least, Law 382 put supervision of terrestrial broadcasting under the Conseil national de l'audiovisuel, Law 531 gave the cabinet the right to grant or revoke licences to broadcast news and political coverage by satellite. In this matter the cabinet was not required to refer to parliament. Thus it is at the power-centre of the Hariri government of the mid-1990s that answers can be found as to who was behind Lebanese satellite television, what they expected to get out of it and the resources that enabled them to get involved. Given that Rafiq Hariri was able to make his particular contribution to Lebanon's post-war reconstruction because of his multiple external connections, especially with Saudi Arabia, Syria and France, it is perhaps not surprising that the first satellite channels launched from Lebanon had backing that was not exclusively Lebanese.

Under Law 382/94, no individual or family was allowed to hold more than 10 per cent in a television company. Licences could only be granted to Lebanese joint stock companies, owned by Lebanese nationals, who were not permitted to hold stock in more than one broadcasting company. Stations applying for a licence had to commit themselves to covering the whole country and broadcasting for a minimum of 4000 hours per year, ensuring that 40 per cent of their programming was locally produced. Insofar as Lebanon's satellite channels could claim they had bases outside the country, it seems they were not subject to these regulations. For example, Prince Alwaleed bin Talal bin Abdel-Aziz, the Saudi prince with a 30 per cent shareholding in ART, told an advertising journal in an interview published in 1999 that ART, through its parent company Arab Media Corporation, had a 50 per cent share in LBC's satellite arm, LBC-Sat. In the same interview he also referred to his share in the terrestrial station, Murr TV, one of LBC's competitors on the domestic Lebanese scene.[113] Although Murr TV was in theory allowed neither a foreign shareholder nor one with a stake in another Lebanese television station, the fact that Prince Alwaleed's maternal grandfather was Riad al-Solh, Lebanon's first post-independence prime minister, seems to have made him a special case. Whereas nationality for ordinary people in both Saudi Arabia and Lebanon is derived from the father rather than the mother, Prince Alwaleed, a partner with Rafiq Hariri in the insurance group, Medgulf Strikers Holding,[114] was granted Lebanese citizenship by decree.[115]

LBC's terrestrial station was founded in the 1980s, during the Lebanese civil war, as the official organ of the Maronite Lebanese Forces under the majority ownership of a Maronite Christian, Pierre Daher. It went on air in October 1985 with the financial and technical support of the Christian Broadcasting Network headed by the televangelist Pat Robinson.[116] French disapproval of the US televangelists' influence led to an arrangement whereby LBC also acquired rights to transmit large amounts of French programming. The variety of LBC programmes and its mainly professional and commercial approach established it as the country's leading television broadcaster, a status that was also made possible by the composition of its board. This included notables with known connections to the Syrian government, including Suleiman Franjiyeh (health minister under Rafiq Hariri), the wealthy MP Issam Faris, and businessman Nabil Boustani. Being relayed by 11 transmitters across the country, LBC's terrestrial service, consisting of light comedy, films, news (including retransmissions from American and French sources), talkshows, serials and televised church services on Sundays, could be received not only in Lebanon but across the border in parts of Syria and Israel.

When its satellite operations began in 1996, comprising two channels, one free to air and the other available by subscription, LBC had been in the terrestrial broadcasting field for a decade. LBC-Sat, relying mainly on ART's production and satellite transmission facilities at Avezzano in Italy, considered itself 'not really a Lebanese station' and therefore exempt from the requirement of Law 382/94 that 40 per cent of programming should be locally produced.[117] LBC-Sat's flamboyant and uninhibited programmes contrasted sharply with those of ART. It appears, however, that ART's majority shareholder, the Saudi business-man Saleh Kamel, believed he was exerting some control behind the scenes. Asked in 1998 how he reconciled the ART–LBC-Sat connection with the fact that LBC 'does not necessarily uphold Islamic values', Kamel asserted that he had 'been able to influence the choice of pro-gramming at LBC'.[118] Direct Syrian controls were also brought to bear, sometimes more obviously than others. For example, the Syrian govern-ment reacted negatively to LBC's programming priorities in July 1998, which they felt to have detracted from the impact of President Hafez al-Asad's visit to France that month. That August, a long-standing friend of Syria's military intelligence chief in Lebanon was appointed to supervise LBC's coverage.[119]

A combination of Saudi and Syrian influence is something the newly launched LBC-Sat shared with Future International, the satellite offshoot of Future TV. Rafiq Hariri, Lebanon's prime minister from 1992 to 1998 and Future TV's most influential shareholder, is both a Lebanese and Saudi national. Before entering Lebanese politics, he made his fortune and became close to King Fahd by successfully completing several prestigious construction contracts in Saudi Arabia. One of his companies, the Luxembourg-based Techniques Audiovisuelles, has holdings in two major media operations, Future TV and Radio Orient, the latter broadcasting from Paris as well as Beirut. Although he was officially obliged to reduce his own stake in Future TV in accordance with the Audiovisual Media Law, the reduction was regarded by most Lebanese as merely cosmetic, since other shares in the company were held by Hariri's associates. In the same way that Mr Hariri used his personal wealth and business acumen to kick-start post-war reconstruc-tion in Lebanon, he appears to have wanted to use Future TV during his premiership to advertise the country as a thriving services centre and tourist resort deserving every dollar of investment Gulf Arabs and others would be prepared to put in. Future TV managers stressed their mission to promote 'civil peace, reconstruction and the consolidation of Leba-non', and contrasted their satellite channel's programming with that of LBC, saying that Future aimed to be 'challenging without being vul-gar'.[120]

Concerns about the implications of Rafiq Hariri's links with the Saudi leadership appeared to be vindicated in late 1997 when he quickly responded to complaints from unnamed officials in the Gulf about political programmes carried by Lebanon's two satellite channels. The complaints coincided with a spate of controversial programmes, or advertisements for programmes, on LBC and Murr TV, involving one interview with Beirut MP Najah Walim about corruption and another with the exiled General Michel Aoun. Hariri's information minister at the time, Bassem al-Sabaa, told Radio Lebanon in December 1997 that the broadcasts had brought an adverse reaction from 'some Arab information ministers, especially in the Gulf'.[121] In January 1998 the Lebanese government, using its powers under Law 531, banned LBC-Sat and Future International from transmitting news. The ban remained in force for more than nine months. Daher, LBC's executive director, denounced the ban as having been instigated by Hariri at King Fahd's request. He said the action had been taken because LBC-Sat was on the verge of overtaking MBC as the most-watched television newscaster in Saudi Arabia.[122] This allegation was corroborated by the only viewing figures available. The *TV Update* for November 1997 released by the Pan-Arab Research Centre in Dubai put LBC-Sat and MBC neck and neck in terms of their share of the audience in Saudi Arabia (see Table 5). Unlike LBC, Future TV did not protest against the ban, describing it instead as a means of safeguarding continued Gulf investment in Lebanon.[123]

**Table 5:  Leading satellite channels' audience share in three Gulf states, 1996–97**

*(Percentage of total; November data unless otherwise stated)*

|               |         | LBC-Sat | MBC | Future |
|---------------|---------|---------|-----|--------|
| Saudi Arabia  | 1996    | 33      | 43  | 39     |
|               | 1997    | 45      | 45  | 35     |
| UAE           | 1996    | 9       | 13  | 14     |
|               | 1997[1] | 17      | 16  | 13     |
| Kuwait        | 1996    | 19      | 25  | 19     |
|               | 1997[2] | 30      | 34  | 25     |

[1]  March figures were the latest available when *ArabAd* published its comparison.
[2]  Figures for 'Summer 1997'.

Source: PARC data published in *ArabAd* 8/2 (March 1998), p 10

Future TV's commitment to positive reporting about Lebanon appeared to wane somewhat after Rafiq Hariri was replaced by Selim al-Hoss as prime minister in 1998. After repeated bouts of criticism of government policy on Future TV during 1999, Hoss lashed out against a 'local satellite station ... affiliated with a prominent opposition figure', accusing it of broadcasting distorted, negative news about Lebanon that was having the effect of discouraging tourism and investment.[124] However, many other politicians implied that Hoss, like Hariri before him, had over-reacted to critical coverage. Hariri meanwhile found it convenient to play the part of convert to the cause of media freedom. Yet his conversion was belied by evidence of Future TV's continued self-censorship, implicit in Hariri's continued good relations with the authorities in Damascus. Had the Syrian government, then responsible for one of the harshest internal censorship regimes of any Arab country,[125] deemed any material on a Lebanese satellite channel to be politically threatening, it would have cracked down on it, as it did on LBC in August 1998. Sulaiman al-Firzli of the Paris-based *Al-Hadath al-Dawli* commented in August 1999, a propos of recent contacts between Hariri and Hafez al-Assad's son Bashar: 'The Lebanese Hariri, the Saudi Hariri and the Franco-American Hariri are all vital assets for Damascus ... but it is his Saudi prop that is Hariri's first and perhaps ultimate passport, the brightest of all the colours of his public persona.'[126]

Indeed Hariri's pivotal role in the Lebanese–Syrian–Saudi power triangle of the 1990s was reflected particularly clearly in the fortunes of the Lebanese satellite media. For, under his premiership, Lebanon's state-owned broadcaster, Télé-Liban, remained almost the only Arab state television company not to be broadcast by satellite. This was despite the fact that it was technically and logistically equipped to do so, and despite the popularity of some of its programmes, including one or two serialized dramas ranked by discerning viewers with the best of Egyptian and Syrian production. It was not until October 1999 that the cabinet found the political will to earmark money intended specifically for satellite broadcasting by Télé-Liban and not to be used towards paying off the company's accumulated debts.[127] With a potentially unifying state institution sidelined in the international arena by two private broadcasters linked to the country's political leaders, the particularities of Lebanon's political make-up and the involvement of external forces in Lebanese politics were projected onto the regional satellite television landscape.

### News or nuisance?

If the dominant themes of satellite channel ownership in the Middle East in the 1990s were the protection of vested interests and observance of editorial taboos, Qatar's Al-Jazeera Satellite Channel gave a very definite impression of breaking the mould. Al-Jazeera, dedicated exclusively to news and current affairs, swept onto television screens across the region by breaking taboos. It did so as part of a wider shift away from earlier Qatari norms that began when Shaikh Hamad bin Khalifa Al Thani ousted his father and took over as emir in June 1995. Within four months of his takeover, Shaikh Hamad's government announced that it planned to end press censorship, and in February 1996 it set Qatar apart from other Arab states by abolishing the Ministry of Information. The official explanation for the move was highly unusual by regional standards. The outgoing information minister, Hamad Abdel-Aziz al-Kuwari, said he was pleased that Qatar had become the first Arab country to take such a step. It was an experiment which, he said, would serve those in positions of responsibility by doing away with secrecy and enabling them to 'feel the people's pulse'.[128] Later that year Qatar became the first Arab country to agree to the local 24-hour relay of BBC programmes in Arabic and English on FM and arrange BBC training for local radio and television personnel.[129]

To assess exactly how far and where the government of Shaikh Hamad bin Khalifa Al Thani wished to 'do away with secrecy', its media policy needs to be viewed against the emirate's situation before and after the 1995 coup. Qatar is unusual in several ways, not least in terms of its size and wealth. The emirate's total population stood at just 560,000 in 1998, including only around 155,000 native Qataris, making it by far the smallest Arab state. Its GDP per head, at nearly $17,000 in 1998,[130] was one of the highest in the region. With a well-funded welfare system, including enviable pupil/teacher ratios in schools, free tertiary education and advanced healthcare provision, the kind of dissatisfaction expressed by the small community of Qataris has generally had more to do with bureaucratic inefficiency or inadequate infrastructure than deeper issues of political liberalization and representation. Nevertheless, the new emir's political reform initiatives were generally welcomed by a population that had started to question his father's inertia. In foreign policy, meanwhile, there was continuity. The ruling Al Thani had acted independently of other states in the Gulf Co-operation Council (GCC) even before the 1995 coup, re-establishing links with both Iran and Iraq in the early 1990s.

The experiment in uncensored television that began with the launch of Al-Jazeera was only one element of the new emir's agenda for change. By March 1999 the top-down reform programme had resulted in the first Qatari elections for municipal councils, in which women as well as men were allowed to stand for office and vote. Four months later Shaikh

Hamad appointed a committee to draw up a new constitution with provision for an elected parliament. By combining municipal elections, political rights for women and the promise of legislative elections, Shaikh Hamad's programme set Qatar apart from every one of its five neighbours in the GCC, namely Saudi Arabia, Kuwait, Bahrain, Oman and the UAE. But differences between the Qatari government and its co-members of the GCC had long been apparent. They surfaced at the first annual GCC summit after the Qatari coup, when the Qatari delegation walked out of the meeting. One reason for rancour, apart from the support some GCC governments gave to Shaikh Hamad's father after he was deposed, was Qatar's territorial dispute with Bahrain. This concerned the Hawar islands off the Qatari coast, claimed by Qatar but controlled by Bahrain. In pursuit of Qatar's territorial claim, the emirate's radio and press played host to Bahraini dissidents even before Al-Jazeera was launched. Unhappy with support for Bahrain's position from other Gulf states,[131] Qatar used its media to score political points in the dispute, giving Mansour al-Jamri of the Bahraini opposition movement opportunities to air his grievances in public.[132] Cynics might say there was a certain logic in developing this small-scale tactic into a fully fledged policy of acquiring leverage on the Gulf political scene by injecting a nuisance factor into regional satellite television. It so happened the emir and his ministers could do this by taking a principled stand on freedom of expression.

Although the Qatari government eventually staffed Al-Jazeera with BBC-trained professionals rendered jobless by Orbit's April 1996 cancellation of BBC Arabic news, the first news of the channel's creation came with an emiri decree issued on 8 February 1996. Under that decree the state-owned venture was capitalized at QR 500 million ($137 million).[133] Start-up was scheduled for 1 November 1996, with broadcasting initially limited to six hours a day. The man put in charge of Al-Jazeera was Shaikh Hamad bin Thamir Al Thani, who was still being referred to as under-secretary at the Ministry of Information and Culture at the time of Al-Jazeera's launch, as the Ministry's actual abolition did not take place until February 1997. Shaikh Hamad bin Thamir made it clear that Al-Jazeera would deal predominantly with news and current affairs, establishing a network of correspondents around the world. But the government deliberately distanced itself from the operation by keeping the Al-Jazeera logo devoid of any mention of Qatar.[134] It said the start-up funds for the station were a loan, to last five years. By 2001, if new funding were to be needed, alternative sources would have to be found.

By making this money a loan rather than a direct subsidy, the government could dissociate itself from Al-Jazeera's editorial content.

With editorial staff representing several Arab countries and without the institutionalized censorship mechanisms in force in those countries, Al-Jazeera started to cover subjects studiously avoided by the rest of the Arab media. This process developed a momentum of its own. By creating regular slots for televised debates with titles like *Akthar min Ra'i* (More than One Opinion) and *Al-Ittijah al-Muaakis* (The Opposite Direction) the stage was set for controversy and the presenters of these shows became potential rivals in seeking public attention. Viewers, stunned at first, gradually became used to loud arguments and confrontations, with Islamists and anti-Islamists pitted against each other, as well as people of all political persuasions and dissidents from Morocco to Egypt and Palestine to Bahrain. Once the first furious complaints from Arab governments had flooded into the offices of Al-Jazeera and Qatar's emir, the recipients learned to ride out the storm. Al-Jazeera's director could say, with some justification, that freedom of expression may be unusual in the Middle East but is not unusual in the developed world.[135] At the same time the station discovered that, by gaining privileged access to Baghdad, it could establish a niche for itself as a provider of television pictures to international agencies.

Critics of the experiment claimed that the emirate was giving itself the freedom to tackle topics that were sensitive in other Arab countries while keeping controversial aspects of domestic politics off limits. The foreign minister, Shaikh Hamad bin Jassem bin Jabr Al Thani, refuted this criticism in a press interview in October 1999, citing instances in which he and Qatari government policies had come under attack, including on Al-Jazeera. Judging from the amount of criticism, he said, 'you would think that [Qatar's] population numbered 50 million rather than half a million'.[136] Indeed, the Qatari emir's willingness to provide media outlets for local complaints served to reinforce Al-Jazeera as a means of asserting Qatar's independence from less receptive Gulf regimes. This was demonstrated when local radio aired grievances about allowances paid to members of the Al Thani, which one caller described as a 'big emotional and financial weight on the nation and its people'.[137] The talkshow host, Abdel-Aziz Mohammed, said the debate proved there were 'no more red lines' for the Qatari media. However, the breaking of taboos was not proof of the absence of media manipulation at the highest level of the Qatari government. With the emirate's political reform programme having been devised by the emir himself, and with Al-Jazeera seen as an element in that programme, an alignment between the state and the satellite channel was perceived both internally and externally.

Al-Jazeera's launch at the end of 1996 was followed within a few months by that of a second all-news channel, Arab News Network (ANN). There was never any doubt that this was privately owned. It was established in May 1997 in the heart of London's West End by Sawmar al-Asad, son of Rifaat, the estranged brother of Syria's then president, Hafez al-Asad. For most Middle East analysts, there was little mystery about who was behind ANN and why it had been set up. The station was started at a time when the possibility was looming that the ailing Hafez al-Asad might cease to be president within the next few years. As commander of the Defence Brigades during the early 1980s, at a time of political instability in Syria exacerbated by Hafez al-Asad's ill-health, Rifaat had built up a power base which Hafez then chose to dismantle while forcing Rifaat to remain outside the country for two years. Rifaat did not abandon his ambitions, however. He continued to see himself as a contender for high office and, on these grounds, ANN was seen as paving the way for his eventual bid for power.

In other words, Sawmar al-Asad, a French national, was put in charge of ANN on his father's behalf. Since Sawmar al-Asad was just 26 when ANN was founded, there seemed little doubt that his investment in the station had come out of family funds. Moreover, his father had already demonstrated his readiness to use the media to shore up his position inside Syria. He produced a magazine in Syria, called Al-Forsan (The Cavalry), which ceased publication in 1991, and a daily newspaper which closed a year later. During the 1980s he tried to launch an FM radio station serving the Paris region, but was unable to obtain a frequency.[138] For a while, Sawmar himself published a weekly magazine in Paris, under the title Al-Shaab al-Arabi (The Arab People). This closed in 1999. The potential benefits for Rifaat of having his own satellite channel were demonstrated, within a few weeks of ANN going on air, when pictures of a meeting he had held in Damascus with Crown Prince Abdullah of Saudi Arabia were shown repeatedly on ANN on 4 July 1997. Hafez al-Asad clearly disapproved of this footage receiving such attention, as became apparent when Zubayda Muqabel, the member of Rifaat's staff who had shot the film, was taken from her car in Damascus by security forces and held at an unknown location for eight months.[139] Rifaat al-

Asad was himself stripped of his position as Syrian vice-president in February 1998. Republican Decree No 8, issued by Hafez al-Asad, relieved Rifaat of all his official duties, thereby formalizing a situation that had prevailed informally for some time.[140] Nevertheless, via ANN, Rifaat was able to keep the limelight on his political manoeuvres. He attended the funeral of King Hassan of Morocco in July 1999, which Hafez al-Asad did not attend. A few days later Sawmar al-Asad visited Yasser Arafat, the head of the Palestinian Authority, in a move that, in view of persistent difficulties in Palestinian–Syrian relations at the official level, was seen in Damascus as deliberate provocation on Rifaat's part.[141]

Just as the reasons for ANN's creation were fairly plain, so was the fact that ANN was spending around $30 million a year[142] without any obvious source of funding beyond the accumulated resources of Rifaat al-Asad. In this case, therefore, the question posed throughout this chapter – as to the means employed by satellite channel owners to run their channel – calls for an answer that gives as much prominence to powerful personal contacts and technology as to money. Access to a satellite with a footprint well positioned over the high-spending television viewers of the Gulf is a pre-requisite for a channel that expects to build up its advertising revenue. ANN's management screened no advertisements in the channel's first six months and refrained from seeking a place on Arabsat, sensing that ANN was likely to be viewed as a Syrian opposition station and consequently refused.[143] Gradually, however, the means of reaching a wider Middle Eastern audience for a longer time materialized, accompanied by shifts in editorial coverage. These shifts were limited in scope since ANN, being licensed as a UK-based station by the Independent Television Commission (ITC), was bound by the ITC's code of impartiality. Nevertheless, whereas ANN either ignored Syrian government news in its early months or reported it frostily, a softening of this approach was noted after the station started 24-hour broadcasting in 1997 and expanded during 1998.

When, in early 1998, ANN suddenly found $40 million to rent a 12-year lease on the brand new Hot Bird 4 satellite,[144] rumours circulated to the effect that Crown Prince Abdullah was helping to foot the bill. Given the media ventures of so many other Saudi princes, this explanation had credibility. Abdullah's involvement would allow him to influence ANN's editorial stance, boost ANN's ability to challenge the popularity of Qatar's uncensored Al-Jazeera Satellite Channel and provide an alternative to the 24-hour news channel which MBC had by then decided to scrap from the bouquet of MBC channels being prepared for Al-Rawwad. A few months after the move from Hot Bird 2 to Hot Bird 4, ANN gained the promise of a place on Arabsat 3A,[145] which was eventually launched in February 1999. The links ANN established during this period went some way to helping it survive in late 1999, when Rifaat al-Asad's private port in Latakia was demolished by the Syrian government on the grounds that it was used for smuggling,[146] and Rifaat's own funds started to dry up.

In any event, ANN, like other privately owned Middle Eastern 'émigré' satellite channels reviewed here, was clearly born out of the need for a political player in a specific Middle Eastern country to pursue his bid for power from a foreign base because of the constraints on political activity at home.

### Virtual Kurdistan

For decades, television has been a weapon in the struggle over Kurdish autonomy, a struggle that has been fought out mainly in the four countries – Turkey, Iraq, Iran and Syria – where the majority of Kurds live. As a propaganda weapon it has not always been used in the most obvious way. When Iranian assistance to Iraqi Kurds ceased under an Iraq-Iran agreement of 1975, and the Iraqi government forced thousands of Kurds to relocate away from their homes, truck-loads of colour television sets were distributed as sweeteners to Kurdish officials and their families to encourage them to co-operate with the uprooting.[147] But while television sets were to be found in many homes, Kurdish-language programming was not. It was not available at all in Turkey, Syria or Iran, while Iraqi television broadcasts in Kurdish were strictly government-controlled until after the Kurdish uprising that followed the 1991 Gulf war. At that point more than ten local television and radio stations began to operate in the Kurdish enclave in northern Iraq. These were run by the Kurdish Democratic Party (KDP), Patriotic Union of Kurdistan (PUK) and other smaller Kurdish political parties.[148]

In 1994, an expatriate Kurdish group obtained a ten-year licence from the UK's ITC to broadcast by satellite under the name MED TV, derived from the ancient name for ancestors of the Kurdish people, the Medes. The Turkish government immediately interpreted the move as an intensification of the struggle for Kurdish secession by the Kurdish Workers' Party (PKK) in south-eastern Turkey. It claimed MED TV was merely PKK TV in disguise. MED TV representatives put up a campaign to counter the Turkish one, accusing the Turkish authorities of pressuriz-ing satellite operators and other potential business partners not to collaborate with MED TV. They published a letter from the ITC, dated 30 August 1995 and addressed to Lord Avebury as chair of the UK Parliamentary Human Rights Group, providing information about communications received by the ITC from the Turkish authorities. The letter appeared to confirm that the ITC had received Turkish requests to investigate the ownership licensing and content of the MED TV serv-ice.[149]

Despite Turkish pressure, the channel started test transmissions in March 1995, showing Kurdish cultural programmes and films and live debates from the MED TV studio in Brussels. From then on its transmis-sion time increased gradually to 18 hours a day, with material broadcast in Kurdish dialects as well as Turkish, Assyrian, Arabic and English to Kurds throughout Europe and the Middle East. The response among Kurds in the Middle East was reflected in the sprouting of satellite dishes in even the most remote Kurdish villages, especially in Turkey.[150] Given the overwhelming obstacles to creating a unified Kurdistan on the ground, the Kurdish satellite channel seemed to create a kind of Kurdis-tan in space. But this virtual Kurdistan was a vulnerable entity. MED TV found itself accused of money laundering. Its funds in a Luxembourg bank were frozen from 1996 to 1998, when a Luxembourg judge ruled they should be released. Premises of the company's Belgium-based production arm, Roj NN, were repeatedly searched by Belgian police and its employees held for questioning, but never formally charged.[151] Meanwhile the ITC, encouraged to monitor MED TV content especially closely, warned the station several times that it was breaching the ITC Programme Code and fined it £90,000. In November 1998 the Commis-sion formally notified MED TV that unless it adhered to the Programme Code its licence would be revoked. Six months later the closure came to pass. In March 1999 the station's licence was suspended and it was given three weeks to put its case for remaining open. On 23 April the ITC served notice that it was not convinced: MED TV's service would remain suspended for the 28 days remaining before its licence was finally revoked.[152]

Sarah Thane, the ITC Director of Programmes and Cable, acknowl-edged that the ITC had received complaints about MED TV content from the Turkish authorities but said the decision was prompted by the ITC's own responsibilities under UK law. As evidence, the Commission showed a clip from a MED TV news broadcast reporting a call for action

by Kurds in Europe and Turkey to protest about the Turkish government's seizure of the Kurdish rebel leader, Abdullah Ocalan, in Kenya in
February 1999. According to the ITC transcript, the call for action
warned the 'patriotic masses in Europe' not to cross the 'boundaries of
democratic measures', but urged Kurds in Turkey to 'adopt all kinds of
fighting methods without losing any time'. Thane said it was these 'calls
to direct violence and criminal actions' that breached the ITC code.[153]
Even after MED TV was taken off the air, however, the Turkish authorities kept up the pressure, calling the attention of the UK Foreign Office
to the allegedly pro-Kurdish output of another ITC licensee, Cultural
Television (CTV), based in Essex. CTV's director, David Goodenough,
agreed that, as a producer of 'culturally oriented documentary programming',[154] his company was 'very sensitive' to groups like the Kurds who
have been 'drastically alienated' but he distanced it from MED TV.[155]
The ITC, for its part, dismissed any likelihood of CTV being shut down.

This was not to be the last of Europe-based Kurdish satellite television. A reincarnation, named Medya TV, prompted Senkal Atasagun,
the head of Turkish national intelligence, to speak in late 2000 in favour
of ending the long-standing ban on Kurdish television broadcasts inside
Turkey.[156] Thus both the territorially linked rationale behind MED TV
and Medya TV, and their territorially linked limitations, remained clear.
The project that Kurdish viewers liked to think of as their 'nation in the
sky', may have looked to some like a perfect example of deterritorialization. But it could not operate independently of state-based licensing
regulations in Europe, or of Turkish politics.

## Conclusion

In Appadurai's model of global cultural flow, people, machinery, money,
images and ideas follow increasingly non-isomorphic paths with a speed,
scale and volume so great that the disjunctures between them have
become central to the politics of global culture.[157] This chapter, by
applying the non-state-centric analytical approach advised by Strange[158]
(aimed at discovering who is exercising authority, for what purpose and
by what means), was able to trace the paths travelled by people, machinery, money, images and ideas in relation to some of the leading Middle
Eastern satellite channels launched during the 1990s. In this field it is
self-evident that technology, images and money must follow an isomor-
phic path, since that is both the raison d'être and chief characteristic of
satellite broadcasting. But this chapter has also thrown up striking

evidence of close alignments between people, money and ideas in the
Middle Eastern satellite television sector, held tightly together by the
nature of power relations inside Middle Eastern states. Although many
of the people watching these satellite channels may have been doing so
from outside Middle Eastern territory, and although some channel
owners chose bases outside the region, the exercise of power through the
satellite channels was far from deterritorialized. Accepting the need to
deconstruct the notion of state control does not preclude the possibility
that governments, or their proxies, allies or backers, may prove to be the
chief source of authority over satellite television, as over any other
activity.

Satellite television is often seen as a facet of globalization because, in
an age when people and capital move more freely around the globe, it
has the potential to foster notions of a global community of consumers.
But this is not the only possibility. Transnational television also lends
itself to use for nationalist or nation-building purposes, as demonstrated
in Egypt's case. The Egyptian minister of information, Safwat al-Sharif,
made no secret of his determination to see that Arabic-language satellite
channels would be used to promote 'positive' rather than 'negative'
aspects of Egyptian and Arab society. Official pronouncements such as
these made the umbilical link between the ERTU satellite channels and
government objectives abundantly clear. In the Saudi case there was
greater complexity, because of the sheer number of princes in the Saudi
ruling family and the various ways in which their interests converge and
diverge. Nevertheless, the Al Saud role in each venture maintained a
direct link between it and the exercise of political power and access to
capital inside the kingdom itself. Meanwhile the dominant role adopted
by Lebanon's two private satellite broadcasters, at the expense of the
state-owned Télé-Liban, reflected that country's political system and the
role played in it by foreign governments. Qatar's high-profile experiment
in uncensored satellite television, conducted via Al-Jazeera, was undertaken at the behest of the Qatari emir as part of a top-down campaign of
carving out a distinctive regional niche for his tiny state. The two
London-based operations, ANN and MED TV, came into being as a
direct result of political power struggles, between branches of the
president's family in Syria and between the Turkish government and its
Kurdish opponents. As demonstrated by the financial difficulties of
ANN and the licensing difficulties faced by Kurdish television in exile,
these stations' fortunes could be traced directly to developments inside
Syria and Turkey.

In fact it was precisely the recognition that the study of power should not be confined to governments and politicians that revealed how much power Middle Eastern governments and politicians wielded over the regional satellite channels established in the 1990s. It showed that they used this power in pursuit of their own domestic and foreign policy objectives. It turned up little evidence of the 'disjunctures between economy, culture and politics'[159] so central to the global cultural economy envisaged by Appadurai. In these circumstances it must be questioned how far transnational television in this regional context was either an agent or a symptom of globalization. It looks rather to have provided a novel vehicle for interaction between contenders for power inside and among Middle Eastern states.

# CHAPTER THREE

# Points of Contact between Regional Channels and the Rest

The previous chapter put the case for seeing Middle Eastern satellite channels as inextricably bound up with regional power structures and the politics of individual states. It seems unlikely that this characteristic is unique to channels owned by interest groups with their primary bases in the Middle East, but it is beyond the scope of this book to make comparisons with Western, Asian or Latin American satellite television companies. At issue in the present chapter is the question of whether, in view of the national power struggles and security concerns at play behind the evolution of transnational television in the Middle East, this sector is implicated to any great extent in the spread of interconnected forces and institutions implicit in the term globalization. Conceivably, Middle Eastern satellite channels merely support the thesis that, despite the growth and widespread adoption of new communication technologies in the 1990s, the globalization phenomenon – for all the overtones of universality inherent in the term – actually remained far from global. Such a possibility is implicit in David Held's and Anthony McGrew's view that globalization can be understood as having the two dimensions of intensity and scope. On one hand, they say, the concept has a spatial connotation, in that a multiplicity of linkages and interconnections are becoming 'stretched' further across the globe. On the other, it involves an intensification or deepening of 'interaction, interconnectedness or interdependence' among states and societies in the contemporary world.[1]

An understanding of globalization as a partial and incomplete process is also implicit in those theories that measure interdependence in terms of specific criteria and indices. This is the case with the model of 'complex interdependence' that Robert Keohane and Joseph Nye developed in the 1970s and revisited over the next 20 years. Keohane and Nye challenged realist assumptions about the dominance and coherence of state actors in world politics, and about those actors' preoccupation with defending their territory and interests from real or perceived threats. In doing so they pictured a world in which actors other than states participate directly in world politics, in which a clear hierarchy of issues does not exist and in which force is ineffective as an instrument of policy. They presented these three features as the main characteristics of complex interdependence,[2] and in doing so established criteria for distinguishing different parts of the world from each other.

Across Arab countries, for example, there may be multiple channels of contact at both the formal and informal levels, based on labour migration and financial flows. But it could not be said of the collective Arab agenda in the last part of the twentieth century that there was yet an absence of hierarchy among issues. Security was always dominant, arising from the Arab–Israeli conflict and from Gulf states' long-standing suspicions of Iraq and Iran. As for the third characteristic of complex interdependence, the military option was likewise ever present when it came to resolving Arab territorial disputes. The 1980–88 Iran–Iraq war and Iraq's invasion of Kuwait in 1990 were prominent examples. Summing up their own original model in 1998, Keohane and Nye acknowledged that the concept of complex interdependence, 'in which security and force matter less and countries are connected by multiple social and political relationships' applied only in certain parts of the world.[3] The information revolution had, they said, vastly increased the number of channels of contact between societies. But it had not led to dramatic changes vis-à-vis the two other conditions of complex interdependence, because 'information does not flow in a vacuum but in political space that is already occupied'. Despite the passage of time, Keohane and Nye concluded that, 'outside the democratic zone of peace, the world of states is not a world of complex interdependence'.[4]

A similar dichotomy, between the world of complex interdependence and the world beyond, underlies Robert Cooper's distinction between 'modern' and 'post-modern' states. Cooper argued, in a study published in 1996, that the world had come to be divided quite differently from Cold War days. It was divided into three types of state: pre-modern, modern and post-modern.[5] Analysing changes in Europe since 1989, Cooper saw in the new European order, and in Japan, signs of a post-modern world distinct and separate from the 'old world of state sovereignty in which others do not interfere'.[6] The post-modern world is made up of pluralistic, complex states where the media, individuals, and interest groups, including transnational ones, play a part in determining foreign policy alongside the state.[7] The 'modern' state, in contrast, is characterized by the importance it attaches to state sovereignty and prohibiting external interference in domestic affairs. Pre-modern states, in Cooper's definition, are those where the state is so fragile that it cannot claim a legitimate monopoly on the use of force.[8]

The divisions depicted in these accounts cannot be drawn in bold lines on a map. They are divisions and demarcations that reflect modes of government, security concerns and the intensity of cross-border contacts, all of which are reflected in, and contribute to, the functioning of the media in different settings. Importantly for the present analysis, the demarcations envisaged in these three compatible theories about interconnectedness are neither fixed nor final. On the contrary, global-ization as a process involves the stretching and deepening noted by Held and McGrew.[9] The demarcations thus provide an underlay against which the creation and intensification of cross-border connections can be charted. What is more, they provide indices with which the intensity of contacts can be measured. Keohane and Nye saw coherent and exclusive 'inter-state' relations on the one hand and complex interdependence on the other as two extremes, with most situations likely to fall somewhere between them.[10] On this basis, a high intensity of contacts would mean that transnational non-governmental actors are involved, whereas a low level of intensity would mean contacts are restricted mainly to govern-ments. A further index of intensity can be drawn from Cooper's observation about non-state media 'interference' in policy: high intensity would mean transnational television companies are potentially capable of influencing government policy, whereas low intensity would mean governments still control transnational television.

Newly launched Middle Eastern satellite channels appeared to open up many opportunities for the stretching and deepening of cross-border contacts. No review of such contacts can ever hope to capture more than a glimpse of a much bigger network of relationships. Yet it is reasonable, from those glimpses, to record whether the contacts identified were primarily personal, institutional or governmental; where they started and how far they reached; and how the television business fitted into the wider picture. Drawing on the information about channel ownership already established, it is proposed to start by scrutinizing the transna-tional interests of four prominent channel owners and then to examine programming links between the world's leading media conglomerates and Middle Eastern satellite companies. The focus in this part of the study is on Arab channels.

## Media moguls

As the role of individuals in the restructuring of the Western media industry was documented in the 1980s and 1990s, the term 'media mogul' gained wide currency.[11] The restructuring increased the assets and revenues of certain companies so dramatically that, before the end of the decade, five integrated global media giants (Time Warner, Disney, Bertelsmann, Viacom and News Corporation) clearly dominated the scene.[12] Subsequent deregulation in the USA allowed further mergers and acquisitions, creating even larger conglomerates as CBS and Viacom announced plans to merge in September 1999, while AOL and Time Warner followed suit in January 2000. As the mergers took place they drew attention to the role of individual stakeholders in the merging companies, confirming that the 'older patterns of personal ownership', identified by Graham Murdock a decade earlier,[13] still prevailed. Viacom, for example, was still majority-owned by Sumner Redstone, the world's tenth richest man in 1999,[14] who was expected to remain at the helm of Viacom after its planned merger with CBS. Like Redstone, Rupert Murdoch, owner of News Corporation, gained a reputation for micro-management, travelling constantly to put his personal imprint on the myriad components of his media empire.[15] An element of personalized rivalry or antagonism between heads of different media empires at this time was revealed in comments made about Rupert Murdoch by Ted Turner, the Time Warner vice-chairman who had founded CNN.[16]

The Middle Eastern magnate with the most extensive links to figures like Redstone and Murdoch, when their empires were being consolidated in the 1990s, was Prince Alwaleed bin Talal bin Abdel-Aziz. Owner of Kingdom Holdings Company of Saudi Arabia, Prince Alwaleed was also part owner of the satellite television company Arab Radio and Television (ART) and shareholder, via ART, in the Lebanese Broadcasting Corporation's satellite arm, LBC-Sat. By mid-2000, the prince's investment portfolio in media and telecommunications technology, including stakes in Rupert Murdoch's News Corporation, Silvio Berlusconi's Mediaset and Leo Kirch's Kirch Media, was estimated at $8.2 billion.[17] Ranked by *Forbes* magazine in June 2000 as the sixth richest person in the world (not counting heads of state), Prince Alwaleed was higher up the *Forbes* list than many of the Western company heads he was dealing with at that time. Analysis of Alwaleed's background shows that he was able to build by turns on his status within the Saudi ruling family and his alliances with billionaire Western entrepreneurs to expand his own business empire, maintaining a high media profile for himself as head of his company and cultivating personal contacts in a world where deals are crafted on yachts in the Mediterranean and luxury hotels. While the prince himself frequently emphasized his preference for a life in business rather than in government, his kinship ties to the Saudi monarchy and sense of duty to Saudi Arabia as his home country emerged equally frequently from the many press interviews he gave in 1998–2000.

**Table 6: Media owners' net worth, 2000**

(*Rank refers to Forbes' ranking of the world's richest people*[1])

| Rank | Name | Net worth ($ billion) | Country |
|------|------|------|------|
| 1 | Bill Gates | 60.0 | USA |
| 6 | Prince Alwaleed bin Talal | 20.0 | Saudi Arabia |
| 14 | Silvio Berlusconi | 12.8 | Italy |
| 17 | Sumner M. Redstone | 12.1 | USA |
| 19 | Leo Kirch | 11.5 | Germany |
| 23 | Rupert Murdoch | 9.4 | USA |
| 30 | Ted Turner | 8.3 | USA |
| 112 | Saleh Kamel | 4.0 | Saudi Arabia |
| 137 | Rafiq Hariri | 3.5 | Lebanon |

[1] Excluding heads of state.

Source: *www.forbes.com*, June 2000

Alwaleed's father, Prince Talal, was one of 45 sons born to the founder of Saudi Arabia and thus a half-brother to King Fahd, Crown Prince Abdullah and many other senior members of national and provincial government in the kingdom. Talal's career took a somewhat different path from theirs, however. In the 1950s and 1960s, he championed constitutionalism, representative government and social justice, for which his passport was withdrawn in 1962.[18] He and the three brothers who joined him in the Free Princes movement were later allowed back into Saudi Arabia on condition they refrained from challenging the political status quo.[19] During the 1990s, however, as head of Agfund, a Riyadh-based development agency for Gulf states, Prince Talal became more outspoken on internal Saudi matters. He indicated in foreign press and television interviews in 1999 that he did not support the official Saudi candidate for the post of director-general of the United Nations Educational, Scientific and Cultural Organization (UNESCO) on the grounds that Saudi Arabia could not live up to UNESCO's commitments on human rights and women's rights.[20] These views did not seem to jeopardize his relations with Crown Prince Abdullah, who was at that time taking increasing responsibility for day-to-day government from the ailing King Fahd. On the contrary, Prince Talal was one of 18 members of the Al Saud appointed to a new royal family council established in June 2000.[21] Meanwhile Prince Talal's son, Alwaleed, while declaring himself proud to be a member of the ruling family in Saudi Arabia,[22] expressed reservations similar to those of his father regarding some of the kingdom's social mores, including the ban on women driving.[23]

Prince Alwaleed, then, belongs to an outward-looking and modernizing branch of the very extended ruling family of Saudi Arabia. But, as noted in Chapter 2, he is also partly of Lebanese extraction, his mother being Mona al-Solh, daughter of Lebanon's first prime minister, Riad al-Solh. Born in 1957, he was educated in the USA, gaining a master's degree in social science from Syracuse University in New York, and made his first major overseas investment in Citicorp in 1991, using money accumulated through business and share dealing in Saudi Arabia.[24] After the Citicorp deal, Alwaleed made many diverse investments but his next most publicized deal involved a rescue package for the Disneyland Paris theme park in France, a country where he has other investments and spends much of his leisure time.[25] He approached the leisure group Euro Disney, owned by the Walt Disney Company of the USA, a few days before the company called an extraordinary meeting to announce a refinancing package. A Disney official indicated at the time that the company had already arranged financial restructuring with banks and other parties and that Prince Alwaleed's rescue deal was the prince's own idea.[26] Its outcome was that he acquired a 23.6 per cent stake in Euro Disney, promising to reduce his share to half of the Walt Disney Company's own 39.2 per cent stake in Euro Disney within a year. In September 1995, however, Walt Disney Company agreed to defer this obligation for a further five years.[27]

With the Disney link established, further acquisitions brought Alwaleed into contact with more of the world's biggest media investors. In 1995 he bought a 4.1 per cent stake in the Italian television company, Mediaset, from Fininvest, the holding company of the former Italian prime minister, Silvio Berlusconi, who had left office in December 1994. Berlusconi and Alwaleed reportedly discussed the deal in person at Berlusconi's country house outside Milan on a Sunday in late May 1995.[28] The Italian magnate had earlier held a similar face-to-face meeting with Rupert Murdoch. Also involved in the Mediaset negotiations was Johann Rupert, whose Swiss-based luxury goods conglomerate Richemont was involved in the pay-TV market through its association with the South African company MultiChoice. MultiChoice was the company chosen in the mid-1990s to manage subscriptions for ART,[29] and its M-NET channel was included in the ART bouquets beamed from Nilesat in 1998.[30]

Prince Alwaleed subsequently aligned himself directly with Rupert Murdoch. He declared Murdoch's News Corporation, along with Disney, Viacom and Time Warner, to be one of the 'four big giants' but the only one positioned to benefit from an impending opening of news and entertainment markets in countries such as India and China.[31] On a single day in October 1997 Alwaleed bought a 5 per cent holding in Rupert Murdoch's News Corporation, another similar-sized stake in Netscape, the Internet browser company, and about 1 per cent of Motorola, the satellite and telephone company. Commenting on the purchases, Alwaleed told *Time* magazine that communications, technology, entertainment and news were the future; he described News Corporation as the 'only truly global news and entertainment company'.[32] The prince later worked with Murdoch on a bid to invest in Germany's Kirch group,[33] being himself also poised to take a stake in Kirch Media jointly with Mediaset.[34] His holding in News Corporation was increased to a total value of $800 million in 1999.[35] Meanwhile Netscape was bought by AOL and, in January 2000, AOL merged with Time Warner, making Alwaleed a stakeholder in the biggest ever merger in the USA. In addition to all these involvements, the prince chose in 1998 to invest $200 million in Teledesic, the satellite telecommunications company part-owned by Microsoft's multi-billionaire chairman, Bill Gates. In October 2000, Microsoft in turn negotiated with Rupert Murdoch to buy a stake in the News Corporation satellite television subsidiary, Sky Global Networks.[36] This was in addition to its existing partnership with America's largest satellite broadcaster, DirecTV. One way or another, Prince Alwaleed established links with all eight of the media multi-billionaires listed, besides himself, in Table 6.

Extensive as they were, these investments in media and communications formed only one part of the prince's numerous acquisitions, many of which facilitated tie-ups between Western companies he bought into and other investors – both private and public – in the Middle East. For example, Four Seasons Hotels and Resorts and Mövenpick Hotels and Resorts, both part-owned by Alwaleed, landed important hotel management contracts in the region.[37] The same was true for companies involved in construction and retail. By virtue of these multiple interests, the prince put himself in a position to help others to do deals; in one interview he readily described himself as a 'deal-maker'.[38] 'They call us because we are Saudi and royalty', he explained in another.[39] The record of his manoeuvres, from his support for the Ghanaian government vis-à-vis the private mining company Lonmin,[40] to his $1 billion agricultural investment in the Egyptian government's controversial Toshka development scheme,[41] shows his willingness to do deals both with governments and private entrepreneurs. On one occasion the prince compared his approach to that of international business tycoons and philanthropists such as Warren Buffett and George Soros. He told an interviewer in 1998: 'I'm a billionaire and I'm international – a Buffett, Soros type – yet I'm an Arab and a neighbour. I'll leverage my assets as best I can. I have alliances with everybody and I don't have enemies.'[42] In another interview the prince said his donations to 'Islamic causes' in Saudi Arabia and the Arab world amounted to $100 million a year, supporting 230 charitable institutions in the kingdom alone. He said he had financed the building of 80 mosques in Saudi Arabia and had designs pending for another 30, in addition to having financed and installed electricity power generating units in different parts of the kingdom.[43] To yet another reporter he revealed that he had volunteered proposals for economic and educational reforms in Saudi Arabia, confirmed that he had offered to rebuild Lebanese power plants bombed by Israel and noted that, so far in his career, he had met with more than 40 heads of state.[44] In November 1999 Alwaleed was received in the Oval Office at the White House by the US president, Bill Clinton. He was accompanied on the visit by his son, Prince Khaled ibn Alwaleed, the deputy chairman of Kingdom Holding Company.[45]

As regards the role played by Alwaleed's satellite television investments relative to the multifarious transnational contacts initiated or nurtured through his Kingdom Holding Company, the prince's own candour makes this easy to assess. In one press interview he intimated that his interest in media generally, including transnational television, was the corollary of his high public profile and extensive government and business contacts. He told the Beirut-based monthly, *ArabAd*:

> Media is a powerful investment tool. I realised this fact early on in life and therefore decided to open my doors to all media people, welcome them and establish a very strong rapport with key figures in the industry.

Media helps me pave the way for new investments and strengthens existing ones.[46]

Telling as this is, in terms of the kind of cross-border media contacts
likely to be forged in pursuit of ever-higher returns on privately owned
capital, it is made even more telling by the fact that the expansion of
Prince Alwaleed's media empire in the Middle East did not go unre-
sisted. From 1997 to 1999, the Lebanese publishing house, Dar al-
Sayyad, resisted the prince's claim to a 50 per cent share. The claim was
based on financial support he is said to have given the publishing house.
Dar al-Sayyad, publisher of the daily newspaper *Al-Anwar* and the
political weekly *Al-Sayyad*, finally announced in November 1999 that
Lebanon's Supreme Court had upheld four previous rulings of the Court
of Appeals and Court of First Instance against Alwaleed and his Lebanese mother, Mona al-Solh, and in favour of Dar Al-Sayyad.[47]

Featuring alongside Prince Alwaleed on the same 2000 *Forbes* magazine list of the super-rich was the Lebanese media mogul Rafiq Hariri.
Hariri's wealth, accumulated in part through his contracting company
Saudi Oger, was estimated at $4 billion in 1999 and $3.5 billion in 2000.
In terms of Lebanese-owned satellite television, Alwaleed's alignment
with LBC-Sat put him on a different side of the fence from Hariri's
satellite television company, Future International. On the other hand,
his joint ownership with Hariri of a major Middle East insurance group,
Medgulf Strikers Holding,[48] suggested that the two men's respective
media interests in Lebanon had more to do with a mutually advanta-
geous sharing of the cake than head-to-head competition. Just as
Alwaleed enjoyed the benefits of mixed Saudi–Lebanese parentage,
Hariri could boast dual Saudi and Lebanese nationality. Just as Alwaleed
had a hot line through his father to the Al Saud family council, Hariri
could claim a hot line to King Fahd. It was Hariri who, in 1977, helped
Fahd, while the latter was still crown prince, to build a luxury hotel and
conference centre in Taif in just nine months. The contract for the hotel,
due to become an Intercontinental, had been turned down by other
contractors because of the tight deadline. Rafiq Hariri's Oger company
took up the challenge, finished the work and earned Fahd's lasting
gratitude. Hariri, born in Sidon in Lebanon, gained a Saudi passport.
Saudi Oger was set up and went on to win many more contracts to build
and repair royal palaces.[49] Hariri's son Saad was later to become the
company's general manager.

As is the case with Alwaleed, Hariri's investments and business contacts extend well beyond the Middle East. He acquired the Luxembourg-
based Mediterranée Investors' Group in 1983, which he used to channel
investments into financial institutions inside and outside the Middle
East, over and above his stakes in Arab Bank, Banque Paribas and
Compagnie de Suez.[50] His friendship with the French president, Jacques
Chirac, and the honorary titles he received in France in the 1980s, were
linked by at least one observer to his role in facilitating French involvement in construction work in Saudi Arabia.[51] President Chirac received
Hariri in Paris in January 1999, a few weeks after he had ceased to be
prime minister of Lebanon, a post he had held since 1992. His closeness
to the Syrian government during this period led many to predict that
Hariri would return to power in Lebanon before long and, in 2000, this
prediction was fulfilled. In or out of power, however, his economic
interests continued to straddle the Saudi–Syrian–Lebanese triangle.
When Bashar al-Asad replaced his father as Syrian president in 2000,
Rafiq Hariri's Saudi Oger, together with Saleh Kamel's Dallah Albaraka,
formed half of a four-company consortium offering to invest $100
million in 'opening up' the telecommunications and hotel industries in
Syria.[52] One commentator, considering Hariri's role as broker in Syrian–
Saudi co-operation, said he was

> like a rainbow, with one base in the Saudi desert, another on the Leba-
> nese coast, one face looking east from Syria to Malaysia, another facing
> west from France to America. He is a chess game in his own right, as well
> as being a pawn in a bigger game.[53]

Rafiq Hariri's media interests form an integral part of the chess game, as
can be judged from the dovetailing of his business activities and government responsibilities during his first six years in office. After playing a
central role in the 1990 conference in Taif, Saudi Arabia, that ended the
Lebanese civil war, he became prime minister but did not retire from
business. On the contrary, he took a 7 per cent stake in Solidère, the
company charged with rebuilding downtown Beirut, and encouraged
political and business allies to join him. As a major shareholder in Four
Seasons Hotels and Resorts, Prince Alwaleed bin Talal joined the
Solidère development with plans for a $250 million Four Seasons hotel
and residential complex.[54] With the reconstruction of Lebanon promising large profits but also needing a great deal of faith and foreign loans
and investment, the temptation to suppress negative media coverage of
the Hariri government's policies was strong. Under his premiership,

Hariri's terrestrial television station, Future TV, licensed under Lebanon's 1994 Audiovisual Media Law, was given the mission of promoting Lebanon. Future TV's president, Nadim Munla, said in 1998:

> We are proud to be a channel that promotes Lebanon. We are very keen to portray the real image to other Arab countries. This will make Lebanon stronger and give incentives to people to invest, by telling them that life is back, Lebanon is healthy, there's fun and entertainment and it's beautiful.[55]

Transnational broadcasting was obviously essential to spreading the message about Lebanon to potential investors, tourists and trading partners, as Hariri acknowledged through the creation not only of Future TV's satellite channel, Future International, but also of Radio Orient, a Paris-based venture he managed to acquire in the early 1990s despite the obstacles to foreign media ownership in France at that time. Radio Orient was originally owned by Raghid al-Chammah, a French national of Lebanese origin whose family, like Hariri's, came from Sidon. Chammah and his family were sole owners of Radio Orient until 1993, from which point ownership was gradually transferred to Hariri's Luxembourg-based company, Techniques Audiovisuelles.[56] According to documents and other information gathered by a Lebanese academic, Bassam El Hachem, the transfer was the culmination of a process that had lasted up to ten years. It seems that Hariri had already decided during the early 1980s to launch an international radio station and that he and Chammah had started co-operating well before the date in 1987 when Radio Orient received its official permit to broadcast in France. Hariri reportedly subsidized Radio Orient from that point and took a keen interest in the content of its news bulletins. In 1991 the station applied to the French authorities for permission to increase its capital nine-fold and transfer 90 per cent of its shares to Techniques Audiovisuelles. Permission was granted in 1993.[57]

Radio Orient's affiliate in Lebanon was one of 16 commercial radio stations licensed in 1996 under the 1994 Audiovisual Media Law, obtaining its FM licence in the name of Future TV. But those involved with the station in Lebanon maintained that the Paris base meant that Radio Orient in Lebanon was exempt from local Lebanese programming quota requirements.[58] Radio Orient also became the only Lebanese FM station to cover Syria via its own transmitter right on the Lebanese–Syrian border. Radio Strike, a competing FM popular music station, whose owner benefited from connections to Bashar al-Asad, boosted its transmitters in Lebanon to cover parts of Syria in 1996 but was forced to close 18 months later, after its application for a formal Lebanese licence was denied. Meanwhile Radio Orient enjoyed a privileged relationship with Syria's sole advertising agency, the Arab Advertising Organization, whereby the AAO sold airtime on its behalf. This arrangement indicated to advertisers that Radio Orient was an officially approved medium in Syria.[59] In the circumstances it is not surprising that Radio Orient's management decided voluntarily to do their bit towards observing the Lebanese government's 1998 ban on the televising of local political news by private stations.[60]

Out of office, Hariri continued to use his media companies for political ends. Inaugurating a book fair organized by his charitable foundation in Sidon in February 1999, he warned the new prime minister, Selim al-Hoss, not to put pressure on media that were criticizing the government. Yet only two months later he instructed Future TV and Radio Orient to refrain from broadcasting controversial political programmes and news commentaries.[61] These companies' ambivalent editorial stance was revealed by Maguy Farah, a presenter with Future TV, in an interview with a Lebanese magazine. She declared that she had 'absolute freedom' in her position, but conceded that the link between Future TV and Mr Hariri meant she would be unlikely to host Selim al-Hoss, the current prime minister, on her show.[62] In the ratings war with competing Lebanese terrestrial stations, Future TV was able to rely on substantial funds to outbid other Lebanese stations for rights to sporting and other events. It paid close to $3 million for the right to broadcast Formula One races with Arabic commentary for five years from 2000, challenging Murr TV which had secured the rights in French until the end of 2001.[63]

The same geographic and sectoral diversification of assets that emerges from a study of Rafiq Hariri and Prince Alwaleed is also apparent in the many businesses of Shaikh Saleh Kamel, the majority owner of ART and part owner, through ART's parent company, Arab Media Corporation, of LBC-Sat. Just as Hariri and Alwaleed profited from their economic power and political influence in Saudi Arabia, Lebanon and further afield, Saleh Kamel's power base was built on his manifold interests in Saudi Arabia, Egypt, Lebanon, Jordan and beyond. He began his business career as a contractor in the kingdom in the 1970s. His holding company, Dallah Albaraka, founded in the early 1980s and based in Jeddah, had already grown to cover 30 countries by 1990.[64] By the late 1990s it had accumulated total assets of around $7 billion. Some $4 billion of this was accounted for by the group's financial services division, which had operations in places as far apart as Switzerland, Sudan and Albania.[65] In 1998 the financial division was licensed to set up an offshore holding company in Bahrain to control Dallah Albaraka's worldwide network of banks operating on Islamic banking principles. In addition to this network the group encompassed ventures in manufacturing, trade, shipping, farming and tourism as well as Shaikh Saleh's media holdings.

It is said in some quarters, including by people with no loyalties to Saleh Kamel himself, that Kamel first had the idea that led to the creation of MBC in London in 1991. His involvement in MBC was not to last. His partners in the project, both brothers-in-law of King Fahd, wanted to do things their way. One of them, Walid al-Ibrahim, became the major shareholder and Saleh Kamel was eased out, selling his share for a generous $60 million when he realized the full extent of King Fahd's financial control of the station through his son and Walid al-Ibrahim's nephew, Prince Abdel-Aziz. Saleh Kamel went on to set up ART, but the split ultimately had an effect on MBC's Saudi advertising and public relations company Tihama, in which Saleh Kamel was a major shareholder. Instead of renewing its five-year marketing contract with Tihama when it expired in October 1996, MBC handed the contract to Walid al-Ibrahim's ARA Media Service (AMS), which was already handling media sales for MBC FM.[66] Tihama's profits dipped as the loss of MBC business dented its turnover.[67] In 1999 the company's Jeddah operations were restructured and put under the executive control of Antoine Choueri,[68] whose Beirut-based Choueri Group was handling advertising for LBC. ART was to be a different business from MBC, however, placing less emphasis on advertising and aiming to rely on subscription revenue. The received wisdom inside the company held that the total value of Middle East advertising would scarcely support one satellite station, let alone several. On this basis ART channels were pitched at an audience of Arabic-speaking professionals occupying a market segment just one notch below the elite of affluent English-speakers targeted by Orbit.[69] In contrast to the large number of Orbit channels supplied by Star TV and others, ART limited its non-Arabic material to input from Cartoon Network/TNT. One of Saleh Kamel's early moves was to acquire the rights to a sizeable library of old Egyptian films.[70]

Within five years of its establishment, ART, jointly owned by Prince Alwaleed and Saleh Kamel, could claim in its publicity brochures that its production and broadcast facilities spanned the globe, 'from Tennessee to Tunis'. Its multiple channels were being beamed to Europe, the Middle East, America and Latin America, Asia and Australia by 11 satellites. Its 'nerve-centre' at Avezzano in Italy contained a 24-hour production facility with ten digital studios, edit suites and a range of equipment capable of handling more than 50 separate satellite signals simultaneously to broadcasters around the world. This capacity gave Saleh Kamel a bargaining chip in dealings with several other Arab satellite broadcasters. It helps, for example, to explain his role in LBC-Sat. The fact that ART was able to handle the relay of an encrypted version of the Egyptian Space Channel and the specialized Nile Drama Channel from Avezzano[71] is also likely to have been significant in terms of the company's extensive presence in Egypt. The Avezzano complex was said to be complemented by offices in three European cities (Paris, Rome and Dusseldorf), eight Arab cities (Amman, Beirut, Cairo, Damascus, Dubai, Jeddah, Riyadh and Tunis) and one in the USA, namely Tennessee. With the easing of Libya's international isolation in 1999, following agreement on the trial of two Libyans suspected of involvement in the bombing of a PanAm flight over Lockerbie in Scotland in 1987, ART also made arrangements to open an office in Tripoli. This was said to be warranted by the large number of Libyan subscribers receiving the ART service by cable. The move into Libya was somewhat in keeping with the 1st Net brand which ART sought to establish for its digital bouquet of channels. The name 1st Net was intended to reflect the idea that ART was a trendsetter in the Arab world, creating channels that were all the first of their kind in some way. When subscribers became confused about the relationship between the 1st Net and ART brands, the former was played down.[72]

Of all the ART offices, Saleh Kamel appeared particularly committed to those in Egypt. His wife, the Egyptian actress Safa' Abu Soud, became a presenter of ART shows. Kamel also appointed Milad Bisada, an Egyptian Copt, to take charge of the station's live shows and variety programmes. Viewers noted the prominence of Egyptian presenters on ART channels, remarking that, when ART talkshows focused on social issues they tended to be issues related to Egypt rather than Saudi Arabia or the Gulf.[73] At one point the growing number of personnel from Egypt's state broadcaster, the ERTU, who were moonlighting for MBC and ART so irked the Egyptian information minister, Safwat al-Sharif, that he and the ERTU director, Abdel-Rahman Hafez, were moved to launch a policy they dubbed 'media nationalism'. By this they meant that Egyptian media personnel should apply their talents for the benefit of the Egyptian rather than the Saudi media and stop using ERTU facilities to make programmes for Saudi broadcasters.[74] It also seems that an attempt by Saleh Kamel to buy into Media Production City, a complex of film and television studios built by the Egyptian government near Cairo, was rebuffed. The result was an expansion of ART facilities in Beirut, under the direction of two Lebanese producers, the brothers Fouad and Ahmad al-Achi, and in Amman, where senior staff were recruited from the state broadcaster, Jordan Radio and Television,[75] and studio facilities hired from the 51 per cent state-owned Jordan Company for Television, Radio and Cinema Production.

Saleh Kamel nevertheless continued to strengthen ART's presence in Egypt, locating ART's worldwide marketing office in Cairo and spending $19 million to build five six-storey units at the company's Kafr al-Nassar centre, near Media Production City. These were to be leased to other television companies operating in Egypt as well as ART.[76] As a major employer of graduates in television production from the Egyptian Cinema Institute and the American University (AUC) in Cairo, and an important source of 'moral and financial support' to AUC's Adham Center for Television Journalism, Shaikh Saleh was named an associate of the Center.[77] He was also able to have ART accepted as a cable and satellite broadcaster in France in mid-1997, after two years of negotiations with the French regulatory body, the Conseil supérieur de l'audiovisuel (CSA).[78] This agreement was reached about a year after the Egyptian Space Channel became the first Arab satellite channel to do what one French journalist described as 'pierc[ing] the defences of a suspicious CSA'.[79] The CSA's decision to authorize cable distribution of carefully selected Arabic-language channels followed a rapid increase in the installation of very large satellite dishes by Arabic-speaking immigrants in France. This had alarmed the French authorities, who interpreted the immigrants' desire to receive non-French television programming as an affront to the country's policy of culturally assimilating immigrant communities. It had also fuelled concerns about the rise of Islamist militancy in France. ART's negotiations with the CSA were conducted by a Tunisian film producer, Tarek Ben Ammar, manager of Prince Alwaleed bin Talal's investments in the Italian company Mediaset, and designated editorial director of ART's operations in France.[80] The five-channel ART package for subscribers in France was launched on the all-digital Télévision par Satellite (TPS) service in May 1997.

In 1998 ART studios in different capitals were put to use on behalf of the Rome-based UN agency, the Food and Agriculture Organization

(FAO), to broadcast a global Arab satellite fund-raising 'telethon'. The eight-hour event, arranged to encourage viewers to donate money to farmers in low-income Arab and Muslim countries, was aired from Cairo, Beirut and Rome, with ART centres in Cairo, Jeddah and Dubai working in tandem with FAO telephone lines in Rome and the USA to take callers' pledges of aid. The initiative arose from an approach made by FAO to ART in 1997 in the context of FAO's TeleFood '98 campaign. Preparations for the event were delayed somewhat when Saleh Kamel underwent emergency treatment in a specialist cardiology unit in the south of France in the summer of 1998.[81] When they got under way about six weeks before the event, ART presenters and producers worked hard to publicize the issues as well as the work of the FAO and to enlist the support of Arab celebrities, diplomats and intellectuals.

In staging a telethon, ART was emulating not only the many events in this genre held in the West, but was also following in the footsteps of MBC. MBC had organized its first telethon for Bosnia in 1993, at a time when many Arabs and Muslims were feeling frustrated that governments seemed to be doing very little on this foreign policy front.[82] Despite his departure from MBC, Saleh Kamel avoided presenting ART as a competitor to MBC, not least by staying out of the business of broadcasting news. He remained linked with MBC's chairman, Walid al-Ibrahim, via the SARAvision MMDS (wireless cable) project for Saudi Arabia, which was planned to carry ART channels. ART's and MBC's different business orientations were soon evident, however, in terms of geography, management and programming strategy. In contrast to ART's production presence in Arab capitals, MBC made its name as part of a conglomerate with major elements located in the USA and UK. Shaikh Walid's personal empire, while apparently backed by King Fahd's personal fortune of some $28 billion,[83] is based on his ARA Group International Holding Company. He acquired United Press International (UPI) at a Bankruptcy Court auction in New York in 1992, owns ANA Radio and Television, distributing Arabic-language news and information from Washington DC, and part-owns Spectrum 558 AM, a radio station serving London and south-east England.[84]

Soon after its inception, MBC was made available terrestrially in Bahrain through the good offices of the head of Bahraini television and under-secretary at the Bahraini Information Ministry, Hala Omran. In 1996, when a new Bahraini information minister made personnel changes in his ministry, Walid al-Ibrahim appointed Omran as managing director of MBC. Omran, a graduate of the American University in

Beirut, stayed in the post for two years. In early 1998, however, with MBC's owners anxious to cut costs and boost revenue, a new British managing director took over and set about arranging redundancies for about a third of the company's staff. This 'down-sizing' exercise was on a scale familiar in the UK but not at all familiar in the Arab world. The staff reductions were not the only changes instituted by Ian Ritchie. As recounted in Chapter 2, he hired two British colleagues to oversee marketing and news and production and set about boosting the proportion of entertainment in MBC's schedules. One move, which institutionalized contacts with the UK and US entertainment industry, was to increase the output of popular music and gameshows. The Pepsi Muzika chart show, adapted from the worldwide Pepsi Chart programme format, was introduced in June 1999, aimed directly at teenagers interested in both Arabic songs and Western pop groups.[85] In a bid to maximize ratings during Ramadan of 1998/99, MBC turned to the UK company Action Time to produce Arabic versions of formats that had proved successful with UK audiences, including *Spellbound*, *Wipeout* and *Hilarious Hits*. MBC's link-up with Action Time (a Carlton subsidiary) apparently fitted in well with the latter's aim of extending its gameshow licensing and production activities beyond Europe and some Asian countries, including India and Japan.[86] While the presenters for these shows on MBC obviously had to be Arabic speakers, the executive producer for all three was a non-Arab.[87] The programming trend established by Ritchie continued after he left MBC in 2000; in November that year MBC proudly announced that it had secured the exclusive Arabic rights to another Western gameshow, *Who Wants To Be a Millionaire*. The deal was signed with the owners of the format, Celador.[88]

The signing of contracts with companies like Action Time and Celador marks a good point at which to stop and review the characteristics of contacts forged between Arab satellite channels and interest groups based outside the Middle East. The picture emerging from the account presented here is one of links between big business conglomerates that were driven primarily by links between individuals. On the Middle Eastern side, each media mogul is seen to have been the prime mover in expanding his network of media holdings within and beyond the region. There was no evidence of a concerted Western media invasion of the Middle East via the channels established by these entrepreneurs. The outward expansion process certainly seems to qualify spatially as a form of 'stretching', to use the terminology adopted by Held and McGrew.

Interestingly, however, the stretching is seen to have encountered resistance, both inside and outside the Arab world. As to measuring the depth or intensity of contacts in terms of whether the main players were government or non-government actors, each of the four business empires examined demonstrated just how closely government and private business interests can be intertwined. This type of interpenetration casts doubt on the social 'depth' of the cross-border relationships established. It points instead to concentration of resources and collaboration among members of a super-rich elite.

## The CNN factor

If Arab media moguls were pushing the boundaries of their empires outwards, what about traffic coming the other way? The investors in question may have had certain rationales for creating television company structures, but these structures in turn created their own imperatives, in the sense that airtime had to be filled. Tangible outcomes of those imperatives represent another facet of cross-border contact, one usually addressed within the discourse of cultural globalization. The problem with the literature on cultural globalization is its tendency to lose focus, seeing certain cultural forms and styles as the 'hybrid' products of multidirectional cultural flows. The hybrids in question are then conveniently said to belong to 'no particular locality'.[89] While there is every advantage in being alert to multidirectional influences, there is also a danger, in overemphasizing notions of hybridization, of losing sight not only of the source of programmes and programme models but also of the interest groups who promote or adopt them. In other words, the fact that cultural globalization may indeed be a two-way process does not mean that power relations involved in the process cannot be traced.

This much has been demonstrated by Western-owned media conglomerates. News Corporation and the Walt Disney Company were prepared, in their eagerness to do business in the vast Chinese market, to adjust their programming to accommodate Chinese government sensitivities. Rupert Murdoch pulled BBC news services from his Star TV network in 1994 and was given permission to start a cable TV station in the Chinese province of Guangdong.[90] Michael Eisner, chairman of the Disney group, met senior officials in Beijing in October 1998 for talks aimed at overcoming problems caused in China by a Disney film based on a Tibetan theme.[91] Examples such as these lend a less than comforting meaning to words like 'indigenization' and 'hybridization'. John

Tomlinson has homed in on the problem of specifying 'the cultural' when the media are studied within a wider context of political and economic domination. He points out that the discourse of media imperialism 'often tugs back to one of economic domination, in which the specific moment of the cultural seems forever to recede'.[92] Perhaps one way to capture the specific cultural moment, without losing sight of the political and economic context, is to track the editorial choices made in the establishment of Arab satellite channels and to unpack any hybridization perceived to be at work. An undertaking on these lines might also uncover further evidence of the 'stretching' and 'deepening' by which globalization proceeds. In what follows, the part played by CNN in triggering and sustaining the Arab satellite revolution is assessed.

When academics study CNN they are often attracted by what has come to be known as the 'CNN effect'.[93] Philip Taylor, for example, remarks that, by 'providing a public forum to the traditionally secretive world of diplomacy', CNN appeared during the 1991 Gulf war to be 'quite simply changing the rules of international politics'.[94] In comparison with this assertion, CNN's effect on Middle Eastern media was just a sideshow. But it was an important sideshow nonetheless. Chapter 1 recounted how CNN's live international broadcasts from Baghdad during the 1990–91 Gulf crisis marked a turning point not only in establishing the genre of 24-hour satellite television news but in bringing Middle Eastern viewers' dissatisfaction with terrestrial television news coverage to a head. Unlike the BBC, which undertook to supply an Arabic news service to the Saudi-owned pay-TV station Orbit, CNN apparently rejected the idea of tailoring a Middle East news service for Saudi-owned satellite channels because of the potential political difficulties.[95] In the absence of CNN in Arabic, Arab broadcasters felt compelled to produce a replica. MBC in particular was explicit about wanting an Arabic version of CNN.[96] Explaining why stations serving the Middle East would want to follow the CNN formula, Sami Raffoul, general manager of the Pan-Arab Research Centre in Dubai said:

> CNN came on the scene presenting 'pure, untainted, spontaneous' news, with a disclaimer clearly attached to pictures saying they were unedited. They were telling people to see and make their own judgement. The public found this unusual. It was unprecedented for them to be asked to use their own powers of interpretation. It was a turning point.[97]

In the Middle East audience CNN found an intense hunger for reliable, up-to-date regional news. This appetite had been growing for at least two generations through a combination of regional crises related to the Arab–Israeli conflict and superpower involvement and a lack of uncensored information generated locally. In the decade and a half following the October war of 1973, the practice of sampling a range of foreign radio stations and other different news sources in order to piece together an understanding of current events may have subsided somewhat. During the Gulf war of 1991 it resumed with a vengeance. With the discovery that, through CNN, viewers could see breaking news stories covered on screen, the context for all Arab print and broadcast media changed. Having sampled this impression of spontaneity and immediacy in political and economic news broadcasts, it seems Gulf viewers wanted it in lifestyle programming too.[98] From the beginning, the MBC schedule was publicized as containing not just news, religious programming and television drama but coverage of 'fashion, money, sport, health and tourism'.[99]

Just as the proliferation of Arab satellite channels was driven by the copycat syndrome, whereby governments felt compelled to respond to the use of the new medium by outsiders and then by each other, the same happened with the model of the 24-hour news channel. Ted Turner, the American who launched CNN in the USA in 1980 on the back of Turner Advertising, the family firm, said himself that the idea of a 24-hour global news network was 'uncharted waters'. But, he told an interviewer in 1999, 'when I saw we were going to make it, we started spreading all over the world, like a virus'.[100] The virus was catching. Similarity between the names of Arab News Network (ANN) and CNN is no coincidence. Qatar's Al-Jazeera was set up to specialize in news and current affairs, while Egypt created Nile News as one of the Nile Thematic Channels. Hassan Hamed, executive director of the Nile Thematic Channels, cited CNN as a benchmark when he told a reporter in 1997: 'We know that news is very expensive and we cannot think of becoming CNN overnight. So I expect us to be as CNN was when it first started broadcasting.'[101] In reaching agreement with the BBC for an Arabic news service, it is believed that Orbit originally intended the service to develop into a 24-hour operation.[102] But while models are one thing, actual content is another. The BBC Arabic service was kept to only eight hours per day and was then axed because of disagreements over news stories about Saudi Arabia. Despite this, Orbit's management acknowledged that the rationale for running an Arabic-language all-news channel had not gone away.[103] MBC similarly had to wrestle with assumed demand for non-stop news and the editorial dilemmas involved in such a project. It originally planned to include an all-news channel in the bouquet it was to have distributed via the SARAvision or Al-Rawwad wireless cable network in Saudi Arabia. It was only in 1998, after the viewing public had become familiar with the controversial Al-Jazeera, that the MBC news channel was dropped. An insider suggested at the time that the choice of news headlines presented MBC's management with too great a headache, because of the potential for disapproval on the part of King Fahd and his ministers.[104] He also indicated that the management might be waiting to see how long Al-Jazeera would survive without making obvious editorial compromises.

It was not just the model of 24-hour news that set a standard for Arab satellite channels to follow. There was also a certain style of no-nonsense, live delivery. This was even more challenging for Middle Eastern journalists subject to tight censorship constraints. Studies of the effects of CNN presentation on Egyptian state television news bulletins after the Gulf war suggested that only minor, cosmetic changes had resulted. Mahmoud Sultan, head of news readers for the ERTU in 1991, said CNN's style had been expected to influence ERTU news output but, in the end, the ERTU was 'still using slow rhythm, long introductions, unneeded shots', with the order of news items the same in the early 1990s as it was in 1960. Despite the supposed impact of CNN, he said, 'we never go straight to the point'.[105] Nevertheless there was a recognition that CNN's captivating live reports had to be emulated in some way if local stations were to keep their audience. According to Sami Raffoul of PARC, the CNN style 'filtered down to news reels of all stations in the region, whether state-owned, terrestrial or whatever ... The *Larry King Live* genre of talkshow [was] replicated and reinvented locally.'[106] Indigenization of this genre offers an insight into the extent to which the stretching and deepening of globalization via satellite television was assisted by CNN and both assisted and resisted in the Middle East.

The first local version of *Larry King Live* was shown in January 1996 by Orbit on its in-house *Al-Thania* channel. The initiative, launched before Orbit's split with the BBC, suited the company's bid to boost its audience against competition in the pay-TV market. Imad Eddin Adeeb, editor-in-chief of the Egyptian *Al-Aalam al-Yowm* (The World Today), was chosen to host the talkshow, which was given the title *Aala al-Hawa* (On the Air). Adeeb identified himself as an opponent of media censorship.[107] The guests on his show included Binyamin Netanyahu after he became Israeli prime minister, and the Libyan leader, Muammar Qaddafi. The programme format encouraged viewers to phone in and ask questions – apparently freely – without giving their names. The scale of the experiment should not be overestimated, given that Orbit channels were available only to paying subscribers, not all of whom were living in the Middle East and who still at that stage numbered in the tens of thousands. Around 18 months after the start of Aala al-Hawa, a maximum of 75,000 subscribers were paying the $600 a year needed to receive Orbit's basic package.[108] Nevertheless, Orbit's chief executive, Alexander Zilo, was convinced that his station's competitors were watching the programme. Drawing explicit parallels between Aala al-Hawa and Larry King Live, and noting that both shows had brought out the copycat tendency among Arab satellite channels, Zilo told one interviewer in 1997:

> We launched the region's first Larry King-type show with live call-ins; now everyone's trying to produce one ... We're planning innovative programming new to the region ... no doubt within three months of our production somebody else will adopt the same concept.[109]

Zilo was referring to Al-Jazeera. As the latter increased its hours on air during 1997, it adopted the live talkshow genre enthusiastically, launching examples such as Al-Ittijah al-Muaakis (The Opposite Direction) and Akthar min Ra'i (More than One Opinion). These steered clear of discussions to do with Qatar but enraged governments elsewhere in the region by giving airtime to opposition activists, from Bahraini dissidents and Polisario guerrillas to members of the Palestinian Islamist resistance movement in Gaza and so on. Anecdotal evidence suggests that word-of-mouth recommendations about these talkshows were a major factor in the spread of satellite access, especially in Lebanon, as households arranged satellite connections specifically to watch political discussions on Al-Jazeera. One veteran media researcher cited the example of an interview conducted with the Iraqi foreign minister, Tariq Aziz, by Al-Jazeera's Sami Haddad, as a kind of television not previously seen on Arabic-language channels or CNN. When Larry King interviewed Aziz, some Arab viewers familiar with Western media interview techniques felt Aziz had been treated too kindly. Haddad, in contrast, by virtue of his wide personal knowledge of Arab politics and the unprecedented editorial room for manoeuvre allowed to him by Al-Jazeera's management, was perceived to be far more challenging.[110] The editorial licence enjoyed by Al-Jazeera presenters was not unlimited, however. In one incident in April 1997, Rachid Ghannouchi, a Tunisian opposition figure living in London, was suddenly cut off while contributing by telephone to the regular Al-Jazeera programme *Al-Sharia w'al-Hayat* (Sharia [Islamic law] and Life). Later investigation of the event suggested that the Qatar authorities had intervened after Tunisian government officials made urgent telephone protests to the Qatari embassy in London while the programme was still on air.[111]

With Orbit and Al-Jazeera having demonstrated that talkshows in the *Larry King Live* genre could attract audiences, others also followed suit in their own way. At its launch in May 1997, ANN said it intended to debate socio-economic issues ignored by other Arab media, such as housing, education, children, marital problems and other Arab social phenomena.[112] The salient feature of the live talkshow, however, is not necessarily its subject matter but the fact that it is broadcast live, thereby reducing the opportunities for censorship. This was the nub for ERTU producers who were urged by their government in 1998 to match the 'liveliness' of the Orbit and Al-Jazeera programmes but without necessarily broadcasting live. One Egyptian writer and broadcaster, whose own programme on Egyptian terrestrial television was terminated in 1995 after it irked the powers-that-be, found himself on air again thanks to satellite stations such as Orbit and Al-Jazeera. By mid-1998 it appears Egyptian television had asked him to return.[113] One solution presenting itself to the ERTU was to test out the live talkshow on its English-language satellite channel, Nile TV. In early 1999 Video Cairo Sat, the private Egyptian company which had been filming *Aala al-Hawa* for Orbit, found itself with a new contract, to film three live shows per week for Nile TV.[114]

By restricting the new format to a small, mostly expatriate, audience, the ERTU, like all but one of the other broadcasters considered here, demonstrated that the CNN stimulus would not be permitted to penetrate all parts of the Middle East with equal ease. Thus it can be argued that a phenomenon we may call the 'CNN factor', as distinct from the 'CNN effect', contributed to the spread of certain foreign broadcasting practices among Arab satellite channels. Yet the result was a hybridization in which two separate sets of traits were still clearly visible. Or – to mix metaphors – to the extent that non-traditional practices were resisted, adapted or manipulated in accordance with political priorities, a form of local immunity was developed to the globalizing 'virus' of CNN.

## Supply chains

A third window onto business relationships and programme formats linking Arab satellite channels to foreign media is provided by pro-gramme supply deals. The aim here is not to provide a compendium of contracts but to locate a few of the main interconnections between major sellers and buyers of satellite and cable television programmes. Not surprisingly, perhaps, a trawl through the trade press reveals the chief sources of supply to be four of the world's biggest media conglomerates: AOL Time Warner, Disney, News Corporation and Viacom. CNN, merged into Time Warner in 1996 and thus into AOL Time Warner in 2000, struck a deal with the ERTU in 1990 to supply Egypt's cable network. When Orbit and Future TV started up in the mid-1990s they looked to Disney. Meanwhile News Corporation's Star TV signed up in September 1996 to supply a tailored package of channels exclusively to Orbit, launched under the name Star Select in January 1997. Viacom created the Showtime bouquet in partnership with the Kuwait Invest-ment Projects Company (KIPCO) in mid-1996. It had already by that time established a presence on Egyptian cable via its music channel, MTV.

Cable Network Egypt, launched in January 1991, a month after the start of the Egyptian Space Channel, was the direct outcome of a plan to make CNN available to tourists and other foreigners in Egypt before satellite dishes became commonplace. It was originally a private initiative on the part of a small local group of entrepreneurs, including Abdullah Schleifer,[115] former Middle East bureau chief for NBC News and co-founder of the Adham Center for Television Journalism at AUC. Schleifer later became a consultant to Saleh Kamel of ART. Schleifer's group made contact with executives of CNN International in the summer of 1988 and gained CNN support for an approach to the Egyptian government. As it happened, the ERTU proved ready to contemplate using its own spare channel capacity to send CNN as an encrypted signal not only to hotels for the benefit of foreign tourists, but to other consumers as well. Preliminary agreement was reached in October 1989 for an entity called Cable News Egypt to be licensed to receive and distribute the CNN news service in Cairo. However, instead of the ERTU holding a 40 per cent stake in Cable News Egypt, as initially envisaged, it insisted on keeping control with a 50 per cent share. The chairman of the ERTU board consequently doubled as chairman of CNE, with the remaining seven members of the CNE board of directors including four from the ERTU.[116]

The licensing agreement subsequently signed by the Egyptian government with CNE and CNN in June 1990 provided explicitly for reception of the CNN satellite signal in Giza and direct transmission from the Moqqatam area of Cairo without censorship of any sort.[117] CNE was to pay CNN 20 per cent of gross sales during the first four years of the contract and 25 per cent of gross sales during the final four years.[118] The contract was renewed in 1999.[119] The ERTU seems to have been attracted to the arrangement by the promise of income from subscriptions charged for the CNE service. Egyptian subscriptions were not expected to be particularly numerous, since the fee for Egyptian households was set at £E 360 per year, at a time when the average wage was below £E 2500 per year.[120] Instead the prime target market consisted of individual foreigners, hotels and embassies, banks and international organizations with offices in Cairo. Besides the prospect of an additional source of income for the state broadcasting institution, the government was also attracted by a promise from CNN of some free advertisements for the Egyptian Ministry of Tourism and the satisfaction of knowing that foreign tourists in Egyptian hotel rooms would no longer feel cut off from the outside world.[121]

In the event, while the free advertisements were forthcoming, subscription revenue fell well below budget. More than a year passed after the preliminary agreement of October 1989 before the CNE service started. When it did start, it was rushed out suddenly, days ahead of the start of the Gulf war on 15 January 1991, before preparations to encrypt the signal, market the decoders or collect subscriptions had been completed.[122] Instead of bringing in money, the service was provided free for two and a half months to all televisions in the Cairo area. At the same time, instead of providing normal international news updates for tourists, the service provided round-the-clock coverage of the war. When arrangements to operate the paying service were finally in place several months later, the war to end the Iraqi occupation of Kuwait was over and the spread of satellite dishes across the region had begun, making CNN available without subscription. Thus the main beneficiary of CNE in its first phase was no doubt CNN, which had become a household name across the Middle East through its coverage of the war – coverage that had been brought to Egyptian households courtesy of the ERTU. As for the subscribers who paid for the encrypted CNE service when it finally started up on 1 August 1991, they numbered well short of 3000, representing a mere fraction of the 60,000–100,000 expected by the ERTU's chairman at that time and hardly sufficient to cover the start-up costs.[123]

Although the link with CNN provided the original rationale for the creation of CNE, it is pertinent to a debate about the globalizing effects of satellite television to note that the initial connection to CNN turned out to be a springboard to interaction with several other outside interest groups. When CNE's encrypted service, consisting exclusively of CNN, failed to attract subscribers in the two years after its launch, it was decided that the only way to boost sales was to add an entertainment and/or a sports channel. Viacom's MTV, Music Television, the channel started for cable distribution in the USA in 1981, was added to the CNE package on 1 May 1993, reportedly bringing in 1400 new subscriptions to the service in six months.[124] These were mainly from Egyptians rather than expatriates. The thoroughly Western material carried on MTV, which caters mainly to people in their teens and twenties, was not the kind that had originally been envisaged as suitable when CNE was formed. Nevertheless, the evident popularity of MTV among young Egyptians was not lost on the other pay-TV operators, ART and Orbit, who subsequently introduced Arabic music channels of their own.[125] As for the CNE package, it continued with just two channels until June 1994. At that point the company added a third in the form of Kuwait Television, for which it received an annual fee of $1 million but attracted few additional subscribers.

The wholesale relaunch of CNE finally took place in November 1994, after a contract had been signed with the South African giant MultiChoice, to take charge of reconfiguring the package, promoting it and collecting subscriptions. This it did through a subsidiary, Multi-Choice Egypt, which MultiChoice regarded as 'the first step' in its expansion into the Middle East and North African market.[126] Announcing the deal with MultiChoice, the CNE chairman, Amin Bassiouny, said it had come about because CNE needed more channels and better encryption technology.[127] Channels added to the package included MultiChoice's own 24-hour film channel M-Net, a 24-hour sports channel called SuperSports International, together with Showtime Egypt, which came from the same source as MTV. Non-paying subscribers were cut off and new decoders introduced at lower prices. Satellite services were added to the terrestrial cable bouquet, enabling the addition of some encrypted channels from ART and Showtime, although there was a hiccup in this operation when ART abruptly switched from Panamsat to

Arabsat in August 1997.[128] This sudden shift meant that Showtime and ART could not be received together until nearly a year later, when both hired transponders on Nilesat. Despite the interruption, Khalid Abu Nuwar, general manager of MultiChoice Egypt, was able to report a five-fold increase in the subscriber base in the four years from the beginning of 1995 to the end of 1998.[129] This represented a total of some 20,000 decoders.

The Egyptian government effectively put its weight behind the MultiChoice marketing drive by imposing a ban on imported decoders other than those authorized by the ERTU. The ban, which also included a ban on advertisements for decoders, was announced by the Council of Ministers in July 1995 on the grounds that Law No 13 of 1979 entrusted the ERTU alone with all matters to do with radio and television transmission so as to 'preserve and safeguard society's values, ethics and traditions'.[130] Various explanations were later suggested for the decoder ban. Some said it was an attempt to halt the circulation of decoders able to pick up the Turkish subscription channel Cine 5, known for its late night erotic programming.[131] Others saw it as 'priming the market' for the impending arrival of digital services from Nilesat, which was ordered in 1995 and originally due for launching in 1997.[132] Yet another possible reason was reaction to competition from new arrivals on the pay-TV market, since both ART and Orbit had started up in 1994.[133] Whatever its motivation, the ban kept Orbit's Scientific Atlanta decoder officially off the market, keeping the field clear for CNE. In other words the authorities alternately accelerated and slowed the intensification of transnational link-ups resulting from the existence of satellite and cable channels. While the CNE initiative, itself a reaction to the global spread of CNN, developed a momentum of its own, based on financial imperatives and drawing in a widening circle of non-government players, the ERTU did not allow the momentum to go unchecked.

The ERTU was not alone in struggling to assemble a viable package of cable channels. As already argued in Chapter 2, Arab satellite channels were not started for business reasons. There was certainly no surfeit of existing Arabic-language television programmes waiting to be aired. When channel representatives met in Amman for a five-day conference in October 1997, it did not take them long to conclude that the problem was not what to screen but how to build up stocks of programmes.[134] The switch to digital technology in the mid-1990s exacerbated the programming gap, since most broadcasters calculate that they have to fill 7000 hours per year for every channel they run. If this figure is compared with the output of the Egyptian film industry in the mid-1990s, the dearth of local content can be assessed, as Egypt has traditionally accounted for around three-quarters of Arab films. From 96 films made in 1986 the number of Egyptian films dwindled to 76 in 1993 and a mere 22 in 1995, the lowest figure since the 1920s.[135] Executives seeking to fill their channels had the choice of commissioning new material or teaming up with other content providers, or both. The former option favoured vertically integrated companies (whether in the public or private sector) with interests ranging from production and advertising sales through to programme distribution. The latter option favoured bulk deals with global media giants such as Disney and Viacom. After Orbit started up in 1994 and Showtime followed in 1996, contracts followed thick and fast to secure access to Western content and Arabize existing Western shows. These were interspersed with a few specially commissioned programmes, particularly during the fasting month of Ramadan and the holiday period at the end of it. Thus news that the pay-TV operators had supply contracts with the distributors of American series such as *Ricki Lake*, or *ER* or *Friends* was mixed with items about Orbit showing the Syrian-made serialized television drama *Khan al-Harir* or organizing its annual four-day live musical extravaganza, the Arabic Song Festival. Showtime's contribution was a weekly one-hour music programme, called *Mashaweer* (Errands), aimed at an Arab audience. Described as MTV 'with an Arabic feel',[136] *Mashaweer* was produced in Beirut, and later also in Cairo. It consisted of half an hour of Arabic music and video clips and half an hour of music from other origins.[137]

Overall, the bulk of Orbit's channels were obtained from Star TV, based in Hong Kong. In fact Orbit's chief executive, Alexander Zilo, was one of the early associates of Star's founder, Richard Li, before Li sold the network to Rupert Murdoch's News Corporation in 1994. Zilo brought with him the benefit of Star's experience of starting up a digital subscription service and was able to draw on the direct co-operation of Star personnel in getting Orbit on the air.[138] The co-operation continued, with the Star Select package of six, and then nine, channels launched exclusively on Orbit in 1997. This included Star Movies, Star Sports, CNBC, Sky News and Fox Kids Network. Meanwhile Zilo took great pains in press interviews to stress Orbit's Middle Eastern identity, saying that the company wanted to be 'close to its market'. He cited this as one factor behind Orbit's decision to move some of its production activities to Cairo, where it took out a lease on a suite of studios in Egypt's Media Production City in May 1998.

Orbit also negotiated a five-year agreement with Disney, which came into effect in 1997, providing a Disney channel tailored to an Arab audience.[139] At the same time, the inclusion of ESPN Sports in the Orbit package represented a tie-up with Disney, as owner of the ESPN brand. Future TV likewise ensured a steady supply of Disney material, signing a $4 million deal to cover rights on Future's satellite channel in 1996 and agreeing a five-year deal with Disney-owned Buena Vista International in 1998 to supply Walt Disney programmes to the year 2003.[140] As a company associated with family entertainment, Disney seemed an ideal source of material for Middle East satellite channels concerned to observe strict guidelines on programme content. The Disney company's aim has been to maximize its 'universe of subscribers' by producing material that can 'cross nationalities and age groups'.[141] At the same time it was ready to dub in Arabic to achieve regional sales.[142] For Disney, meanwhile, the Middle East market had much to offer. The very high proportion of under-15s in the region makes it a potentially lucrative market for merchandizing of Disney-related products, which forms a major part of Disney group activities.[143] Disney officials estimated in 1999 that the $100-million-worth of annual product sales achieved in the Middle East at the end of the decade could be increased more than five-fold, to exceed $500 million a year in the Gulf region alone by 2005.[144] This growth was jeopardized in the summer of 1999 when Arab governments threatened to boycott the Disney group because of an Israeli exhibit at Disney's Epcot theme park in Orlando, Florida. The exhibit attempted to naturalize Israel's annexation of Arab East Jerusalem by presenting Jerusalem as the indivisible capital of Israel. Shaikh Abdullah bin Zayed al-Nahayan, the UAE information minister, initiated consideration of a boycott of Disney within the Arab League. But the campaign was stopped through the personal intermediation of Prince Alwaleed bin Talal, a major shareholder in Disneyland Paris, with Disney's chairman and chief executive, Michael Eisner. Arab foreign ministers attending the UN General Assembly in New York in September 1999 were said to have accepted Eisner's assurances that Jerusalem would not be referred to as Israel's capital. They were told Disney had drawn up a disclaimer stating that any political message contained in the Israeli exhibit did not reflect the company's views.[145]

The Middle East presence of AOL Time Warner, News Corporation and Disney is complemented by that of Viacom, joint owner with the

Kuwait Investment Projects Company (KIPCO) of Gulf DTH, the firm behind Showtime. Showtime started in June 1996 as a direct-to-home digital satellite network providing English-language entertainment in the Middle East. Peter Einstein, who became president of Gulf DTH a few months later, joined the venture from his former position as head of MTV Networks Europe.[146] The Discovery Channel, which was carried by Orbit from 1994 to 1996, switched to Showtime, enabling the latter to offer nine channels in its first year. Besides Discovery, these were the Movie Channel, Paramount, TV Land, MTV, VH1, Nickelodeon, Bloomberg and Style. A link was established with ART early on, through the Cairo-based company MultiChoice Middle East, which was assigned to handle subscription management for both Showtime and ART. Behind the scenes it appears there may have been direct personal contact between Viacom's chairman, Sumner Redstone, and Prince Alwaleed, the holder of a 30 per cent stake in ART. Evidence of such contact came from Prince Alwaleed himself, who told an interviewer in 1999 that Redstone had asked him that August to broker a possible Viacom purchase of Kirch shares.[147] Although, as already mentioned, the Showtime–ART link-up went through a difficult patch when the two bouquets were offered from different satellites, Showtime was able to expand through the region under its own steam. Its channels formed part of the revamped CNE package and some were also carried on cable networks in Dubai, Qatar and Bahrain.[148]

Unauthorized expansion also occurred in some countries, notably Lebanon, via non-regulated cable networks. In 1999, after the Lebanese parliament passed a bill to protect intellectual property rights, six US film studios, including some with links to Orbit and Showtime, filed criminal charges with Lebanon's public prosecutor against the country's hundreds of small cable distributors of pirated satellite television signals.[149] The Hollywood studios in question were Fox (owned by News Corporation), Columbia Pictures (owned by Sony), Warner, Disney, Universal (then owned by the global beverage group Seagram, which later merged with Vivendi and Canal+), and MGM. The International Intellectual Property Alliance calculated that these film companies had lost around $8 million from illegal copying and broadcasting by pirate operators, who collected just $10 a month for popular bouquets instead of the $60 per month charged by authorized distributors. Intellectual property protection, urged on Lebanon as a prerequisite for membership of the World Trade Organization, seemed designed to curb the availability of foreign programming, at least to those strata of Lebanese society unable to afford the full subscription charge for it. While the protection of intellectual property rights is an aspect of globalization associated with the spread of World Trade Organization rules, it would seem to have the countervailing effect of slowing cultural globalization via satellite and cable television.

Overall, the development of supply links between the world's biggest media conglomerates and Arab satellite and cable networks during the 1990s appears to have been driven as much by the expansion of broadcasting capacity in the Arab world as by the expansionist tendencies of global media giants. It is as if a dearth of local programming and a proliferation of new satellite and cable networks together formed a vacuum which sucked in foreign content. Concern to protect investments in cable or satellite systems contributed to a dynamic that fostered interconnectedness with foreign suppliers, even on the part of a body such as the ERTU with a self-professed mission to ward off a foreign cultural invasion. On the other hand, the depth of that interconnectedness seems to have been limited by the small number of giant media conglomerates involved in supplying programmes and by the relatively small number of subscribers to the pay-TV networks that relied most heavily on foreign material.

## Conclusion

This chapter set out to locate and explore sites of interaction between leading Arab-owned transnational television channels and the wider world. Interaction was viewed in terms of company owners' business contacts, responses to the CNN stimulus, and deals reached with non-Arab content suppliers. Guiding the analysis were indices of globalization based on the concepts of intensity and scope drawn from the work of Held and McGrew. Whereas the scope, or spatial dimension, of interconnectedness is self-explanatory, measures of depth or intensity are not. For that reason, one of the criteria of complex interdependence developed by Keohane and Nye was used to test whether the cross-border links in the satellite television sector were transnational, in the sense of involving an array of non-governmental as well as government actors, or whether they were merely transgovernmental or inter-state.[150] An additional measure was derived from Cooper's differentiation between modern and post-modern worlds; this was to gauge whether the newly created satellite television entities sparked their own policy debates, or whether they served merely as policy instruments.

When interconnectedness via Arab satellite television is analysed on these lines, a picture emerges of a globalization process that stretches far but does not run very deep. ART established production and broadcast facilities spanning the globe from Tunis to Tennessee and itself represents a link between two worldwide business empires, in Saleh Kamel's Dallah Albaraka and Prince Alwaleed's Kingdom Holdings. MBC is part of a group based on interests in the USA and UK as well as Saudi Arabia, while Future TV is just one of Rafiq Hariri's many enterprises in Europe, the Middle East and beyond. Yet it is not clear that these far-flung interconnections involve more than a super-rich elite of individuals whose personal importance to their businesses relies heavily on their own one-to-one connections with each other and to the centres of power in world capitals. It would be stretching a point to call these connections transnational in the sense of involving multiple non-state actors, as defined by Keohane and Nye. It is equally clear, both by the media moguls' own admission and from their actions, that their satellite television interests primarily serve their own political and business agendas. In Prince Alwaleed's words, 'media is a powerful investment tool'.

Similar points can be made about the emulation of CNN and the cross-border interconnections established with content suppliers. Aspects of the CNN model were adopted by Arab satellite channels from Cairo and Doha to London, stimulating interaction on the part of television reporters and presenters with a wider range of issues and talkshow guests. Yet the model was not adopted wholesale. Instead it was deployed to suit the interests of those controlling individual stations, which in most cases meant limiting the model in some way. As for relations with global media firms, the advent of satellite television and digital networks led to spatially globalized outcomes such as the dubbing of Disney material in Arabic, MBC's contact with UK-based gameshow producers, and the link between Orbit in Rome and Star TV in Hong Kong. Yet this was an interconnectedness that was neither complex nor deep. On one side the shrinking number of giant media conglomerates, with their ever-expanding holdings, reduced the potential for a multiplicity of different contacts. On the other, the concentration of ownership in Arab satellite television helped to minimize the number of separate links with foreign suppliers. Choices about content, especially for digital channels, were based on the need to fill space and protect infrastructural investment without breaking editorial taboos. Al-Jazeera was all the more remarkable in being an exception to this rule.

Almost by definition, deeper and more diverse contacts across borders, both inside and outside the region, would have been more
conducive to development. Depth and diversity would be achieved
through the emergence of alternative broadcasters who could challenge
the region's few existing dominant players. How was it that, apart from
Al-Jazeera, potential challengers were suppressed? Chapter 4 looks at
television's role in development and identifies some of the ingredients
needed for transnational television to play a developmental role in the
Middle East.

# CHAPTER FOUR

# Missing Links: Transnational Television and Development

At one time, a multilateral development agency such as the United Nations Development Programme (UNDP) might not have regarded television as having much to do with development. Forums for advocating the civil and political rights of freedom of expression and freedom of information, which are associated with the media, were traditionally distinct from those focusing on the economic and social rights of access to shelter, education, healthcare and employment. During the 1990s this split started to close. The annual *Human Development Report*, launched in 1990 under UNDP sponsorship, started to elaborate a new 'development paradigm' that put people at the centre of development and saw economic growth as 'a means and not an end'.[1] Finally, in 2000, the 11th edition of the report formally declared human rights and human development to be 'two sides of the same coin'.[2] Highlighting the complex political and economic interactions of a 'growing global interdependence', the report warned that the 'era of globalization' brought with it the rise of powerful new actors in the shape of global corporations, multilateral organizations and non-governmental organizations (NGOs). This meant greater transparency and accountability were urgently needed. Providing these, the report said, meant removing press censorship and barriers to freedom of expression and finding the resources to build the infrastructure for an effective system of free media.[3]

Publication of the *Human Development Report 2000* came at a time of increasingly explicit recognition on the part of other multilateral agencies and human rights NGOs that freedom of expression represented a crucial dimension missing from development efforts in the Middle East. If the movement of people, goods and capital depends on the movement of information, it is not hard to see how restrictions on information can inhibit mobility – and hence development – in other fields. As scholars of both international communications and international relations have pointed out, 'nerve' has increasingly replaced 'muscle' in the ability of actors to influence each other.[4] Information has to flow efficiently internally and across borders for investment to follow, but freely flowing information has also to be credible. Establishing credibility means 'developing a reputation for providing correct information, even when it may reflect badly on the information provider's own country'.[5] It is argued that, as channels for the dissemination of information increase and the costs of transmitting data fall, struggles will focus less on control over the ability to transmit information and more on the creation and destruction of credibility.[6] Regulated competition among a plurality of media sources is more likely to generate credible information than a situation where the media are subject to centralized control.

In most Middle Eastern countries, despite the proliferation of satellite television channels in the 1990s, struggles over the basic availability of information remained centre-stage. As one Jordanian academic put it, on hearing a litany of disheartening indicators of the region's lack of development over the previous decade: 'This is a triple tragedy. Not only are the figures bad, but they have to be collated by foreign agencies while governments keep people in the dark.'[7] The 'darkness' image was one frequently repeated in the context of controls on information. In 1999, as the Saudi government strove to introduce legal reforms designed to encourage private investment, without making any amendments to media laws, an editorial in the London-based, Saudi-owned daily *Asharq Al-Awsat* deplored the secrecy surrounding all types of information in the kingdom. 'Without accurate information', it said, 'decision-makers are like the blind who don't know if they are stepping into a pit, or on to a pavement or killer highway.'[8] The Qatari foreign minister, interviewed by the Saudi-owned daily newspaper *Al-Hayat* in late 1999, argued that if Arab Gulf governments wanted their joint organization, the Gulf Co-operation Council (GCC), to get stronger, they had to be honest and open about their differences. All GCC members had a legitimate right to agree or disagree with Saudi Arabia as to how the GCC should be steered, the minister said, and these disagreements should not be kept hidden because 'our people have a right not to be left in the dark'.[9]

Upholding the right to freedom of information has always been part of the UN mission. In its very first session in 1946, the UN General

Assembly passed a resolution stating that 'freedom of information is a fundamental right and is the touchstone of all freedoms to which the United Nations is consecrated'.[10] Under Article 19 of the 1948 Universal Declaration of Human Rights:

> Everyone has the right to freedom of opinion and expression; this right includes freedom to hold opinions without interference and to seek, receive and impart information and ideas through any media and regardless of frontiers.

This guarantee is repeated in Article 19 of the International Covenant on Civil and Political Rights, which entered into force in 1976 and which a majority of Middle Eastern states have signed and ratified.[11] Signing is one thing, however, and implementation another. It is a characteristic of rights that they are usually claimed rather than given, and that where rights are claimed this involves the reform of institutions and modification of laws. As the 1990s gave way to the 2000s, the need for legal and institutional reforms geared to promoting transparency and openness in policy-making was being urged on Middle Eastern governments from several quarters. These even included the World Bank, whose own economists were divided over the extent to which empowerment of social groups could promote economic growth.[12] Addressing the Second Mediterranean Development Forum in Morocco, in September 1998, the World Bank president, James Wolfensohn, spoke in favour of 'democracy and freedom', 'the growth of civil society', 'social justice', 'access to information' and 'transparency'.[13] The Third Mediterranean Development Forum, held in Egypt in March 2000, took place under the highly explicit slogan 'Voices for change, partners for prosperity'. Forum participants were left in no doubt that the 'voices' referred to included those of civil society groups that might be expected to find expression through the media. One of the forum's five plenary sessions was entitled 'Transparency and the Role of the Media' and, in the opening ceremony, the World Bank's vice-president for the Middle East and North Africa region, Kemal Dervis, told the conference: 'The time for designing policies behind closed doors is over; now we have to do it together.'[14] Instead of the World Bank meeting only with economy and finance ministers, Mr Dervis indicated plans for a more inclusive approach, whereby a country's media representatives should also be involved.

To acknowledge a dynamic relationship between freedom of expression and wider economic, political and social development is to pinpoint both the potential and the shortcomings of transnational television in the Middle East. On the one hand, freedom of expression promotes development by creating public awareness of policy issues, allowing them to be debated thoroughly so that informed choices can be made. On the other, development promotes freedom of expression by increasing the number and diversity of channels through which ideas and information can flow. What contribution did the first decade of Middle East satellite television make to the development process? Many people saw the rise of the satellite channels as a benign form of globalization, capable of promoting more immediate, better-informed and more relevant debate of issues affecting individual countries in the region and the region as a whole. By the end of the 1990s satellite dishes had sprouted in their hundreds of thousands everywhere, Al-Jazeera Satellite Channel had succeeded in breaking a wide range of censorship taboos, and viewers had found alternatives to the censored terrestrial fare on offer from government broadcasting monopolies. Some observers of the Middle East even felt emboldened to describe the advent of Al-Jazeera as the 'beginning of a fundamental change'.[15] But, for all this optimism, glaring gaps in the media-development dynamic remained.

The present chapter explores some of these gaps, or missing links, to understand whether or not the rise of satellite television promised to narrow or close them. The analysis acknowledges that it is freedom of expression, not transnational television technology as such, that is crucial to development. Satellite broadcasting provides a platform for greater freedom, but how the platform is used depends on laws, policies and habits. Satellite technology may have drawn attention to the dearth of uncensored media in the Middle East, but it had no intrinsic powers to change this situation. For that reason the first task is to seek out the legal, financial and other factors inhibiting the emergence of non-governmental media, to understand how these were affected by the satellite phenomenon. There is much to be said, for example, about television ratings, advertising expenditure and links between editorial and financial independence. Notions of professionalism and the purpose of news reporting raise other issues. Where signs of change are apparent in television broadcasting, the question arises as to whether they actually reflect government resistance to more fundamental transformation, or whether the satellite medium has indeed been deployed to advance development.

## Struggles for diversity

According to the *Human Development Report 2000*, at the start of the new millennium, the state retained its monopoly on the media in only 5 per cent of countries worldwide.[16] It would be wrong to interpret this statistic as indicating a wholesale move towards media pluralism in the Middle East. While non-government ownership of newspapers is legal in most of the region, in broadcasting state monopolies remained the norm. In other words, the Middle Eastern-owned satellite channels, whether directly or indirectly linked to governments, were operating in a regional context dominated by a single model for broadcasting ownership and regulation. This was the model of state ownership and government control, exercised by information ministers. Change was promised in several countries from the start of the 1990s. By 2000 it had failed to materialize.

In Algeria, for example, the new Information Code promulgated in 1990 abolished the state monopoly on the written press and provided for the eventual establishment of private radio and television. The latter provision was not put into practice because the State of Emergency Law of February 1992 intervened. Yet even if it had been, the Code introduced penalties that would have severely curtailed private broadcasters' editorial scope. These included prison sentences of up to five years and heavy fines for publication of information capable of harming state security or national unity or constituting an insult to the president. Jordan's minister of information in 1996, Marwan Muasher, announced a draft law designed to end the government's monopoly over radio and television and open the way for private broadcasting channels.[17] However, parliament was dissolved before the law could be passed and a new government appointed in April 1997 took a far more conservative approach to both the print and audiovisual media. It was not until 1999 that the privatization issue resurfaced in Jordan. This was despite the fact that the Tunis-based Arab States Broadcasting Union (ASBU), whose membership comprises the radio and television broadcasting institutions of Arab states, had proposed in the mid-1990s that the time had come for governments to ease themselves out of the broadcasting sector. An internal ASBU policy document, written by the ASBU director-general, Raouf Basti, and circulated in early 1995, advised increasing the autonomy of broadcasters in order to give them 'more credibility in citizens' eyes'. It said they should move towards a redivision of labour so as to 'disengage the state gradually from direct management responsibilities and encourage the private sector to take over'.[18]

Until Lebanon's Audiovisual Media Law authorized a few influential personalities to set up private television stations in competition with the state broadcaster in the mid-1990s, examples of licensed non-government broadcasting in the Arab world and Iran were virtually non-existent. Even unlicensed television was strictly limited in terms of location. The mushrooming of unlicensed broadcasters that occurred in Lebanon during the civil war was repeated in the West Bank and Gaza Strip even before the Israeli withdrawal from Gaza and Jericho in 1994. In most cases these operations consisted of a one-room studio in a house trans-mitting only within the immediate vicinity. Yet, besides pirating programmes from satellite channels, they also generated local and community programming. The run-up to elections to the Palestinian Legislative Council in January 1996 was a busy time for the private stations, as they provided airtime for election candidates.[19] By reflecting social and political diversity, the private stations kept alive the hopes expressed by many Palestinians that self-rule in the West Bank and Gaza Strip would bring a new broadcasting formula to the Arab world. This would break decisively with the centralized 'mouthpiece of authority' tradition and introduce a new approach, suited to a 'forward-looking contemporary state' and progressive enough to recognize that a 'clash of ideas' is a 'source of enrichment'.[20] During the second half of the 1990s more than 30 small private television broadcasters (ten of them in Nablus alone) pursued a fraught co-existence with the troubled official Palestinian radio and television operation, as efforts to realize the forward-looking vision clashed with the authoritarian approach of the chairman of the Palestinian Authority, Yasser Arafat, and his own broadcasting ambitions. Although radio broadcasts in the name of Palestine had been transmitted from various parts of the Middle East since the 1950s, it was not until the signing of the Declaration of Principles by Israel and the Palestine Liberation Organization in Sep-tember 1993 that the two sides agreed to discuss the licensing of a Palestinian radio and television station.[21] The birth of the Palestinian Broadcasting Corporation (PBC) itself demonstrated the struggle between authoritarianism and proponents of free expression over everything from resources and management to editorial direction.[22] In early 1996, less than two years after the PBC had gone on air, its head, Radwan Abu Ayyash, was forced to admit that PBC television broadcast-ing would only take place from Gaza (where the chairman of the PA was based) rather than the originally designated studios at Ramallah on the West Bank.[23] This recognition of Yasser Arafat's close control over the PBC was followed in September 1996 by the appointment of Arafat's political adviser, Nabil Amr, as overall supervisor of the PBC.[24] Meanwhile the private Palestinian television stations' legal status was subject to confusion as temporary licences were issued and then withdrawn pending promulgation of a Broadcasting Law.

Apart from the Lebanese and Palestinian examples cited, the only other private broadcaster in an Arab country was Radio Mediterranée Internationale (Médi 1) in Morocco, jointly owned by French and Moroccan investors and launched in 1980. The Moroccan government also allowed a private pay-TV service, 2M, to start operations in 1989. In January 1997, however, with the company on the brink of bankruptcy, the state moved in to buy a 69 per cent share. From that point on, 2M broadcasts were unencrypted. When government control is so entrenched, the problem for those pressing for change is to find acceptable alternative financial and regulatory models. The difficulty of engineering a satisfactory relationship between investment and accountability is apparent in the vague language of some proposals for change. According to the Saudi Press Agency in June 2000, the kingdom's Majlis al-Shura (consultative council) responded to the Ministry of Information's latest annual report by proposing that state television and radio and the national news agency should be turned into commercial organizations with public investment and be given 'sufficient latitude to allow them to progress and develop'.[25] A few months earlier, the head of the Majlis's Cultural and Information Affairs Committee, Fahd al-Urabi al-Harithi, had spoken of the need to face up to challenges created by media developments at the local, regional and global levels.[26] He appeared to be referring to discrepancies between the multiple layers of censorship applied to locally based media and the somewhat lighter touch experienced by Saudi-owned newspapers and broadcasting stations based abroad.

Resistance to any radical departure from centralized state control was evident in the actual plans for private broadcasting discussed in 1999–2000. These served to give the buzzword 'privatization' another airing, but were mostly cautious in terms of time-scale and scope. Of the three countries where plans for private broadcasting received most attention during this period (Egypt, Jordan and Morocco), two (Jordan and Morocco) were undergoing institutional reforms resulting from the accession of a new, comparatively young, head of state. When King

Hussein of Jordan died in February 1999, having reigned for 47 years, the throne passed to his son, Abdullah, aged 37. King Mohammed VI of Morocco succeeded his father, King Hassan, in July 1999 at the age of 36. King Hassan had ruled for 38 years. With various steps towards political liberalization in progress in Morocco, including in the field of human rights and women's personal status, the Moroccan Ministry of Communication hosted an international conference in Rabat in May 2000 on the future of publicly owned broadcasting in the continent of Africa. The general message of the conference was that African countries needed a 'new vision' of public service broadcasting to meet the challenges posed by globalization and technological development. According to one version of the conference proceedings, participants agreed that neither state-owned nor commercial broadcasters could provide a truly public service without the right funding mechanisms and respect for high standards of journalism, democratic values and citizens' right to information.[27] A month after the conference, the Moroccan minister of communication, Larbi Messari, announced that the government was preparing to submit a draft law to parliament allowing the creation of private television channels and radio stations and reducing government censorship.[28] However, a government clampdown on the media before the year was through raised doubts about this promise. In October a French film crew was placed under house arrest for filming a prison camp; in November the Agence France Presse bureau chief in Rabat was expelled with no reason given; and in December three weekly newspapers were banned under Article 77 of the Press Law. Their offence was to have published documents relating to a failed coup attempt in 1972.[29]

The government appointed in Jordan in June 2000 worked swiftly to get the long-awaited media privatization scheme under way. 'His Majesty King Abdullah wants a free and independent media and he will get it', the Jordanian minister of information, Taleb Rifai, announced.[30] But, he warned, the process was more complex than simply selling government shares in media enterprises. Under instructions from the king to ensure that the media would serve the nation rather than an individual or a government, the government had to make sure that divestment would bring independence.[31] This in turn meant devising a regulatory formula to oversee the sale of government shares in newspapers and then moving on to the wholly state-owned Jordan Radio and Television Corporation and news agency, Petra. In the event, the proposed legal changes reserved to government ministers – rather than an independent, non-government body – the right to license private broadcasters.[32]

Whereas in Jordan and Morocco moves towards diversification of broadcasting ownership seemed to come from the monarch and his entourage, in Egypt pressure for diversification of broadcasting ownership came from opposition politicians and local business leaders. These calls were spurred by the wider privatization process urged on the Egyptian government by its international financial backers after the 1991 Gulf war. Credit and debt relief agreements reached with the IMF, World Bank and other lending agencies in 1991 linked cash injections to structural adjustment and economic reform, with the emphasis on promoting the private sector. The necessary legislation was put in place, transferring control over 314 public sector enterprises from government ministries to 16 separate holding companies, in readiness for their eventual sale. Media enterprises were not among them. This did not make the media readily accessible to alternative viewpoints before or during elections. In the 1995 elections for the People's Assembly, the opposition party returned with the most seats was the New Wafd, with just six MPs. It was Ibrahim Desouki Abaza who, on behalf of the New Wafd, applied for a broadcasting licence in November 1995. When the application was rejected on the grounds that the ERTU's monopoly was protected under Law 13 of 1979,[33] the party challenged the constitutionality of Law 13, alleging that ERTU news and information was biased in favour of the ruling National Democratic Party.

Several Egyptian entrepreneurs started at around this time to lobby for media restructuring that would give them a public voice. Despite international pressure on the government to privatize large parts of the economy, it took five years, a change of prime minister and the prospect of the Egyptian economy coming under international scrutiny at the US-sponsored Middle East and North Africa Regional Economic Conference in Cairo in November 1996, for the first offering of a majority share in a public company to be pushed through. As Egypt subsequently rose through the ranks of the IMF's privatization league and privately owned local business empires such as Orascom, Artoc and the Lakah Group expanded, the magnates behind them intimated that they would be ready to take advantage of the satellite revolution if denied the chance to broadcast from home.[34] Their message was reinforced at conferences and in consultancy reports by US and US-related institutions, notably the American Chamber of Commerce, the American University in Cairo and USAID.[35] The minister of information, Safwat al-Sharif, responded by pointing to privately owned shares in media projects such as Nilesat (40 per cent owned by the Egyptian Radio and Television Union), Cable

Network Egypt (50 per cent owned by the ERTU) and Media Production City (50 per cent ERTU ownership). But he steadfastly refused to contemplate privatization of any ERTU ventures. As late as January 2000 the minister flatly ruled out the sale of any of the digital Nilesat Thematic Channels.[36] This was despite suggestions within the ERTU that the six Thematic Channels, by virtue of their number, presented the authorities with a convenient opportunity to start the process of devolving state control.[37] One possible option, as seen from inside the ERTU, was for one or both of the two government-owned daily newspapers, *Al-Ahram* and *Al-Akbar*, to run satellite television news services as partners in the Thematic Channels. From Safwat al-Sharif's perspective, however, the plan for *Al-Ahram* and *Al-Akbar* seemed to be that they should launch satellite channels of their own.[38]

In fact, after Nilesat's launch in 1998, a few small chinks in the state broadcasting monopoly did begin to appear. Cairo Sat News, run by Mohammed Gohar's private company, Video Cairo Sat, was permitted to send a daily news feed (of pictures only) via Nilesat to 12 Arab satellite stations, including the ERTU.[39] Then, in the early months of 2000, the government joined the regional competition to attract private investment in satellite broadcasting by creating a media free zone. Although most business groups would have preferred to broadcast terrestrially, to attract advertising revenue commensurate with the size of the audience for terrestrial television,[40] the free zone opportunity gave these groups a reason to calculate the likely returns from starting a satellite channel. With the successful launching of Nilesat 102 in August 2000, the supply of digital channels increased yet again and, by the autumn of that year, plans for a private Egyptian satellite channel, backed by businessfolk and called Al-Mehwar, were well advanced.[41]

While struggles for broadcasting diversity were under way in Egypt, Jordan and Morocco, diverse forms of Palestinian broadcasting were coming under sustained attack from the Palestinian police and security forces. When Al-Quds Educational Channel started airing sessions of the Legislative Council in early 1997, its broadcasts were jammed by the authorities. In May that year the man behind the channel, Daoud Kuttab, was arrested and detained without charge for a week. The arrest was reported to have taken place on the direct orders of Yasser Arafat, who objected to references made during a televised Legislative Council session to a company allegedly owned by his wife.[42] Broadcasting of the council sessions was suspended, as the political climate made critical reporting of internal Palestinian affairs ever more sensitive.[43] Many temporary closures were forced on television stations from 1996. Those affected included Al-Watan TV, Nawras TV and Al-Nasr TV.[44] Fragmentation of non-government television in the West Bank and Gaza, with many small operators barely surviving from day to day, lessened the sector's ability to pose a serious challenge to the region's dominant model of television as government mouthpiece.

## The free zone fad

Given the extent to which government-decreed restrictions on television station ownership and content still persisted in early 2000, the 'media free zone' concept – a Jordanian brainwave instantly copied by other Arab states – elicited a mixed response from potential users. The idea was to capitalize on the fact, amply demonstrated by the 'émigré' media in London, that when broadcasters and publishers operate transnationally they can be flexible in choosing where to be based. While the English-language Jordanian press toyed with the meaning of 'media free zone' by shifting the adjective 'free' from zone to media, thereby emphasizing a different kind of freedom, cynics decided the zone in question would probably end up being 'media-free'. In any event, the basic issue appeared to be whether media free zones could harness satellite television to development. In theory they were expected to do so by encouraging broadcasters, production companies, advertising agencies, distributors and others to cluster together in a hot-house environment of advanced technology, plentiful employment and creativity.

The two separate notions of 'free media' and 'free zone', and the respective ideals of political freedom and economic initiative, lay at the heart of the struggle over the project as conceived in Jordan and implemented elsewhere. In contrast, it was the technology of satellite television and proliferation of satellite channels serving the region that provided the project's rationale. Observers wondered how long so many separate Saudi-owned satellite channels – MBC, Orbit, ART – could go on spending more than they earned. In 1999, in the wake of MBC's budget cuts during the previous year, and with merger talks having been attempted between Orbit and ART, it seemed that one way these stations could reduce their costs would be to uproot themselves from expensive European capitals and relocate in cheaper cities in the Middle East. Eventually it was a pan-Arab newspaper that led the way. Early 2000 saw the Saudi-owned daily newspaper, *Al-Hayat*, move most of its operations out of London to Beirut, where the title was first registered. MBC and Orbit indicated their intention to follow suit, but to different destinations. MBC started letting parts of its London premises in readiness for a move to Dubai's newly launched Technology, Electronic Commerce and Media Free Zone in 2001. On 24 January 2000, Orbit's owners, the Mawarid Group, signed an agreement with the Bahraini Ministry of Information to move Orbit's headquarters from Rome to the Bahraini capital, Manama.[45] The incentives for this decision were said to include the absence of corporate, personal or withholding taxes in Bahrain and the absence of customs duty on certain imports and re-exports. After the company's long-running argument with the Italian tax authorities, the prospect of a tax-free, duty-free environment was clearly attractive.

The Jordanian authorities had been hoping that MBC and Orbit might be attracted to Amman. When MBC's Shaikh Walid al-Ibrahim visited the kingdom in late 1999, Amman appeared to be high on his list of possible alternatives to London. In October 1999 King Abdullah instructed the Jordanian government to draft a law offering satellite broadcasters and production companies investment and relocation incentives such as tax and customs exemptions, support services and residence permits. These would apply in a free zone to be established on a tract of land near the premises of JRTV, the government-controlled broadcaster. In a country with unemployment unofficially estimated at up to 25 per cent,[46] the scheme's economic dimension was paramount. Local press reports suggested it could create 10,000 jobs,[47] especially for unemployed university graduates, and dramatically boost inward investment. But alongside the advantages there were also drawbacks and dilemmas. Not least of these was the likelihood that introducing different standards for media companies inside and outside the free zone would focus attention on the anomalous status of JRTV. The free zone, if successful, would (as ART had already done) attract employees away from low-paid jobs at JRTV, even though it was planned that Jordanians working for free zone companies would still pay income tax at local rates. At the same time, by enabling pan-Arab satellite companies to operate more profitably inside Jordan, the free zone would help the satellite channels in their bid to woo Jordanian viewers away from JRTV. In these circumstances, revitalization of JRTV through some means such as part-privatization, took on added urgency.

At the same time it was not clear exactly how much broadcasting freedom companies in the free zone would enjoy. For one thing it appeared that they would be free to transmit only outside Jordan. For another it seemed the government intended to retain powers to penalize programme-makers deemed to have abused free zone hospitality. The 21-article draft law, released on 17 January 2000, indicated that the prime minister would appoint the chairman and six-member board of the entity running the free zone and that contracts signed between this entity and investors would require the latter to observe a code of ethics.[48] Officials said this code would be based on one adopted by the Arab Federation of Journalists, which in turn replicates many elements of Arab countries' existing censorship laws. Ayman Majali, speaking as deputy prime minister and minister of information in October 1999, had said that the code would ensure that broadcast material did not contradict Jordan's culture or criticize religion.[49] At the very least it seemed unlikely that Jordan would risk being blamed for programmes considered hostile to Gulf governments, especially in view of the diplomatic efforts exerted to restore Jordan's relations with these countries after the 1991 Gulf war.

Ironically, it was Jordan's parliamentary process that delayed passage of the free zone law just long enough for other countries with less active opposition groups in parliament to jump on the bandwagon and announce free zone projects of their own. Egypt's information minister, Safwat al-Sharif, announced in January 2000 that private Egyptian companies would be allowed to broadcast by satellite from a free zone of 3.5 km² linked to the Media Production City studio complex near Cairo. Egypt made no attempt to compete with Jordan in offering more editorial freedom, however. Sharif stressed that the Ministry of Information reserved the right to censor both news and entertainment broadcast by private channels operating in the free zone.[50] As for the media free zone bill approved by the Lebanese government in February, this charged the zone's management board with drafting an 'honour agreement' requiring companies operating in the zone to respect the ethics, public morals, habits and customs of Lebanese society'.[51] Most people saw this as a thinly veiled injunction to avoid criticism of Syria.

## Table 7:  Trends in television ownership in the 1990s

(*Number of televisions per 1000 people*)

|              | 1990 | 1996–98 |
|--------------|------|---------|
| Algeria      | 68   | 68      |
| Bahrain      | 424  | 419     |
| Egypt        | 107  | 127     |
| Iran         | 66   | 157     |
| Iraq         | 72   | 82      |
| Israel       | 259  | 318     |
| Jordan       | 76   | 52      |
| Kuwait       | 432  | 491     |
| Lebanon      | 349  | 352     |
| Libya        | 99   | 143     |
| Morocco      | 102  | 160     |
| Oman         | 657  | 595     |
| Qatar        | 392  | 808     |
| Saudi Arabia | 249  | 260     |
| Sudan        | 73   | 141     |
| Syria        | 60   | 68      |
| Tunisia      | 81   | 198     |
| UAE          | 344  | 480     |
| Yemen        | 274  | –       |
| *For comparison* |  |         |
| USA          | 772  | 847     |
| Greece       | 194  | 466     |

Source: UNDP, *Human Development Report 2000*

### Advertising issues

Even without the mass of legal and political obstacles, non-government television ventures faced serious problems of funding. These could be attributed in large part to wide-ranging government controls over advertising budgets and state bodies' self-serving resistance to the gathering of credible statistics on television-viewing habits. Financial independence is the *sine qua non* of editorial independence. State broadcasters in the Middle East have long been saved from grappling with this equation by local distaste for television licence fees. Dependence on licence fees makes broadcasters accountable to fee-payers. A lack of accountability represents another missing link between television and the development process. While government broadcasters, and satellite stations allied to government figures, could dip into state budgets or their sponsors' financial reserves, any independent competitor needed to swim against the tide to establish a steady flow of advertising revenue or other business-related income. Here the challenges would be manifold. Not only do advertisers need evidence of the relative popularity of channels and particular programmes; the majority of companies based locally in the Middle East have also yet to be convinced that spending money on television advertising is worthwhile. Despite increases in the ownership of television sets in some countries during the first half of the 1990s, levels measured in terms of individual viewers rather than households remained far below other regions (see Table 7). Moreover, if companies are seen to be advertising on a channel that may be popular with audiences but is unpopular with governments, their contracts from government departments may be jeopardized.

The lack of reliable or consistent data on satellite access in a populous country like Egypt illustrates the point, especially if private broadcasters are allowed to transmit from Egypt only by satellite. Kamilia Ahmad, director of Promoseven Egypt, a major private advertising agency, said in 1998 that her company still had 'no clue' about the number of satellite dishes in Egypt.[52] She knew only that it was very low and definitely 'still in single figures in percentage terms'. Kamilia Ahmad was not alone. In 1999, Professor Farag Elkamel, head of the Centre for Communication Training, Documentation and Production in the Faculty of Mass Communication, Cairo University, said he knew of no authoritative study of satellite penetration among Egyptian households apart from a doctoral thesis being carried out at that time under his supervision.[53] Jon Alterman, author of a monograph on new media in the Arab world, published in 1998, resorted to quoting a Kuwaiti estimate of Egyptian satellite access.[54] Due to changes in survey methodology, the annual Eutelsat survey showed the number of Egyptian homes with television rising from 7.7 million to 11.6 million between 1997 and 1998 but the number of homes with satellite access decreasing from 669,000 to 650,000 over the same period.[55] Such results simply drew attention to the difficulties of obtaining raw data from which to extrapolate trends. PARC started collecting audience data informally in Egypt in the early 1990s but did not start to release it until 1998. As a six-monthly report based on responses from 1000 families about their television viewing over the previous six to eight weeks, the *Egypt Media Index* of the late 1990s was inevitably less sophisticated than might have been possible elsewhere. But shortcomings in research into media use in Egypt pale by comparison with those in Syria, where the state monopoly, the Arab Advertising Organization, insisted on censoring the first detailed media market research questionnaire prepared for distribution under its auspices in 1998.[56]

**Table 8: Results of satellite and cable access surveys in ten countries, 1997–99**

*(Total satellite and cable access measured as percentage of homes with TV)*

| Country | 1997 | 1998 | 1999 |
|---|---|---|---|
| Algeria | 37.5 | 37.5 | 80.0[1] |
| Egypt | 8.7 | 5.6 | 7.5 |
| Israel | 69.4 | 69.4 | 69.4 |
| Jordan | 14.4 | 14.9 | 14.7 |
| Lebanon | 8.3 | 41.3 | 42.5 |
| Morocco | 24.8 | 25.8 | 24.7 |
| Saudi Arabia | 50.4 | 69.7 | 65.4 |
| Syria | 26.4 | 19.9 | 29.7 |
| Tunisia | 3.4 | 7.1 | 10.0 |
| Turkey | 9.0 | 19.5 | 17.9 |
| *Average* | 20.1 | 23.0 | 27.2 |
| *For comparison* | | | |
| Western Europe | 42.8 | 43.8 | 48.5 |
| Eastern & central Europe | 22.7 | 16.7[2] | 25.1 |

[1] New statistical series.
[2] Change of methodology.

Source: Eutelsat (based on surveys conducted mid-year by fieldwork institutes including PARC, Stat-IPSOS and others)

Any doubts surrounding data on satellite access were inevitably compounded when it came to assessing which of the leading Arabic-language free-to-air channels widely available from 1997 onwards were the most widely watched. In the absence of television metering systems in all but a few Arab countries, such as Morocco and the UAE, even the most senior of advertising executives had to admit that no advertiser could be 100 per cent sure what they were getting for their money. The resulting situation was one in which satellite channels would rely on self-administered audience questionnaires (such as the one circulated by MBC in 1997) along with anecdotal evidence from viewers' telephone calls and faxes as the best means of judging their impact. For the purposes of canvassing advertising revenue, longevity and the personal clout of channel owners thus tended to substitute for reliable up-to-date evidence about the size of audiences and their purchasing power. In other words, the link between popularity and advertising income was missing. Al-Jazeera Satellite Channel, having commissioned its own audience surveys, maintained in 2000 that 46 per cent of all satellite viewers watched Al-Jazeera at some point between 6pm and midnight. The next highest percentage was said to be the 23 per cent enjoyed by MBC.[57] Previous studies, in 1998, had also indicated that Al-Jazeera was ahead of MBC even among Saudi viewers during the latter part of the evening, while Al-Jazeera's live discussion programmes were being aired.[58] Yet this ranking was not reflected in the two stations' advertising results. While PARC estimated MBC's advertising revenue in 1999 at $91.5 million, its equivalent estimate for Al-Jazeera was $8 million – a figure not disputed by well-informed Al-Jazeera staff. The disparity can be attributed to several factors, including MBC's assured position as a general channel providing entertainment as well as news to wealthy viewers in Saudi Arabia and other rich Gulf states. Al-Jazeera, by contrast, as a news and current affairs channel, had a more specific appeal and attracted audiences of less interest to advertisers. Its most avid viewers were believed to include Palestinians in the West Bank and Gaza Strip. A poll conducted by the Palestinian newspaper Al-Quds in late 1999 suggested that 75 per cent of Palestinians with satellite access preferred to watch news and current affairs programmes on Al-Jazeera rather than on the local Palestinian channels.[59] Besides these factors, however, are the effects of government influence over the spending of advertising budgets, even in the so-called private sector. Where government ministers and civil servants have links to business either through family connections, professional ties or as potential customers, they have the power to steer advertising expenditure away from broadcasters of whom they disapprove.

Whatever advertisers' reasons for choosing one satellite channel in preference to another, overall advertising expenditure placed with satellite television channels in 1999 was still not sufficient to fund the full number of channels in operation. The total spend in 1999 was up to an estimated $463 million, from a notional $360 million in 1998, which in turn represented an increase of 73 per cent over the previous year. However, not only were these figures somewhat inflated, being based on channels' stated advertising rates without any allowance made for discounts, they remained small compared to the combined cost of all the active satellite channels. Addressing a conference of advertising professionals in late 1997, the president of Future TV, Nadim Munla, commented that advertising spend would have to rise considerably from current levels to pay for the number of satellite stations in operation. He indicated that a sum of $600–700 million would be 'barely enough for 10 large TV stations', implying that the average annual running costs of a general satellite television channel at that time were around $60–$70 million.[60] Thus total advertising expenditure with pan-Arab television was barely sufficient for six channels in 1998. In 1999 only three stations, LBC-Sat, Future International and MBC, appeared to have covered the bulk of their costs from advertising income (see Table 9). Al-Jazeera is meanwhile known to have supplemented its advertising revenue with earnings from leasing equipment and facilities and selling film footage.

### Table 9:  Advertising revenue received, 1998–99

*($ million; at 'rate card', i.e. excluding discounts)*

|                         | 1998 | 1999  |
|-------------------------|------|-------|
| LBC-Sat                 | 93.3 | 166.5 |
| Future International     | 88.0 | 114.2 |
| MBC                     | 76.9 | 91.5  |
| Egyptian Space Channel  | 26.7 | 36.4  |
| Emirates-Dubai TV       | 20.8 | 22.3  |
| ART                     | 26.5 | 21.4  |
| Al-Jazeera              | 3.2  | 8.0   |
| Syria Satellite TV      | 1.8  | 1.9   |
| Jordan Satellite Channel| 0.7  | 0.6   |

Source: Pan-Arab Research Centre, Dubai

In sum, by 2000, the majority of satellite channels had yet to build the crucial link between financial and editorial independence. At the same time their prospects for doing so were not encouraging. For one thing, precisely because they cover a large geographical area, satellite channels lend themselves to advertising only certain types of goods and services. The most obvious examples are internationally known brands of detergents and soft drinks, or luxury goods such as cars or cosmetics, or cross-border services such as those offered by airlines and banks. Transnational television is not best suited to promotion of domestic products which vary from country to country. For example, the top ten brand names advertised on pan-Arab television in 1998 included a strong showing on the part of the American multinational Procter & Gamble, owner of the Pantene, Pampers, Ariel and Pert Plus brands.[61] Moreover, even a big percentage increase in advertising spend from Arab sources would have a limited impact, given the low starting point. According to Munla, advertising spend per head of population in the Arab world in 1997 was equal to only $6, compared with $10 in Turkey, $75 in Cyprus and more than $140 in Israel. Whereas advertising expenditure was equal to 1 per cent of GDP in Israel, 0.7 per cent in Cyprus, and over 0.5 per cent in Turkey, it amounted to only 0.25 per cent of GDP in the Arab states. Munla's proposed solution to the funding shortfall included collaboration in producing and acquiring programmes, with the aim of sharing expenses and lessening the kind of competition among stations which could drive up programming costs.[62] Similar points were made by Hala Omran, the outgoing managing director of MBC, interviewed shortly before she handed over to Ian Ritchie in 1998. She noted that a large number of satellite channels were chasing a limited amount of content and that more and better-organized advertising was needed to fund efforts to fill the 'content gap'. Complaining at steeply rising prices for the rights to sports events and concerts, Omran urged the advertising industry to be 'aggressive enough to help us cater for the expansion'.[63]

From the potential advertisers' point of view, however, there was the added complication of how best to target viewers of digital channels. The successive launches of Nilesat 101 in 1998, Arabsat 3A in 1999 and Nilesat 102 in 2000, all of them equipped with digital technology, resulted in a dramatic increase in channel capacity, with these satellites able to transmit scores of channels where previous generations could transmit relatively few. With digitalization came the creation of countless separate thematic channels for news, sport and drama alongside the numerous general interest channels. One implication of this trend was a fragmentation of audiences into so many diverse segments that their viewing preferences would be almost impossible to track. At the global level, the digital revolution presented major challenges to experienced advertisers and advertising agents. In the less-developed advertising industry in the Middle East there was apprehension that the challenges would act as a deterrent.

## Blaming the messenger

With so many Middle Eastern satellite channels created in pursuit of particular political agendas (see Chapter 2), their commitment to reporting news for its own sake or promoting policy debates was not something that could be taken for granted. This situation created a further gap in place of a link between transnational television and development. It is debatable whether the missing link should be described as that of media professionalism. Media scholars in Europe long ago problematized the ideology of media professionalism, according to which journalists are assumed to strive after objectivity and impartiality in their reporting. Even when subject to minimal legislative controls, the media are not a neutral channel for the direct exchange of information between governments and citizens. Peter Golding argued in the 1970s that, since all media institutions are 'wedded to social and political processes', the Western professional ideal of impartiality in communication was probably unattainable.[64] John Keane has likewise identified internal 'blindspots' of classical theories of press freedom. These neglect the complex practical processes whereby newspaper owners and their employees set agendas, frame content, censor themselves, negotiate and compromise in an uneven marketplace to produce and distribute to a public differentiated by varying levels of literacy and wealth.[65]

This is not to say, however, that the editorial policies of specific institutions cannot be scrutinized for evidence of attitudes to neutrality and professionalism, as demonstrated in their approach to covering news. In the case of Middle Eastern satellite channels, contrasts between Al-Jazeera and its competitors on this single issue throw their respective editorial policies into sharp relief. When Al-Jazeera reported news and views governments preferred not to hear, blame was invariably heaped on Al-Jazeera for performing the role of messenger.

In contrast, editorial policy at the Egyptian Space Channel and the Lebanese-owned Future International was based firmly on the belief that satellite channels in particular have a duty to tell 'good' rather than 'bad' news. The rationale for such an approach lies in the channels' relationship to those responsible for maintaining a certain image of Egypt or Lebanon abroad, especially among potential foreign investors. In the view of Sana Mansour, the head of ESC who joined it in 1995, terrestrial and satellite television have distinct roles. Whereas terrestrial channels may be given some leeway to bring attention to local matters of concern, airing complaints if necessary, it is incumbent on the Egyptian satellite channels, ESC 1 and 2 and Nile TV, to be ambassadors for Egypt.[66] This means being 'choosy' about the appearance of people and buildings, and certainly not screening documentaries of the 'warts-and-all' variety. Nadim Munla, chairman of Future TV, shared a similar vision during

Rafiq Hariri's premiership in the 1990s. Given Mr Hariri's dual role as prime minister of Lebanon and prime mover behind Future, Mr Munla saw it as Future's duty to promote Lebanon to Gulf investors, to 'tell people that life is back'.[67] 'Life' in this context was taken to mean fun and entertainment, not searching interviews with Lebanese politicians. Hariri's cabinet put programmes in the latter category out of bounds for Lebanese satellite channels at the start of 1998.

Nor were government officials alone in their concern to present a glossy, modern, cohesive image abroad. In the early days of satellite television a large section of Egyptian public opinion, both inside the country and among Egyptian expatriates in the West, showed itself equally in favour of portraying an idealized Egypt to the rest of the world. When a BBC 2 documentary, called *Marriage Egyptian Style*, was shown on UK television in 1991 and at the Ismailiya film festival in Egypt in 1992, it provoked a furore. An Egyptian anthropologist, Reem Saad, who had advised the film-maker,[68] interpreted the outcry as illustrating 'how the nation's reputation becomes a cause which seeks to be sacred and unnegotiable'.[69] Analysing the protests contained in a flood of letters and articles in the press, Saad drew up a list of icons she believed to signify Egyptian civilization (*hadara*) to the people outraged by the film-maker's decision to focus on a woman who earned her living as a cleaner. Besides the pyramids, the Sphinx and the Nile, the list included the Cairo Opera House, traffic flyovers, high-rises, five-star hotels, educated professional women, including female ambassadors, and a homogenized entity called 'the people', whose moral qualities and 'authenticity' can be celebrated, provided their hardships and idiosyncrasies are kept from view.[70]

Splits over the acceptability of washing a nation's linen in public were repeatedly exposed by Al-Jazeera's news and current affairs coverage once this became accessible to a wide audience from November 1997. Al-Jazeera management departed from regional norms when they adopted a news agenda determined by criteria such as newsworthiness, and set out to beat CNN and BBC World at their own game by obtaining 'exclusives' and 'scoops'. Government-controlled media in the region responded by echoing government suspicion that this novel approach to Arabic-language news reflected ill-will from their Qatari counterparts. Al-Jazeera's director, Mohammed Jassem al-Ali, summed up the opposing approaches as follows:

> We are not against any government. All we do is tell the truth and nothing but the truth ... After all, we are not doing anything different from

what others do in Europe and the USA. Maybe it's unusual in the Third World, but not elsewhere ... When you watch Egyptian TV or Saudi TV you know it's Egyptian or Saudi because it says so. In the case of Al-Jazeera, it doesn't have a country identity. It's not Qatar TV.[71]

This message was reiterated many times in exchanges between Qatari representatives and the leaders of other Arab states, who took personal offence at Al-Jazeera's output. In some cases this was translated into a ban on Al-Jazeera news-gathering activities in the country concerned. One of the most public bannings was that imposed in Jordan at the end of 1998. In November that year the Jordanian Ministry of Information, through the Press and Publications Department, cancelled the accreditation of Al-Jazeera staff in Amman in protest at a panel debate screened by Al-Jazeera from Doha. The debate in question took place in the *Al-Ittijah al-Muaakis* (The Opposite Direction) series chaired by the Syrian presenter, Faisal al-Qassim. It brought together a Jordanian and Syrian to discuss the Jordanian–Israeli peace treaty, signed in 1994. The Jordanian was Kamel Abu Jaber, a former foreign minister and head of the Jordanian–Palestinian delegation to the multilateral Arab–Israeli peace talks in Madrid in 1991. The Syrian was Mohammed Khalifa, described on the programme as a writer and researcher but said privately by sources involved in the programme to be head of Syrian intelligence in Scandinavia.[72] While Kamel Abu Jaber defended Jordan's peace treaty with Israel on the grounds that Arab countries generally were moving in this direction, Mohammed Khalifa harked back to the creation of Jordan, and suggested that the state had been established to absorb Palestinians so as to facilitate the creation of Israel. Khalifa then accused Jordan of colluding with Israel to deprive Syria of water resources, an allegation which Abu Jaber robustly denied.[73]

Although the attack on Jordan was mounted by an individual guest in a panel debate, the Jordanian authorities equated the views expressed by a single person with the editorial policy of the entire satellite channel. The Jordanian minister of information at the time was Nasser Judeh, son-in-law of Crown Prince Hassan. He told the daily *Jordan Times* that cancelling the accreditation of Al-Jazeera staff would effectively close down the channel's Jordanian office. 'I am not interested in having an office whose sole concern is to level personal insults against the country', he said.[74] In a statement reported by Jordanian Television, Judeh said the programme had 'enraged all sectors of the Jordanian public' and that a pattern of 'repeated offence' indicated that Al-Jazeera had a 'clear policy

[of] targeting Jordan'. He said he expected the Al-Jazeera administration to apologize officially and publicly, adding that 'those who do not like our decision are not part of Jordan and do not belong to it, and that is their business'.[75] Surprisingly perhaps, given this denunciation, Kamel Abu Jaber was himself among those who advised Nasser Judeh not to close the Al-Jazeera office. Despite being unhappy at the way the programme had been organized and chaired, Kamel Abu Jaber is known to have regarded the closure as an over-reaction. It took a respected member of the Jordanian media, speaking a fortnight later under protection of an international conference, to put what he called the Al-Jazeera 'debacle' in context. Addressing an audience of academics, media professionals and public figures in Amman at the end of November, the *Jordan Times* editor, Abdullah Hasanat, argued that, by stifling free debate for so many years inside the kingdom, Jordan's 'hierarchical and patriarchal system' had left too many citizens ignorant of their country's history and ill equipped to put up a factual or intellectual defence of the national cause. The Jordanian media had not only failed, he said, to explain to Jordanians the 'actions and ambitions of the leadership or the blessings of peace versus war'. They had also failed to 'create a breed of free-minded intelligentsia capable of defending the country at crucial junctures'.[76]

Despite dissenting voices inside Jordan, others elsewhere in the Arab world regarded closure of Al-Jazeera facilities as the natural reaction to contentious views aired on the channel's debates. A few days after the Jordanian information minister took his decision, a campaign started in the semi-official Egyptian press calling on Nasser Judeh's Egyptian counterpart, Safwat al-Sharif, to follow suit. At that stage, however, Al-Jazeera had no official Cairo office. Instead it was left to newspapers like *Akhbar al-Youm* and *Al-Usboua* to criticize Al-Jazeera for being anti-Egyptian, because of its controversial choice of talkshow guests. These included people charged in absentia with conspiracy to carry out terrorist attacks. In the light of a very public disagreement between Qatar and Egypt in 1997 over Egypt's decision to boycott a regional economic summit meeting held in Doha, Al-Jazeera's actions were widely interpreted as indicative of a Qatari campaign to embarrass the Egyptian government. As in Jordan, however, experienced media professionals saw Al-Jazeera's output from a different perspective. Mohammed Gohar, managing director of Video Cairo, commented that audiences were simply unused to hearing such debates in Arabic. 'They'll listen to it on CNN', he told the *Middle East Times* in 1998, 'but when you put it in

Arabic, that's something else.'[77] Two years later, however, the Egyptian authorities had still not become inured to Al-Jazeera's editorial style. When the Egyptian president, Hosni Mubarak, hosted summit meetings in Egypt in October 2000, to try to end Israeli–Palestinian clashes, Al-Jazeera provided a forum for those opposed to the summit meetings to air their views. Opposition commentators and Palestinian Islamists criticized the Egyptian leadership for not being tough enough with their Israeli counterparts. This was too much for Safwat al-Sharif. He accused Al-Jazeera of focusing its broadcasts 'only on attacks against Egypt and its president', called on it to stop and threatened to cease all co-operation with the channel. By this he meant forbidding it from having studios or correspondents in Egypt or broadcasting from Egypt by satellite.[78]

While members of the Egyptian government felt they were being targeted by Al-Jazeera, Kuwaiti ministers apparently felt the same. They objected strongly to the channel's coverage of US and British bombing of Iraq at the end of 1998, seeing it as biased in Iraq's favour. In mid-1999 Al-Jazeera was banned for six weeks from reporting from Kuwait after an Iraqi (apparently living in Norway) called up a live phone-in show on the channel to vent his anger about the presence of Western forces in Kuwait. The caller criticized the Kuwaiti emir for 'embracing atheists and allowing foreign armies to enter Kuwait'.[79] Visiting Kuwait some months after the incident, the Qatari emir was reported in the Kuwaiti daily *Al-Watan* as defending Al-Jazeera's output. In his view the problem had stemmed from hostility between Iraq and Kuwait, not from the existence of Al-Jazeera. The emir, Shaikh Hamad, said that if Al-Jazeera did not shed light on contentious issues, other media would. He reassured the Kuwaitis that Al-Jazeera had not been set up to spite them and pointed out that Qatar had not banned Kuwaiti newspapers when they criticized the Qatari government.[80]

Instead of taking advantage of Al-Jazeera to air their own views, however, many officials in the region preferred to boycott it. When the Kuwaiti Ministry of Information withdrew the work permits and press accreditation of Al-Jazeera staff in mid-1999, it also urged Kuwaitis not to appear on any Al-Jazeera programmes produced outside Kuwait.[81] After the channel hosted two leading members of the Palestinian Islamic Resistance Movement, Hamas, in 1998, the secretary-general of the Palestinian Authority (PA), Tayyeb Abdel-Rahim, requested PA representatives to refrain from taking part in televised exchanges with Hamas leaders abroad. Nabil Amr, information adviser to Yasser Arafat, consequently refused to take part with Mohammed Nazzal of the Hamas Political Bureau in an edition of the Al-Jazeera programme *Akthar min Ra'i* (More than One Opinion).[82] A similar stand was taken by the Moroccan government. It objected to interviews on Al-Jazeera with representatives of the Polisario Front fighting for independence in territory claimed by Morocco.[83] It also complained that Al-Jazeera had omitted to cover a visit to Washington by the Moroccan king.[84]

For the Saudi authorities, Al-Jazeera's less forgivable offences included its coverage of Iraq, its reporting on King Fahd's illness, its exclusive interview with the exiled Saudi-born militant Usama Bin Laden, and a report on the release in June 1999 of three dissident shaikhs who had been imprisoned during a demonstration in the Saudi town of Buraydah in September 1994. In July 1999, Crown Prince Abdullah of Saudi Arabia ordered coffee shops in the capital to stop showing satellite television altogether and to restrict themselves to Saudi terrestrial channels. Given the coffee shops' function in providing young male Saudis in and around Riyadh with a place to meet in groups of two to six to talk or watch television until the early hours of the morning, the ban on satellite channels and the additional order for coffee shops to close by midnight had many critics. Those affected by the crackdown were aware that forthcoming sporting events, to be screened exclusively on satellite television, would be likely to see a de facto end to the ban, especially when Saudis were taking part in the events.[85]

The people behind Al-Jazeera had forthright responses for these official and semi-official objections. The channel's chairman, Qatari ruling family member Shaikh Hamad bin Thamer al-Thani, said it had simply opted for freedom of expression. 'Free expression is a human right', he said in 1999. 'It is difficult to control information when the world has become a small village.'[86] Defending Al-Jazeera after it had been censored by Kuwait, he pointed out that the channel was not in the business of allowing itself to be 'used as a platform for attacking anyone'.[87] In one of his many interviews with interested observers, Al-Jazeera's director, Mohammed Jassim al-Ali, referred to the notion of professionalism. 'Of course we are working as professionals', he said, 'with a difference between news and debate.' He went on:

> Debate on our channel is always controversial, that is what makes for interesting television. Sometimes if we bring someone on who supports this or that argument, there will be others who disagree. These are the opinions of both people, but it doesn't mean it is the view of Al-Jazeera. I will

leave a space for them to talk. If it is news we have a responsibility to give accurate information, but as every news broadcaster knows, there is always false news, gossip and malicious information about. We have to treat this with great caution.[88]

On another occasion, he said Al-Jazeera was a 'unique experiment that respects the intelligence of the Arab viewer'.[89]

Quantitative and qualitative audience surveys conducted in Saudi Arabia between April and June 1998, just a few months after Al-Jazeera had become more widely available by broadcasting on C-band, suggested that viewers generally appreciated having their intelligence respected. The quantitative survey, conducted by PARC through face-to-face interviews with 3453 Saudis and Arab expatriates, indicated that Al-Jazeera and LBC-Sat were equally popular, but at different times of the evening, and that Al-Jazeera ratings were higher than those for MBC from around 21:45 onwards.[90] In the qualitative study 551 respondents were asked to associate statements with specific satellite channels. Nearly three-quarters of those questioned (73.7 per cent) agreed that the statement 'People often talk about the arguments raised by its programmes' applied to Al-Jazeera. Two-thirds agreed that Al-Jazeera had a 'professional team of programme presenters' and was 'outspoken and even-handed' (65.9 and 65.3 per cent respectively) and 82.4 per cent said it presented 'daring programmes about hot Arab issues'.[91] Al-Jazeera's uniqueness in fitting this description earned it a loyal and ever-growing following as more people realized that the channel's representatives regarded themselves as messengers, not as originators of the message.

## Types of training

The training of media professionals working with Middle Eastern satellite channels is a major factor in the quality and character of the channels' output and thus their role in the development process. As the number of channels increased, creating more and more jobs for journalists and presenters, attention was drawn to opposing trends in training and recruitment. On one side was the traditional approach, cultivated and led by Egypt, with an emphasis on rules and 'ethics'. On the other was a move towards a form of journalism described by its advocates as 'independent' and 'investigative'. Satellite channels based outside the Middle East naturally tended to hire journalists already employed in Europe in a professional capacity. In some cases these people had worked for the foreign-language services of European public service broadcasters.

The ethics learned by such practitioners were not always compatible with those advanced in their countries of origin. There the concept of ethics was used more often to carry a sense of duty to those in authority than to the viewing public at large. Different understandings of the journalist's role were thus introduced into pan-Arab television stations by their staff. In a climate of competition among stations, both for audiences and for popular presenters, the struggle over definitions of professional competence and ethics came to be reflected transnationally – in adjustments to staffing procedures and greater availability of Western-sponsored training.

While many senior people in the Arab satellite channels have impressive professional backgrounds and experience, their scope for exploiting such experience is constrained by the environments in which they work. At the same time it should not be forgotten that they also exert some influence over their environments. A comparison of the biographies of three Egyptians, one in Al-Jazeera and two in the Egyptian state-run satellite sector, shows how the training media practitioners receive can influence their interaction with the structures in which, and through which, they work.

Salah Negm became editor-in-chief at Al-Jazeera from a background in journalism in Egypt and Europe. In the 1970s he worked on a university newspaper in Cairo, *Saut al-Gamaa*, and then in Egyptian broadcasting. He moved from there to the Netherlands Arabic-language radio service, which became one of eight Dutch foreign-language services to be axed in 1995. That was when Negm moved to the BBC Arabic television service set up to serve Orbit, the Saudi-owned pay-TV station based in Rome. In 1996, however, the service was brought to a sudden halt after it screened a BBC *Panorama* documentary on beheadings and other aspects of the Saudi justice system. Having already been contacted by Qatari representatives seeking recruits for Al-Jazeera, Negm moved within weeks to Doha to set about preparing Al-Jazeera for start-up in November that year. Gradually, other editorial staff of the BBC Arabic television service did likewise, including Sami Haddad, a Jordanian, and Faisal al-Qassem, a Syrian, who both rose to prominence on Al-Jazeera as presenters of lively panel debates. Together the members of this team, whose work for the BBC had mainly involved translating material already created in English, now had their first opportunity to initiate television programmes. They also had more airtime in which to do it. Whereas the BBC service was limited to eight hours per day, Al-Jazeera's daily schedule increased in stages to 24 hours. As the station developed, its staff came to represent – in an individual capacity – almost all Arab countries except Libya and those in the Gulf. One Saudi who joined briefly was recalled after two months. This group's collective efforts, based on training and experience gained inside and outside the region, shook up the Arabic-language satellite television sector.

Sana Mansour, head of the Egyptian Space Channel and Nile TV, started as a journalist with the leading semi-official Egyptian daily, *Al-Ahram*, and moved from there to the state-run Middle East Radio in Cairo. She went to France on a scholarship in 1968 to study child psychology and, in 1973, at the age of 26, became one of the founding staff members of a new French radio station for the Middle East, Radio Monte Carlo-Moyen Orient (RMC-MO). Broadcasting for only four hours initially, the station was soon called on to increase its output in response to the outbreak of the Arab–Israeli war of October 1973. In doing so it established itself as a favourite foreign radio service among young people in Arab countries. As a direct competitor to the BBC's Arabic service, RMC-MO distinguished itself through its deliberately relaxed, informal and youthful style. Mansour stayed in France for ten years. She cites her involvement with RMC-MO as having accustomed her to working with a small, efficient and motivated team.[92] To assemble such a team for her satellite television channels, she set about hiring the best new graduates of Egypt's institutes of cinema, theatre and photography. Her conditions were that they should be young enough not to have acquired preconceived ideas and prejudices and should be hired for their talent and not their family connections. Her preference for recruiting young staff was endorsed by the minister of information, Safwat al-Sharif. He commented proudly on the ages of Nile TV and Nilesat employees to an international conference in 1998. None was more than 28 years old, he said.[93] Mansour's call for motivated people who would take responsibility and do a full day's work, in place of time-servers appointed for reasons other than their professional reputation, was also accepted by senior management. In 1997–98, as the impact of LBC-Sat, Future International, Al-Jazeera and ANN started to be felt, traditional behind-the-scenes recruitment practices in Egyptian television started to give way to open advertisements, speedy appointments and selection according to perceived competence.[94]

Hassan Hamed, deputy director of the Egyptian Radio and Television Union and executive director of the Nile Thematic Channels (broadcast from Nilesat), is another senior Egyptian broadcaster with experience gained at home and abroad. He spent 15 years overseas, working as a reporter with Radio Japan and Voice of America. In establishing the Nile Thematic Channels in 1998, he took a particular interest in the dedicated news channel, Nile News, developing it to include live talkshows. These represented a break with tradition in Egyptian television, where concerns about content had long created an overwhelming obstacle to live broadcasts. By mid-2000, Nile News had three live talkshow slots per week. In discussions about the Thematic Channels during 1998,[95] Hamed is believed to have emphasized their potential as a training ground. His argument was that specialized channels were an important component in the development of Egypt's media, since they would provide opportunities for staff to concentrate on certain fields and increase their output at the same time. The plan was that a 'new generation of media people' working on the Thematic Channels would learn to handle subjects 'with courage' and get used to dealing with producers and technicians in the private sector. Keeping Nile News, as one of the digital Thematic Channels, separate from the established ERTU News Department was a major step towards breaking new ground in programme formats and styles. A readily available source of media graduates for the Egyptian satellite sector at this stage was the expanding Adham Center for Television Journalism at the American University in Cairo.

Major staffing cuts at MBC in London in the summer 1998 freed a large number of Arabic-speaking television professionals again, just as happened with the collapse of Orbit's BBC service in 1996. But net growth in demand for experienced people, and the perceived political impact of satellite channels, appear to have played a part in boosting the prestige attached to television journalism in the Arab world. It also increased television journalists' career choices. Al-Jazeera, for example, established a network of ten bureaux, each with a staff of around four, together with enough part-time correspondents to cover 38 countries. As Abu Dhabi Satellite TV stepped up its recruitment drive in London and elsewhere in 2000, it began to compete for the same personnel. Meanwhile the state authorities in Bahrain and Dubai acknowledged major growth in the television industry by establishing new training facilities. The first training courses in radio and television started at a new centre in Bahrain in May 2000, three months after Orbit signed its agreement with the Bahraini government to move its base from Rome to Manama in 2001. At the same time, as back-up to the new Internet City and Media Free Zone in Dubai, Shaikh Mohammed bin Rashed al-Maktoum, the Crown Prince of Dubai and defence minister of the UAE, lent his personal support to the promotion of local journalism training. He opened a press club, offering journalists free access to international news agencies and the Internet for 14 hours a day,[96] donated a headquarters for the newly created UAE Journalists' Association and set up a fund to support journalists and their families on the grounds that this would reinforce journalists' 'freedom and rights'.[97] The UAE information minister, Shaikh Abdullah bin Zayed publicly praised Shaikh Moham-med's support for journalism and the 'exchange of ideas'.[98] One of the Dubai Press Club's first initiatives was to create a raft of internationally recognized awards for Arab multimedia journalism. These were to be modelled on the Emmy Awards presented by the International Council of the National Academy of Television Arts and Sciences.[99] Significantly, given the sensitivity shown in some quarters to Al-Jazeera's focus on newsworthiness, the categories chosen for the new awards included best coverage of breaking news.

In this way, recruitment and training changes both contributed to the satellite television phenomenon and were influenced by it. They may also have been influenced to some degree by foreign-backed journalism training initiatives. As satellite channels gave the impression of altering the regional media landscape in favour of more credible and professional journalism, foreign donor governments showed an increasing interest in supporting this trend by funding media training. In any event, the task was left to individual countries after the European Union's multilateral Med Media programme ended in 1995. Med Media had been an early outcome of a new set of EU policies towards the Mediterranean that culminated in the Barcelona Declaration and creation of the Euro-Med Partnership at the end of 1995 (see Chapters 5 and 6). Aimed at promot-ing exchanges among journalists in European and Mediterranean countries, it set up around 30 joint projects in just two years. Although hopes for its relaunch were disappointed, two regional organizations spawned by Med Media continued to operate in the Maghreb and East Mediterranean. One of these, the Jemstone Network, based in Amman, adopted the slogan 'Supporting media supporting development'. It conducted diverse training workshops for journalists in both the print and broadcast media, including a series of workshops on independent and investigative journalism in 1999–2000. By this time, developments in the expatriate Arab media and in the satellite field had created a cadre of journalists both in the Arab diaspora and inside the Arab world who could play an important role in such events. A similar exercise in investigative journalism was piloted by two Lebanese universities in Beirut in early 2000, with support from the Washington-based International Center for Journalists. A shared aim of these training schemes was to help journalists find ways of working within the law to obtain information, good or bad, without resorting to unethical or sensationalist approaches. Their common rationale was the link between free and active journalism and economic, social and political development.[100]

## Conclusion

A comparison of the Arabic-language satellite channels' potential and actual contribution to wider development in the Middle East and North Africa shows that it is misleading to overstate their role. It is true, for example, that members of the policy-making elite in countries from Morocco to Saudi Arabia were made aware of discrepancies between editorial controls on terrestrial and satellite television and were prompted to try to iron these discrepancies out. But this did not lead them to a speedy or wide-reaching removal of terrestrial controls. On the contrary, the decision by some satellite companies to uproot from their original European bases and relocate in the Middle East held out the possibility that channels which had previously imposed editorial controls on themselves would become subject to formal censorship under the penal codes or codes of media 'ethics' in force in their new host states. In Egypt, pressure for private entrepreneurs to gain a media voice commensurate with their reclaimed role in the economy came from private entrepreneurs themselves. They saw satellite technology as providing opportunities denied them in terrestrial television. In this case satellite television provided the means but not the impetus for change.

The financing of satellite channels is a major factor in deciding their editorial dependence or independence and thus their ability to benefit the public at large. Financial independence requires adequate funding from diverse sources. The satellite channels' mere existence could not boost the pool of funds available for television advertising available in the Middle East. An element of competition among the satellite channels gave rise to more assessments of satellite access and channel ratings. But these evaluations remained unsophisticated and sometimes implausible, with many broadcasters and governments having little interest in improving the status quo. Each time an influential channel owner decided to keep a loss-making operation going, or impediments were placed on the gathering of accurate audience data, these actions served to distort the flow of advertising funds.

Just as transnational television is better suited to the advertising of international rather than local brands, so it has been widely perceived in the Middle East as better suited to disseminating 'good' rather than 'bad' news. The preference for 'good' news has stemmed from a desire to attract foreign or private investment but, in a world where most people want credible and relevant information before they part with their money, this preference may ultimately be shown to have deterred investment instead. Nevertheless it withstood repeated exposure to the type of news broadcast by Al-Jazeera, which made few concessions to sensitive egos worried about tarnished images or ridicule. Instead of learning to live with uncensored Arabic-language news, whether good or bad, several veteran Arab government ministers and their allies were as vocal in their criticism of Al-Jazeera four years after its creation as they were at the beginning. Despite the spread of satellite television, those in power in countries from Egypt, Jordan and Morocco to Kuwait and Saudi Arabia were just as willing to prevent journalists from going about their business in 2000 as they were in 1990. And for as long as most governments retained both a monopoly and direct editorial control over broadcasting stations based in the Arab world, the vast majority of television personnel effectively remained government employees, trained by government-run institutions to toe the government line.

Satellite channels, by creating new jobs in a competitive environment, may have helped to shake up the status quo, making the television journalist's job more demanding and prestigious. Foreign donors may have been inspired by the growth of Arabic-language satellite television to switch from paying for factories to funding media training instead. Such training afforded Arab expatriates new opportunities to transfer know-how to the Middle East. But the developmental impact of these changes would be slow to materialize. In the meantime, by creating an illusion of instant fundamental change and freedom, the proliferation of Arab satellite channels arguably retarded the development process by deflecting pressure on governments to reform their domestic media laws.

# CHAPTER FIVE

# International and Regional Regulation of Satellite Broadcasting

Of all the exogenous influences on satellite television, it might be imagined that international regulation has little impact. There being no coherent, universally agreed set of international rules for satellite broadcasting, the proliferation of channels of Middle Eastern origin in the second half of the 1990s often gave the impression of an international free-for-all. The time has come in the present study to test the accuracy of that impression.

Different UN agencies regulate different aspects of direct broadcast by satellite (DBS) with varying degrees of effectiveness and compliance from member states. For example, activities in outer space are governed by an international treaty of 1967, while regulation of worldwide telecommunications, including the allocation of orbital slots for satellites and the frequency bands needed to make use of them, falls to the Geneva-based International Telecommunication Union (ITU). The issue of prior consent to the cross-border transmission of DBS signals was taken up within the United Nations Educational, Scientific and Cultural Organization (UNESCO), while matters to do with content are covered by the 1966 International Covenant on Civil and Political Rights (ICCPR). Piracy and unauthorized copying and transmission of programmes and events is another fraught area for satellite broadcasting; following the Uruguay Round of world trade talks, intellectual property rights were policed with increasing vigour by the World Trade Organization (WTO). To investigate the effect of these bodies and agreements, it is not sufficient to look at their purpose or even to examine the way states interact with each other through them. While government self-interest may partially explain the effectiveness or ineffectiveness of regulation, other factors, including the strength of domestic lobbies, also need to be taken into account.

For present purposes, the main advantage of existing theories about international regimes is the understanding that regimes may exist even where there is no named international organization or secretariat. That is because effective regulation ultimately depends more on shared expectations and principles than explicit rules. 'Mutual expectations' has long been a key phrase in regime theory,[1] since stable mutual expectations about others' 'patterns of behaviour' are more likely to encourage parties to adapt their own practices to new institutions than any attempt at centralized enforcement of agreements.[2] Stephen Krasner summarized regimes as 'principles, norms, rules and decision-making procedures around which actor expectations converge'.[3] He explained principles as 'a coherent set of theoretical statements about how the world works'.[4] Sandra Braman carried the emphasis on shared values and understandings into the field of communication policy. In her definition, a regime is a set of 'operational definitions, modes of argument and value hierarchies that provide a basis for international negotiations in a policy issue area'.[5] The implication of stressing expectations and values in this way is that effective regimes, if they can be identified at all, will be far from ubiquitous and truly global regimes will be extremely rare.

Attempts by Western powers to regulate electronic commerce and international investment during the late 1990s demonstrated the impossibility of agreeing international regulatory arrangements unless all parties share similar fundamental principles. Negotiations about Internet regulation within a group no larger or more disparate than the seven leading industrialized countries gave rise to press reports strewn with words and phrases such as 'expectations', 'common principles', 'differences of approach' and 'sharp philosophical differences'.[6] Talks aimed at reaching a Multilateral Agreement on Investment (MAI), conducted within the 29-member Organization for Economic Co-operation and Development, collapsed in October 1998 when France withdrew. The negotiations had exposed fundamental differences of principle, between France and Canada on the one hand and the USA on the other, regarding protection for cultural industries. Non-governmental critics of the MAI also complained that the agreement confused rules (such as investor protection) with principles (such as the desirability of sustainable economic growth). They did not regard investor protection as a principle in its own right. By the same token, examples exist in which the concentration or critical mass of shared norms and values is seen to provide the cement for integration. It has been observed that European integration does not rely primarily on its institutional superstructure but operates through a 'rich substructure' of 'values, laws, rules, norms and procedures'.[7]

If such a substructure exists it will be evident in internal as well as external relations. Both the critics and some proponents of regime theory have stressed the role of domestic interest representation as a factor in the existence or absence of international regimes. Susan Strange objected to regime theorists' tendency not only to overlook, but actually distract attention from, the multitude of areas of non-agreement where there is no international regime of any kind. Instead of looking for common factors and general rules, she advised trying to map interlocking and overlapping bargains, including those between governments and domestic interest groups. According to Strange, the key bargains affecting whether international arrangements exist or not may often be struck not between states but inside them.[8] Ultimately, then, as John Vogler argues, regime analysis is about identifying patterns of governance in a system without formal government.[9] Since the term 'governance' covers a wider range of human activity and control functions than formal government,[10] it avoids the trap of state-centrism to which regime theory is prone.

A recognition within regime theory that norms and expectations are as important as secretariats and signatures chimes with the notions of different 'worlds' and different levels of interdependence evoked earlier in this book.[11] Different sets of norms and expectations may well coincide with varying intensities of interaction among groups of countries and different modes of domestic interest representation. Domestic constraints on international bargaining may be far less obtrusive in the formal international dealings of centralized, authoritarian state-systems than in those where government actions are openly constrained by the manoeuvrings of private interest groups and regular democratic elections. Nevertheless, both domestic and regional preoccupations clearly influence Middle Eastern governments' policies on transnational broadcasting and help to explain their stance in international forums. In what follows, international and regional patterns of governance discernible in the field of Middle Eastern satellite broadcasting are explored.

## Outer space

The easiest place to start a review of the international regulation of DBS is in outer space. One of the most basic international agreements in this field is the one establishing that there is no national sovereignty in outer space. Article I [2] of the 1967 Treaty on Principles Governing the

Activities of States in the Exploration and Use of Outer Space, Including the Moon and Other Bodies, declares that outer space is free for use by all states 'without discrimination of any kind on a basis of equality and in accordance with international law'. This agreement, which founded international law in the field of space resources, was signed simultaneously by all the major powers in London, Washington and Moscow. Importantly, the treaty requires states to assume regulatory responsibility for their national entities involved in space industries (Article IV) and guarantees them freedom from interference with the transmission of DBS signals in international space.

The principle of no national sovereignty in outer space underlies arrangements for the allocation of orbital slots and frequency bands for satellites. These arrangements are made by countries grouped within the ITU. The ITU became a UN agency in 1947, having been created as the International Telegraph Union in 1865. Agreements on the use of radio frequencies and satellite orbits are hammered out at regular intervals at World Radiocommunication Conferences (WRCs, or World Administrative Radiocommunication Conferences – WARCs, until 1993). The Final Acts of WRCs have international treaty status. A total of 142 ITU member states were represented at the WRC in 1997 out of a possible 187 at that time.[12] National or regional departures from ITU agreements are regarded as feasible to a degree, as a means of preserving sovereignty while also achieving consensus. These reservations are entered as footnotes to the Final Acts and put into practice through special procedures whereby a country planning to use a given frequency obtains the agreement of all countries likely to be affected. Although ITU rules provide for formal voting, voting is usually conducted informally with formal votes taken only as a last resort.[13] ITU texts use studiously apolitical language and repeatedly emphasize the need for consensus. Nevertheless, the business of assigning space resources for DBS purposes remained as highly charged and politicized in the 1990s as it was throughout the previous three decades, with different groups of countries pursuing incompatible approaches. Indeed, deregulation of the telecoms sector in the USA and Europe during the 1980s, combined with technological advances, increased the commercial value of space resources. Together these developments reinforced Western demands for efficient use of space, as opposed to the equitable access to it sought by countries left behind in the space race. Where Middle Eastern countries were concerned, these opposing standpoints were accentuated by the fact that the first faltering steps towards corporatization and privatization of

Middle Eastern telecoms operators did not start until the late 1990s. While privately owned Western telecommunications corporations were represented at ITU conferences, speaking the language of transnational business, Middle Eastern delegations remained preoccupied with protecting national sovereignty.

For the purposes of relaying radio and television signals, satellites are optimally placed in a geostationary earth orbit, where they are synchronized with the earth's rotation at a height of approximately 36,000 km above the equator. The amount of space that has to be left between satellites in this orbit in order to avoid interference is not subject to any explicit ITU ruling and depends on the user. Satellites serving European countries but belonging to different owners are usually spaced approximately three degrees apart.[14] It is technically possible for satellites to be placed closer to each other, provided users can co-ordinate their frequency bands.[15] A single user can group several satellites at the same location, as demonstrated by the fleets of Astra satellites at 19.2°E and Eutelsat Hot Bird satellites at 13°E. Discussions about the positioning of all satellites, including privately owned ones, are conducted among governments. Article VI of the Outer Space Treaty of 1967 provides that 'State Parties to the Treaty shall bear intentional responsibility for national activities in space ... whether such activities are carried on by governmental agencies or by non-governmental entities'.

Developing countries, traditionally disadvantaged in international forums, availed themselves of a short window of opportunity in the early 1970s[16] to press their demands for equitable allocation of geostationary orbital slots and frequency bands. The practice for assigning these involved then, as now, notification to the ITU's International Frequency Registration Board (renamed the Radio Regulations Board in 1993) of a member state's intention to use a particular slot and set of frequencies. In an effort to prevent countries with ample financial resources and advanced technology from reserving all the best slots and frequencies in perpetuity, it was agreed at the 1971 WARC that existing frequency assignments, even if already in use, 'should not create an obstacle to the establishment of space systems by other countries' and 'should not provide any permanent priority for any individual countries or groups of countries'.[17] This agreement meant that allocations should in principle have time limits attached. The two methods of allocation, one allowing powerful countries to pick and choose their slots and frequencies (by occupying them first and gaining authorization later) and the other guaranteeing an entitlement for all countries, are widely referred to in the literature as the *a posteriori* and *a priori* systems respectively. A *priori* planning characterized ITU operations long before the advent of satellites but was adamantly opposed by the USA as a basis for international negotiations about space. For reasons of self-interest, Western European countries, Latin American countries and Japan supported the US approach.[18] The 1971 agreement effectively placated the *a priori* camp by combining the two potentially incompatible concepts of economical and equitable use.

Allocations of orbital slots and frequencies were agreed in stages at special Space WARCs during the 1970s and 1980s, but these agreements were rapidly overtaken by technological change. The 1977 WARC drew up a plan for Broadcast Satellite Services (BSS) that allocated frequencies but also established the 'national service' rule for BSS systems, whereby states were called upon to minimize spillover onto other countries.[19] The same requirement was not imposed for the Fixed Satellite Service (FSS) arrangements for telecommunications satellites, because the early FSS satellites were not technically capable of television transmissions. However, as technological advances enabled broadcasters to transmit via lower-powered telecommunications satellites, FSS frequencies not covered by the plan started to be used for broadcasting and the BSS national service rule became obsolete.[20]

The allocations contained in the Final Acts of the 1988 WARC were originally intended to remain valid for 20 years from March 1990, unless revised by another WARC before then.[21] The Arab Satellite Communications Organization (Arabsat), being a joint enterprise, was one of a limited number of Common User Organizations, like Intelsat, that were accepted on the basis that their notification procedures vis-à-vis the ITU were handled by a single national administration. It had established positions at 30.5°E and 26°E during the mid-1980s, with the Saudi Ministry of Posts, Telephones and Telegraphs (PTT) acting as the notifying administration. Things were different for Nilesat. Egypt first notified the ITU of its intention to exploit the position at 7°W for a satellite of its own soon after being expelled from Arabsat in 1979.[22] However, the initial order for Nilesat was not placed until May 1995, by which time it had long been clear that revisions to the 1988 BSS plan would be needed well before 2010 and work on a new plan had already begun. The 1992 WARC had called for a future WARC to revise the 1988 BSS plan for Europe and Africa and Asia/Australasia,[23] or, in ITU parlance, Regions 1 and 3 (since North and South America correspond to Region 2). The 1995 WRC, chaired by Sami al-Basheer, head of the Saudi Arabian delegation, adopted the planning principles that would apply to the BSS revision. True to the ITU tradition of achieving what the organization's secretary-general, Pekka Tarjanne, called 'consensus by exhaustion', delegates to WRC-95 kept on discussing through to the last hour of the last night of the four-week conference. Even then they left two articles to be reviewed at the next WRC, in 1997.[24] It was at WRC-97 that the issue of Nilesat's inclusion in the BSS draft plan came up.

The partly state-owned Egyptian company responsible for Nilesat stood to benefit from having the Nilesat satellite system included in the new BSS plan. The main benefit would be in co-ordination with other systems in the plan and protection against technical interference created by future systems, since the onus falls on newcomers to avoid causing interfering to systems already in place. However, the Nilesat system was swept up in a much wider surge in demand for frequency bands and orbital slots. Pressure for a more rigorous approach to dealing with this demand had mounted during the 1990s as industrialized countries privatized their telecommunications sectors. Private telecommunications companies were no strangers to the ITU. Unusually for an intergovernmental organization, the ITU introduced rules as far back as 1868 to allow private companies to join as part of their country's delegation or to join in their own right, provided they contributed to the ITU budget and had the endorsement of their national administration.[25]

WRC-97, responding to calls for a 'use it or lose it' approach to orbital slots and frequency entitlements in order to stop the hoarding habit, addressed the increasing problem of 'paper satellites'. These are so called because they are satellite systems which exist on paper only, having been notified to the ITU with the main aim of reserving satellite slots for future use. The conference decided that, if paper satellites were to be transformed into real ones within a reasonable timeframe, notifying administrations should be required to supply information on a regular basis about the maker of the satellite, the contracted delivery date, the launching company and the scheduled launch date. Arab countries represented at WRC-97 unsuccessfully challenged this approach. They opposed the idea of cancelling the assignment of unused satellite slots after a certain time limit. But other countries refused to leave the process open-ended.[26] Thus, under the rules agreed at WRC-97, the maximum time allowed for satellite plans to be implemented would depend on whether they were already recorded in the Master Register and whether the requisite advance information had been received before or after 22

November 1997. In short, submissions for which advance information had been received before that date were mostly given a maximum of nine years to be brought into service (comprising the previous allowance of six years plus a possible three-year extension). Submissions received by the ITU after 21 November 1997 were made subject to a new time limit of five years between the time of submission and the date of bringing into use, with a possible extension of two years.[27]

Based on these 'due diligence' provisions, the UAE, which in 1996 notified the ITU of its intention to site a broadcasting satellite named Emarsat at 52.5°E, was given until 2004 to bring it into operation.[28] But the new provisions had more immediate implications for some non-Middle Eastern operators with satellites transmitting Arab television channels. The first half of 1998 saw the Paris-based consortium Eutelsat engaged in a tussle with the Luxembourg-based Société Européenne des Satellites (SES), operator of the Astra satellites, over which of the two had properly established the right to position satellites at or near 29°E. While Eutelsat was testing its Hot Bird 4 from the 29°E slot, SES was starting transmissions from Astra 1D at 28.2°E. Acting on behalf of SES, the Luxembourg government lodged an official reservation at WRC-97 disputing Eutelsat's permanent right to a position at 29°E.[29] When the ITU Radio Regulations Board decided that Eutelsat had not brought the 29°E slot into use within the required time period, Eutelsat announced that it would appeal, via the French administration, against the decision.[30] Problems such as this one, arising from the fact that more demands were being made on some orbital sectors than could be accommodated with existing technology, had been foreseen for some years. An ITU official, writing in a personal capacity in 1994, had warned that the development of privately owned multinational radio-communication satellite systems threatened to 'distort the regulatory regime and the sovereign rights of a country over its own territory'. He pointed out that, while the ITU could provide standardization and co-ordination services, the actual regulation of procedures depended on national administrations exercising goodwill and playing a more effective regulatory role.[31]

Against this background, Nilesat's inclusion in the new BSS draft plan adopted at WRC-97 was not a foregone conclusion. The negotiations about its inclusion lasted a whole morning and half an afternoon. They took place in Working Group 4D at WRC-97 and were led on Egypt's behalf by Raga' Mahmoud Aboul-Ela, director-general of technical affairs at the National Authority for Communications and

Telecommunications. The Egyptian team faced the problem that, with the launch of Nilesat only months away, the necessary information had not been confirmed to the ITU's Radiocommunications Bureau in accordance with a cut-off date fixed during WRC-95. Arguing that discussions on BSS planning principles were still under way, the Egyptian papers submitted to Working Group 4D sought to have the whole Nilesat 1-S system included in the BSS plan anyway. Had the Egyptian predicament been unique, it seems many delegates in the working group would have been prepared to make an exception for it. Support for such an approach was forthcoming from the delegates of Lebanon, Syria, the UAE, Israel, Mauritania, the UK and Russia.[32] However the strongest, and ultimately least beneficial support came from the Laotian delegate, who also wanted exceptional treatment for his country's LSTAR 3B-4B system. With the delegates of Australia and India apparently unwilling to make an exception for Laos, and faced with the prospect of putting the whole idea of the cut-off date back into question, the committee voted by 32 votes to 11, with 12 abstentions, against including Nilesat 1-S in the BSS plan.[33]

In the event this technicality did not hinder the launch of Nilesat 101 in April 1998. On the contrary, the general thrust of WRC-97 was to favour countries, such as Egypt and the main shareholders in Arabsat, with satellites already launched or near to launching. They had the advantage over countries unable to see their own satellite projects through to completion within the new, shortened timeframe now agreed within the ITU. African governments planning a joint satellite under the name Rascom reportedly asked the Egyptian Ministry of Information in 1997 if Nilesat capacity could be put to use for African countries pending Rascom's launch. Nilesat's management suggested that the cheapest and most effective form of assistance would be for Nilesat to send material to African television stations which would receive and retransmit. Since Nilesat's footprint does not officially include sub-Saharan Africa, this course of action would require the ITU to be notified that Nilesat was extending its reach.[34]

It is evident from the account so far that, as the 1990s progressed, negotiations over the positioning of satellite systems involved the accommodation of an increasingly wide range of interest groups (national governments, private telecommunications companies, regional satellite operators) via a single regulatory system. Although the government owners of Arabsat and Nilesat were not required to engage with private telecoms operators or broadcasters based on their own territories, their dealings with the ITU and their scope for action were nevertheless affected by the outcome of telecoms commercialization and deregulation elsewhere. In other words the rise of powerful corporate actors based in the West impinged on the workings of the ITU and consequently on all ITU members. On the Middle Eastern side of the equation, satellite positions and frequencies were still being negotiated by government representatives; among industrialized countries, in contrast, the precise locus of 'national' policy-making was sometimes less clear. Regional coalition-building tended to obscure it even further. This was certainly the case in the horse-trading that took place at WARC-92. That conference faced the complex and major tasks of allocating frequency bands for digital sound broadcasting by satellite, mobile telecommunications systems and wideband high-definition television. The first of these tasks was accomplished through an Arab–African alignment.

WARC-92 was the first major frequency allocation conference to take place after 1979. An official preview stated, somewhat ominously: 'The outcome of all ITU conferences is based on a broad consensus as a result of negotiations between national delegations attempting to reconcile a wide variety of often divergent national interests'.[35] The final overview of the same event put the emphasis on consensus again, and on pragmatism. It said: 'Whenever national interests were better served by derogation to the consensus, exceptions were agreed, also by consensus ... No vote took place on any of the substantive issues.'[36] Yet, for all the supposed consensus, WARC-92 has been described as 'unequivocally one of the most contentious' conferences in the ITU's history.[37] The bargaining that took place over four weeks was complex and intense. It is difficult, in analysing the negotiations, to disentangle national interests from regional, sectoral or corporate ones, partly because these interests were often fused to start with, or became intertwined during the proceedings. Analysts reviewing the conference on behalf of the US Congress spoke warmly of good co-operation between US government and private sector representatives, resulting from 'the extensive network of personal relationships ... built over many years'. But, they reflected, sometimes 'it is unclear who is in charge of formulating US international spectrum policy – the Federal Government or the private sector and its consultants'.[38]

For Arab delegates to WARC-92, with no private telecommunications lobby to complicate matters, the issues to consider included state aspirations and traditional alliances. Middle East and African states took their cue from the example set at the same conference by European countries, which forged a unified regional stance to oppose the USA.[39] The US government had added the subject of low earth orbiting (LEO) satellites for mobile telecommunications to the agenda for WARC-92 in 1990, a year after the agenda had officially been fixed.[40] Acting on behalf of Motorola and its Iridium satellite-telephone system, it regarded a global frequency allocation for LEO satellite services as a priority, whereas the European group, reflecting the interests of European multinationals such as Ericsson and Alcatel, favoured land-based networks.[41] By formulating common positions on several issues through the 33-member Conference of European Postal and Telecommunications Administrations, Western and Eastern European countries provided an effective counterweight to US pressure.

African and Arab countries followed suit when it came to deciding which portion of the spectrum should be allocated to BSS-Sound.[42] This service, consisting of digital radio, broadcast by satellite directly to portable individual receivers on earth, needed some 80MHz around either 1.5GHz or 2.5GHz. Existing efforts to develop the service had been conducted at 1.5GHz, but this part of the spectrum was also being used for other purposes.[43] At WARC-92 the chief proponent of digital radio by satellite was a private entrepreneur, Ethiopian-born Noah Samara, whose Washington-based company, Worldspace, had plans to broadcast information and educational programmes to developing countries in three continents. With the USA, Russia and much of Europe opposed to spectrum allocation proposals for BSS-Sound, the issue remained unresolved 24 hours before WARC-92 was due to end. However, Samara, having a background in law and having attended a previous WARC, demonstrated how personal contacts could be brought into play to build alliances. After hosting a party for delegates at a Mexican beach restaurant in the Spanish resort of Torremolinos where the conference was being held, he managed to assemble a coalition of country representatives who were ready to make their approval of the frequency allocations sought by Europe and the USA (including allocations for the Iridium project) contingent on a worldwide allocation for BSS-Sound in the 1.5 GHz band.[44] As a result, 40 MHz of L-band spectrum (between 1452 and 1492 MHz) was allocated for BSS-Sound, with immediate use of 25 MHz (between 1467 and 1492 MHz) subject to co-ordination processes.[45] The USA and some other administrations dissented from the decision, resorting to the practice of national derogation set out in footnotes to the Final Acts.

It is not surprising that Worldspace was able to gain Arab and African support. With financial backing from wealthy Saudis[46] and a licence from the US Federal Communications Commission to operate a satellite system at 21°E, obtained in advance of WARC-92, Worldspace planned that its first satellite, AfriStar, should serve Africa and the Middle East with a range of health and educational channels and local music.[47] Egypt's ERTU was among the few established broadcasters to sign up to use AfriStar before it was launched.[48] In addition to its five-year agreement to use this satellite, the ERTU was also expected to make its services available on the two other planned Worldspace satellites, AsiaStar and CaribStar.[49] The Worldspace–Iridium deal hatched at WARC-92 demonstrated that commercially driven splits among big powers in the ITU could be exploited by smaller players to extract some concessions. It also alerted US negotiators to the possible benefits of forging alliances with non-European states in Region 1 (Europe and Africa) so as to be in a position to undermine future European solidarity. US analysts observed in the wake of WARC-92: 'The experience of WARC-92 showed the effectiveness of making direct contacts with high government officials in other countries. It is at these higher levels that political and economic pressures will be understood and acted on.'[50]

A similar message was grasped by Arab countries, which acted in concert again subsequently, despite being separated administratively as a result of the ITU's reorganization, which took effect in 1993. In its first reorganization since joining the UN system in 1947,[51] the ITU was restructured in line with its three functions of standardization, regulation and development. After the change, Arab countries were split across Regions 1 and 2 as far as the regulation of radiocommunications was concerned, but still formed a single group in dealings with the Development Bureau. Arab ministers meeting in Damascus in November 1997 to co-ordinate policy in readiness for the 1998 ITU Plenipotentiary in Minneapolis decided to accept the split across two regions within the ITU Radiocommunications Bureau in the interests of influence and flexibility.[52] By then it was nearly two decades since the demise of the Arab Telecommunications Union (ATU), which once existed to unify Arab policy in this field. The ATU ceased to exist in 1980, after Egypt's expulsion from the Arab League.

Having witnessed the benefits of coalition-building at WARC-92 but failed collectively to forestall moves against 'paper satellites', Arab delegates to WRC-97 did push successfully for channels to be reserved for Palestinian use under the new BSS plan. Citing the planning principles used in the old plan, which allowed entries to be made for new countries, supporters of an allocation to Palestine managed to achieve a compromise agreement allocating five satellite broadcasting channels and related orbital positions to the Palestinian Authority (PA).[53] The compromise was conditional on Palestine being regarded as an 'entity', not a country. This entitlement, equivalent to half that agreed for full ITU members at WRC-97, recognized the transitional status of the Palestinian self-rule areas under the terms of the Declaration of Principles agreed by Israel and the Palestinians in 1993. It built on resolutions passed at the ITU Plenipotentiary Conference in Kyoto in 1994 regarding Palestinian participation in ITU work and ITU technical assistance to the PA. It also provided a platform from which the question of ITU–Palestinian relations could be revisited at future conferences. Resolution 18 of the World Telecommunication Development Conference in Malta in 1998 referred to the WRC-97 BSS allocation to the PA; it called on ITU members to co-operate with the director of the Development Bureau in assisting the PA financially and technically, and instructed the ITU's secretary-general to report to the 1998 Plenipotentiary Conference on progress achieved on this issue.[54]

Though they were conducted at a time in the 1990s when globalization rhetoric was at its height, it can be seen that negotiations over slots for broadcasting satellites were more contentious than ever and exposed even more clearly the contrasting priorities and principles pursued by different groups within the ITU. While the 'haves' benefited from the 'first come, first served' approach, the 'have-nots' still struggled for equitable access. Judging from the three sets of allocations considered here, namely those for Nilesat, Worldspace and the Palestinian 'entity', it seems that dividing lines between disparate groups became more entrenched during the bargaining process. It was only through the consolidation of regional alliances that those seeking to establish their right to orbital slots and spectrum resources could negotiate more effectively with big powers and transnational corporations.

### Airspace

As the focus of regulatory attention moves from outer space into the airspace through which DBS signals flow, the question of sovereignty comes to the fore. When sovereignty is at stake, conflicts arise between the principles of non-interference in states' internal affairs and the free flow of ideas and information across borders. UNESCO has at various times defended national sovereignty, through the principle of prior consent to satellite broadcasts, and the removal of obstacles to freedom of expression at the national and international levels. Internationally recognized human rights mechanisms exist to uphold the right of independent and private groups to broadcast terrestrially or by satellite from any country, unhindered by government control, and for inhabitants of any country to receive broadcasts from abroad. Yet, as will be shown, these mechanisms are effective only in some parts of the world and do not constitute a global regime.

When Robert Cox and Harold Jacobson reviewed the workings of several major international organizations in the 1970s, they drew a distinction between forum organizations that provide a legitimizing framework for multifarious activities and organizations that provide a service.[55] While the ITU provides a service in arranging physical co-ordination of communication systems, UNESCO is a forum. Even though neither the ITU nor UNESCO encompasses any mechanism for enforcing adherence to resolutions, there are obvious differences between the two. A forum implies scope for the airing of different views with minimal follow-up, while the provision of a service implies the existence of something approximating to a contract. Thus some degree of compliance would appear to be built into ITU membership, irrespective of the fact that the Final Acts of ITU World Radiocommunication Conferences have international treaty status. UNESCO conventions, in contrast, are not binding in international law and have the status of ideals rather than rules.[56] In the absence of follow-up, observance of UNESCO agreements is patchy. Yet even a set of international instruments and mechanisms specifically designed to monitor and promote compliance with international treaties may have only partial success. The right to 'seek, receive and impart information and ideas through any media and regardless of frontiers' is enshrined in Article 19 of the Universal Declaration of Human Rights, signed in 1948, and Article 19 of the International Covenant on Civil and Political Rights (ICCPR). The ICCPR entered into force in 1976 and, 24 years later, had been ratified by 144 states. Signatories' adherence to the provisions of the covenant is monitored by a special treaty body, the Human Rights Committee (HRC), which is charged with reviewing country reports from governments and civil society institutions, commenting on them and providing procedures for hearing complaints.[57] The ICCPR is binding on all states that have ratified it. However, five Middle Eastern states – Bahrain, Oman, Qatar, Saudi Arabia and the United Arab

Emirates – had neither signed nor ratified it by mid-2000, while many of those that had signed simply ignored their obligation under Article 40 of the ICCPR to report on their compliance to the HRC.

The demonstrable lack, in the procedures for ensuring implementation of the ICCPR, of what Hurrell terms 'independent compliance pull'[58] testifies to the absence of an effective global human rights regime. By the same token it underlines the significance of the regime concept. It confirms that regimes and international law are not the same things. Non-compliance with the provisions of the ICCPR is likely to stem from a combination of factors, including governments' lack of internal accountability, weakness of domestic lobbies nationally and internationally, disinterest on the part of powerful states with the means to encourage compliance, and the number of precedents for non-compliance. In other words the fact that the UN human rights machinery lacks teeth of its own is only part of the story. Seeing the wider picture means looking not at the organization itself but seeking out 'compliance-pull' in the form of a regime. That in turn means taking due account of expectations across the board, both inside a given country or group of countries and outside.

There are two sets of regulation to consider with regard to the transmission of DBS signals across the territory of sovereign states: prior consent and media pluralism. Looking first at the question of whether broadcasters are permitted to send DBS signals to other countries without their consent, this has been raised in different international organizations over the years, including the ITU, UNESCO and the Committee on the Peaceful Uses of Outer Space (COPUOS). Several international agreements and declarations call upon states to gain the prior consent of other states before allowing DBS signals to radiate over their territory, but these agreements are open to different interpretations and none are binding. Krasner has pointed out that the spread of DBS has been characterized by co-ordination among states with the 'same preferences and the mutual ability to interfere with each other's broadcasts, such as members of the European Community', but by deadlock between those states, such as Cuba and the USA, which are predisposed to disagree.[59]

The Final Acts of the ITU's 1971 WARC stated that 'all technical means available shall be used to reduce, to the maximum extent possible, the radiation over the territory of other countries unless an agreement has previously been reached with such countries'.[60] The wording of this decision, with its open-ended references to 'all means available' and 'the maximum extent possible', contains obvious loopholes. It had to, since the ITU itself is obliged, under Article 4 of its governing convention, to facilitate unrestricted international communications.[61] Had the ITU ruling been unequivocal there would have been little reason for UNESCO to reiterate the call for prior consent in 1972. Its Declaration of Guiding Principles on the Use of Satellite Broadcasting for the Free Flow of Information, the Spread of Education and Greater Cultural Exchange called for prior consent and was adopted by 55 votes to 7, with 22 abstentions, but remained non-binding. The same year, in response to a proposal from the Soviet Union, the UN General Assembly called on COPUOS to develop a set of principles to govern DBS as the basis for a possible treaty. That UN resolution (2916) was adopted by a vote of 102 to 1, the USA voting against. Its wording indicated that 102 countries regarded DBS as a form of interference and thus as a violation of international law.[62]

A Working Group on DBS had been created within COPUOS four years previously, in 1968. Following the 1972 instruction from the General Assembly it worked on drafting a treaty for the next ten years. It gained agreement that all states should have an equal right to use DBS and that existing international copyright instruments were applicable to DBS. But, partly because it was mandated to proceed by consensus, it failed to reach agreement on prior consent. In 1982, the year of the Second United Nations Conference on the Peaceful Uses of Outer Space (UNISPACE) in Vienna and in the absence of any draft treaty from COPUOS, the UN General Assembly adopted Resolution 37/92 on the Principles Governing the Use by States of Artificial Earth Satellites for International Direct Television Broadcasting. Sponsored by 18 African, Asian and Latin American states, together with Romania, the resolution strongly endorsed the principles of national sovereignty, non-intervention and prior consultation and consent. Articles 13–14 of the Resolution ordered states intending to establish DBS services to notify the proposed receiving states and to proceed with broadcasts only on the basis of agreement. But Article 1 also endorsed the 'right of everyone to seek, receive and impart information and ideas' as enshrined in the relevant United Nations instruments. Article 4 likewise specified that DBS activities should be conducted in accordance with international law, 'including the Charter of the United Nations, the Treaty on Principles Governing the Activities of States in the Exploration and Use of Space ... [and] the relevant provisions of the International Telecommunication Convention and its Radio Regulations'. Resolution 37/92 is not legally binding. The UN Charter reportedly confers no legislative competence on the General Assembly in resolutions which are not related to the internal workings of the UN.[63] It was carried by 107 votes but was opposed by the USA, Japan, ten Western European countries and Israel.[64]

Despite the impasse, and despite (or perhaps because of) the boom in satellite broadcasting in the 1990s, the issue of prior consent was not allowed to become a dead letter. Developing countries, including Arab states, continued to argue in the ITU that agreement to the spillover of DBS signals should not only be sought but should be explicitly obtained. Hot debate at WRC-97 resulted in a resolution that administrations originating DBS services affecting other countries should obtain those countries' prior consent. However, the resolution did not make it mandatory to do so and the rule of procedure was not changed.[65] Technically speaking, the prior consent rule is partially observed insofar as the data supplied to the ITU as part of the official notification of plans to launch a satellite include a description of the satellite's footprint, on the understanding that the signal will not extend beyond the specified area. The ITU, in circulating the footprint data to other member states, acts as the channel through which the notifying administration can claim to have gained approval for its plan, since affected countries have an opportunity at this stage to object or ask for modifications.[66] Yet it is not clear whether, if modifications have ever been requested, they have actually been made. It is a characteristic of satellite footprints that they can expand or contract according to the specifications of the receiving equipment used to pick up signals. For example, dishes of 50–75 cm are sufficient to receive Nilesat signals inside Nilesat's official footprint. However, it is still possible to receive these signals 'outside' the footprint, using a dish of 1 m or more.[67] While some Egyptian officials happily boasted that Nilesat signals could extend beyond the Middle East and North Africa to southern Europe and sub-Saharan Africa, others prudently pointed out that Nilesat's management dutifully observed the prior consent rule. Amin Bassiouny, Nilesat's chief executive, said in 1998: 'When we notify the ITU we have to be clear about our footprint coverage ... We stick to our footprint commitment ... People outside the footprint can [only] get the signal if they make an effort.'[68] According to Bassiouny, there was no problem regarding prior consent from countries inside the Nilesat footprint, because the company kept in 'constant discussion with the affected states'.[69]

Given the long-lasting rift among Arab countries caused by Iraq's invasion of Kuwait in 1990, Arabsat's Saudi-led management believed there was potential for objections from states affected by transmissions from Nilesat. It distributed a circular to states within the Arabsat and Nilesat footprints to draw their attention to the similarity between the two in case they had not already been made aware of it through the ITU.[70] Kuwait, however, studiously avoided public comment on Nilesat's decision in 1998 to lease a whole transponder to the same Iraqi government that had invaded Kuwait. Two days after the Iraqi satellite channel started operations from Nilesat, in mid-July 1998, the Kuwaiti foreign minister stressed that 'Kuwait has nothing to do with Iraqi internal affairs' and that running Nilesat was a matter for Nilesat management.[71] This example demonstrates the tensions inherent in the notion of national sovereignty as justification for prior consent. Egypt's sovereign right to decide who may or may not lease a transponder on Nilesat would appear to clash with Kuwait's sovereign right to deny access to enemy programmes beamed onto its territory. As Krasner has pointed out in another context, the meta-regime of sovereignty contains an inherent contradiction between the 'right of self-help and the norm of non-interference'.[72]

Indeed, it seems from decades of international negotiations over prior consent for DBS that different parts of the world no longer share a coherent set of theories about the principles of national sovereignty at stake. The differences tend to bear out a conceptual map which has a 'post-modern' world of pluralistic, complex states co-existing with an 'old world of state sovereignty in which others do not interfere'.[73] In a world divided along these lines it is not surprising that 'modern' and 'post-modern' states take differing views regarding the acceptability of unimpeded transnational broadcasts. In any event, there is no global consensus on this score.

A contradiction also exists between the call for prior consent on the one hand, and, on the other, internationally agreed rules concerning the right to free expression across borders. Article 19 of the Universal Declaration of Human Rights (UDHR) is binding on all UN members as a matter of customary international law. In stating that everyone has the right to seek, receive and impart information and ideas 'through any media and regardless of frontiers', it guarantees the right to freedom of expression in terms which implicitly encompass DBS.[74] This guarantee clearly endorses media pluralism and outlaws monopoly of satellite broadcasting by governments. Article 19 of the UDHR is repeated in

Article 19 [Paragraph 2] of the ICCPR. But Paragraph 3 of Article 19 of the ICCPR contains loopholes which many Middle Eastern governments consider exonerate them from giving the guarantees contained in Paragraph 2. Paragraph 3 states:

> The exercise of the rights provided for in Paragraph 2 of this article carries with it special duties and responsibilities. It may therefore be subject to certain restrictions, but these shall only be such as are provided by law and are necessary (a) for respect of the rights and reputations of others; (b) for the protection of national security or of public order, or of public health and morals.

The phrase 'the protection of national security' is widely interpreted by administrations in the Middle East to signify the preservation of the government in power. The phrase 'public order' is officially taken to mean the status quo. In the 1980s Jack Donnelly described the human rights 'regime' prevailing outside Europe and the Americas as merely 'promotional' and beset by 'profound discontinuity'.[75] That remained true 15 years on. Of the four regional human rights systems (inter-American, European, African and Arab) that came into existence over the second half of the twentieth century, the Arab system was the latest and least comprehensive. The Arab League's 1994 Arab Charter of Human Rights allowed all rights to be restricted for reasons such as national security, the economy and the preservation of public order.[76]

As regards the ICCPR's implications for satellite broadcasting in the Middle East, discontinuities abound. First, not all Arab states have signed the ICCPR. Those that have are required to comply with it, and all other international conventions they have signed and ratified, under Articles 27 and 46 of the 1969 Vienna Convention on the Law of Treaties. Non-adherence may not be excused by having the treaty declared unconstitutional by a supreme court. Reservations to treaties are allowed provided they receive the consent of other signatories. However, statements of interpretation (based on the principle that states themselves should interpret the convention) reportedly do not require other signatories' consent.[77] For example, Egypt's Supreme Court ruled in 1975 that treaty obligations can be limited by subsequent or more specific legislation.[78] The HRC has meanwhile indicated, through its response to reports submitted to it, that it does not accept interpretations of Article 19 of the ICCPR which protect governments from criticism or ban non-government media.[79] Yet the HRC can only respond to reports it receives. Many reports arrive years late, if at all.

Syria delivered its first report to the HRC in 1978. Its second was due in 1984 but failed to materialize over the next 14 years, despite 25 requests from the HRC, the largest number for any country.[80] Egypt's second periodic report, due in 1988, was delivered in 1992. HRC comments on it focused on measures taken under the State of Emergency and issues relating to freedom of thought and association; they did not mention freedom of expression.[81] The April 1994 and April 1999 deadlines for Egypt's third and fourth periodic reports were not met.[82]

Despite the rise of international non-governmental organizations advocating human rights observance, and the increased attention paid to 'good governance' by lenders such as the World Bank and EU, external pressure to comply with media pluralism requirements remained weak. Mediterranean countries signing Association Agreements with the EU were formally called upon to honour their human rights commitments under the terms of the Barcelona Declaration agreed by 27 European and Mediterranean states in November 1995. The Barcelona Declaration stated that members of the Euro-Mediterranean Partnership should 'act in accordance with the United Nations Charter and the Universal Declaration of Human Rights', as well as their other obligations under international law, in particular 'those arising out of regional and international instruments to which they are party'. It called on members to 'respect human rights and fundamental freedoms and guarantee the effective legitimate exercise of such rights and freedoms, including freedom of expression'.[83]

However, those Mediterranean countries that actually signed Association Agreements with the EU after 1995 had little reason to expect that doing so would bring strong pressure from European institutions to comply with the freedom of expression requirements contained in the Barcelona Declaration. When Tunisia became the first southern Mediterranean state to sign a partnership agreement with the EU under the Barcelona framework in 1995, its poor human rights record was criticized in the European Parliament in Strasbourg in 1996 but in 1997 the criticism fizzled out.[84] It was not until June 2000 that the parliament repeated its concern that human rights, 'particularly with regard to freedom of expression, opinion and association' were being denied by the Tunisian government in contravention of its obligations internationally and as a Mediterranean partner of the EU.[85] When a leading Egyptian civil rights campaigner, Saad Eddin Ibrahim, was detained for six weeks in the summer of 2000 under Egypt's State of Emergency laws, the European Commission and Council of Ministers remained silent. In an appeal on Ibrahim's behalf to the French presidency of the EU, a group of seven human rights organizations noted that the EU's silence was especially regrettable since one of the charges against Dr Ibrahim concerned funds received by his research centre from the EU.[86]

Meanwhile UNESCO started to marshal its resources behind observance of Article 19. The 1990s saw UNESCO's Communications Division paying attention to media pluralism in a way not seen during the previous decade, when its chief preoccupation was to promote a New World Information and Communication Order (NWICO). *Many Voices, One World*, the report of the International Commission for the Study of Communication Problems (the MacBride Commission), published by UNESCO in 1980, had called for a shift of emphasis from 'free flow' to a 'free and balanced flow' of ideas.[87] The NWICO era was short-lived. In 1989, after the USA and UK had withdrawn from the organization, UNESCO introduced what its officials called a 'new communication strategy'. Six days after the fall of the Berlin Wall on 9 November 1989, the 25th session of the UNESCO General Conference undertook to

> encourage the free flow of information, at international as well as national levels; to promote the wider and better balanced dissemination of information, without any obstacle to freedom of expression; and to strengthen communication capacities in the developing countries in order to increase their participation in the communication process.[88]

The fresh emphasis on pluralism and freedom of expression, which was to remain as the basis for UNESCO action to 2001,[89] was followed up with a series of regional seminars, the fourth of which took place in Sanaa, Yemen, in January 1996. This produced the Sanaa Declaration, deploring censorship and intimidation of media professionals in the Arab world and stating, among other things, that:

> State-owned broadcasting and news agencies should be granted statutes of journalistic and editorial independence as open public service institutions. Creation of independent news agencies and private and/or community ownership of broadcasting media including in rural areas should also be encouraged.[90]

As agreed in Sanaa, this declaration on 'Promoting Independent and Pluralistic Media' was duly submitted to, and adopted by, the 29th session of the UNESCO General Conference in Paris in 1997.[91] However, as with the earlier UNESCO declaration dealing with prior consent for sending DBS signals to other countries, this declaration was not binding. Moreover, UNESCO officials working with Arab countries at this time saw their first priority as promoting independent print media, on the grounds that they could 'make a larger impact' in this field than in state-owned radio and television.[92] Egypt, Jordan and Morocco were considered relatively unusual among Arab states in being susceptible to international pressure and were consequently not regarded as 'problem' countries as far as media freedoms were concerned. It is not considered appropriate for UNESCO to insist on any course of action or take sides in disputes over freedom of expression. The UNESCO Secretariat has to wait to be asked for advice or assistance from member states and its staff see no call to get involved in day-to-day affairs. In other words, nothing has changed since James Sewell wrote of UNESCO conventions that they are 'more aptly described as ideals than rules', since member governments are 'most unlikely to be called to account when they fail to do what they had agreed to do'.[93] Where other mechanisms work effectively to make governments accountable for their international treaty obligations, UNESCO resolutions are redundant. Where this is not the case, UNESCO resolutions do not plug the gap.

## Trade and piracy

While the freedom to transmit television programmes across state borders is covered by the UDHR and ICCPR, and nominally by UNESCO declarations and the Euro-Mediterranean Partnership, issues related to trade and foreign investment in broadcasting services and copyright for televised material are overseen by the more recently established WTO. The WTO, set up as a result of the Uruguay Round of negotiations on the General Agreement on Tariffs and Trade (GATT), came into being at the start of 1995. It arrived on the scene with a remit that included removal of protective barriers affecting trade in services and investment and to protect intellectual property rights. Seen by some as the 'third pillar of the global economic management system',[94] its goal was to extend a single regime for trade in both goods and services to all countries and all sectors over time. WTO membership was opened to countries prepared to accept the Uruguay Round in its entirety.[95] Ironically, while the aim of opening services sectors to foreign investment represents a form of deregulation, the protection of intellectual property rights involves the imposition of new regulation which has been strictly enforced.

Five years after its creation the WTO could not claim to be a global organization. A Saudi deputy minister involved in negotiating his country's accession to the WTO pointed out to an international audience in June 2000 that Saudi Arabia was hardly unusual in not yet having gained membership; more than 60 countries were in the same boat.[96] Besides Saudi Arabia, populous non-member countries in the Middle East included Iran, Syria and Algeria. For those countries signing up for WTO membership, the main incentive was the prospect of attracting private foreign direct investment by promising to protect intellectual property rights, treat foreign firms at least as well as national ones, and safeguard private investment. However, as this section will show, not only is WTO membership far from universal, the status of cultural industries under WTO rules remained contested long after the organization was formed. Any Middle Eastern government contemplating membership would have had ample reason to assume that this would not mean opening the broadcasting sector up to foreign involvement, cancelling subsidies to the domestic film industry, or making way for unlimited amounts of foreign programming.

During the course of the Uruguay Round, which began in September 1986 and ended in December 1993, a working document entitled 'Draft Services Trade Framework for Audiovisual Services' was drawn up and discussed. Article IV of the 1947 version of the GATT had provided in general for free trade in film[97] but allowed quotas, as a non-tariff barrier, to be applied to the screening of national films.[98] Disagreement over subsidies and quotas for audiovisual production under the new GATT pitted countries in favour of these devices, such as those in the European Community as well as India and Canada, against the USA. US negotiators, representing the Motion Picture Association of America (MPAA), were implacably opposed to subsidies or special treatment of any kind.[99] In the concluding weeks of the Uruguay Round, from October to December 1993, the split crystallized around European resistance to US media exports. Apparently in response to Europe's new proliferation of commercial broadcasters, US media exports to Europe had climbed from $2.3 billion in 1987 to $3.7 billion in 1992.[100] The eventual stand-off between the EU and USA over treatment of the audiovisual sector led some press observers to deduce that the sector had been left out of the final agreement altogether.[101] Officially, however, the exclusion could be neither total nor permanent. The WTO, spawned by the Uruguay Round, was created to cover all sectors, on the principle that member countries maintaining barriers in respect of specific areas would be required to make these barriers public and work towards removing them eventually.

Thus, under the General Agreement on Trade in Services (GATS), which is binding on WTO members, parties to the agreement must draw up a national schedule specifying which service sectors and activities will be opened to access by other members and indicating where limits will apply.[102] The GATS has four main elements. It favours national treatment, meaning that foreign service companies should receive the same treatment as domestic ones. It provides for most-favoured nation (MFN) treatment, meaning that there should be no discrimination for or against other WTO members. It promotes transparency, so that barriers and restrictions are revealed by means of annexes to the national schedules.[103] It also entails a commitment to continue to negotiate until all services, with the sole exception of air transport landing rights, are covered in all member states.[104] Because there are no customs duties on services, the abolition of discrimination means the end of protection from foreign competition, although internal regulation may still apply. As far as audiovisual services are concerned, the national schedules can cover all, some or none of the various means by which these services can be traded: through investment in the broadcasting sector of the host country, through direct broadcasting from abroad, and through trade in recorded programmes.

Schedules of commitments by 95 members were agreed in Marrakesh in February 1994 and, by the launching of the WTO in 1995, two developed and 11 developing countries had made commitments regarding audiovisual communication. This was almost the lowest total for any single named sector within the 11 groups of sectors identified, namely business, communication, construction, distribution, education, environment, finance, health, tourism and travel, recreation, culture and sport, and transport. The only lower ones were for health services other than hospitals, libraries, archives and museum services, and a few strategically important branches of the transport sector such as pipelines.[105] The 13 countries making commitments on audiovisual services included the USA, Mexico, Singapore, Hong Kong, South Korea, Thailand and Malaysia. Some of their commitments were limited to motion picture or video tape production or distribution, while Malaysia's offer on broadcasting covered only cross-border transmission from abroad, limited to 20 per cent of total screening time.[106]

Apart from these limited early pledges, there was little sign of WTO jurisdiction over trade in cultural products being generally accepted. The national schedules presented by Indonesia, Australia and European Union countries contained no commitments on audiovisual services at all.[107] Canada, which included advertising in its definition of cultural industries, established a precedent for exempting cultural industries from free trade agreements when it signed the US–Canada Free Trade Agreement in 1989, and the North American Free Trade Agreement (NAFTA) in 1994. Yet the value of the precedent was soon questioned. Observers pointed out that the 1989 agreement made subsidies for cultural production a specific target for retaliatory action in terms that reduced culture to a tradeable commodity.[108] Article 2005 (1) of NAFTA stated: 'Cultural industries are exempt from the provisions of this Agreement'. But Article 2005 (2) qualified this exemption by permitting a party to the agreement to take 'measures of equivalent commercial effect in response to actions that would have been inconsistent with this Agreement'.[109] In March 1991 the US Trade Representative, Carla Hills, said of the cultural industries exemption that it was 'no more than an agreement to disagree' and declared that the USA reserved the right to bring cases against Canada.[110] Doubts about the durability of exemptions for cultural industries were vindicated when a Canadian–US dispute over magazine advertising erupted in 1995. A US complaint against Canada on this matter, raised on behalf of US companies including Time Warner, was upheld,[111] being regarded as a dispute over trade in goods rather than services.[112] But broadcasting disputes did arise among WTO members. South Korea agreed in 1995, in response to a US threat to raise the matter with the WTO, to drop restrictions that stopped foreign companies from advertising on television during peak viewing hours. It also promised that its state-run monopoly agent for broadcast advertising would lose its monopoly by the end of the decade.[113]

Bilateral cases such as these hardly signalled an impending wholesale sweep towards removing protection for cultural industries. Article XIX of the GATS calls for successive rounds of negotiation with the aim of achieving ever-increasing liberalization of service sectors. However, no specific group, committee or working party was established under the Council for Trade in Services to continue GATS negotiations on the audiovisual sector. In contrast, such groups were set up for financial services, professional services and maritime transport services.[114] All WTO members are theoretically subject to a trade policy review every six years, but where Middle Eastern members are concerned, trade barriers in other sectors are likely to attract far more scrutiny than those in the audiovisual sector. Moreover, the GATS contains standard exceptions on matters concerning public morality, health and safety and security. The matter of subsidies in services trade is deferred and the need of developing countries to subsidize service sectors in the interests of development is taken into account.[115]

As for safeguards for local content within broadcasting, any developing country need only point to the precedent established by the European Commission through its Television without Frontiers Directive. This Directive, launched in 1989 and renewed in 1997, requires member states to ensure 'where practicable' that 50 per cent of programming is European-made. European countries have likewise withstood US demands, pressed in the closing stages of the Uruguay Round, for curbs on public funding of film and entertainment production. There is also considerable resistance within developed countries to allowing foreign broadcasters to creep in by the back door as a result of convergence between broadcasting and telecommunications. The implications of convergence are demonstrated in the multimedia capabilities of the Internet and the availability of video-on-demand over telephone lines. Sixty-nine countries signed a telecommunications agreement within the GATS framework on 15 February 1997, whereby they undertook to open their domestic markets to foreign competition with general agreement that the offer of access should be 'technology neutral'.[116] Among Middle Eastern countries, only Israel, Morocco and Tunisia signed this agreement. Even some signatories, including the USA itself, continued to impose limitations on market access on grounds of public interest.[117]

Like the battle lines that exist over protection for cultural industries, so there are battle lines inside and between countries over piracy of films and television programmes. Countries receiving inward investment are required under WTO rules to take special measures to protect intellectual property rights. The Council on Trade Related aspects of Intellectual Property Rights (TRIPS) has equal status with the Council for Trade in Services within the structure of the WTO. In this way, the TRIPS agreement bestows enforceability on the century-old Berne Convention copyright standards, tightened and widened by the Universal Copyright Convention in 1952. Under these standards, copyright protection applicable in one signatory country is equally applicable to all. Because of the all-or-nothing nature of WTO membership, the TRIPS agreement applies to all WTO members, whatever their previous observance of copyright rules. Additionally, it can be enforced through WTO dispute mechanisms. It affords exclusive rental rights to producers of sound recordings and films and protects performers against unauthorized recording and broadcasting of live performances. These rights and protection are valid for a minimum of 50 years. Developing countries and transition economies have between five and 11 years to comply with the agreement by amending their domestic laws to ensure that the intellectual property rights of foreign producers are adequately protected and to make piracy of audiovisual material a criminal offence. A US complaint to the WTO against Japan regarding protection of pre-1971 sound recordings was dropped only after Japan amended its domestic legislation.[118]

The TRIPS agreement is significant for television broadcasting because the Berne Convention and the Universal Copyright Convention did not protect television broadcasts from taping for sale or rebroadcast.[119] Although UNESCO and the World Intellectual Property Organization worked to correct this situation in the early 1970s, the 1974 Convention Relating to the Distribution of Program-Carrying Signals Transmitted by Satellite was ratified by very few states. Countries whose nationals complained about piracy generally dealt with the problem on a bilateral basis.[120] In the mid-1990s, in contrast, the issue was brought under the WTO umbrella. Yet the regulation has very different implications for countries depending on the extent to which they either originate or retransmit films and television material.

For example, Egyptian producers generally welcome copyright protection. Moneib Shafei, chair of the Chamber of the Movie Industry, estimated in 1997 that foreign piracy was costing Egyptian film companies $100 million a year in lost royalties and sales.[121] Enquiries made by the head of the Egyptian Space Channel, Sana Mansour, revealed that pirated videos of ESC and Nile TV programmes were openly on sale in Europe and the USA, complete with the original channel logos.[122] Law 38 of 1992, amending Egypt's 1954 Copyright Law, stiffened the penalties for copyright infringement inside the country and a ministerial ruling in April 1994 specifically protected audiovisual material and performance rights, as well as defining personal use. The General Department for Technical Compilations in the Ministry of Culture stores works formally deposited against the event of possible future copyright infringement.[123] Externally, however, Egyptian copyright law carries no weight, while Egypt itself comes under intense pressure from the office of the US Trade Representative (USTR) to enforce its own domestic legislation. Egypt was moved from the USTR's 'watch list' to its 'priority watch list' in early 1997, mainly because of complaints from US pharmaceutical companies and the Business Software Alliance. The MPAA, in contrast, reported an improvement in the copyright situation with regard to piracy of foreign films and videos inside Egypt.[124]

The MPAA responded to reports of piracy in Lebanon in the mid-1990s by sending representatives on a mission to close down a television station called Kilikia, one of dozens of stations that existed before the closures imposed in 1996 under Lebanon's 1994 Audiovisual Media Law. The owner of Kilikia was allegedly rebroadcasting recently released Hollywood films acquired from his local video store. Reports at the time said that, as soon as the MPAA left, Kilikia's owner resumed his piracy, claiming to be resisting American imperialism.[125] The proliferation of small television stations in the West Bank and Gaza, unusual in the region after Lebanon's 1996 clampdown, likewise created a situation conducive to piracy. There is a feeling among some radio and television presenters in the region, including some in Egypt, that that those who pirate and rebroadcast material are providing a laudable service, in the style of Robin Hood, to those unable to afford satellite connections.[126] But people everywhere hold different views depending on their position in the production, distribution and reception chain. When six US film studios raised a case in 1999 against an estimated 1000 illegal cable television distributors in Lebanon, after the Lebanese parliament passed a bill protecting intellectual property rights, the threat of action against the pirates was, not surprisingly, extremely unpopular with the viewing public.[127]

## Regional governance

So far this chapter has focused on regulatory bodies that have a global remit in theory if not in practice. To complete the picture it is necessary to entertain the possibility that regional regimes, whether implicit or explicit, may exist where international ones do not. Regional trade blocs have emerged in all parts of the world since the 1980s and the European Union has provided examples of attempts at supranational rule-making in the field of transnational television, some more successful than others. The EU's Television without Frontiers Directive provides guidelines on programme content and sets broad parameters for national regulation of television advertising and sponsorship. However, the European Commission's attempts to regulate cross-media ownership throughout the EU, started in 1992, ran aground. Proposed changes in the draft directive on ownership, favouring flexibility for member states, drew attention to deep divisions among EU members over the purpose of regulation and whether it should be geared to promoting pluralism or promoting the single market, which are two divergent aims.[128]

Arab countries have many joint organizations that invite comparison with those of the EU. There is an Arab League, a large number of associated pan-Arab bodies, and a long tradition of cross-border interaction, facilitated by a shared language, religion and culture. Yet few scholars have sought to apply insights developed through the study of international regimes to pan-Arab regulation. This may be because of the evident lack of anything approaching a pan-Arab regime. Bahgat Korany, referring to the Arab League, has observed that it is quite possible for an international organization to 'stay imprisoned in its formal structure without being an effective international regime', if it fails to harmonize the attitudes and expectations of its members.[129] Korany has nevertheless also noted the collective, tripartite leadership assumed by three countries – Egypt, Syria and Saudi Arabia – during brief occasions, such as the oil embargo and war effort of October 1973 and the 1976 agreement on stationing Syrian troops in Lebanon, when Arab 'interstate society' witnessed something close to an embryonic pan-Arab regime.[130] Pan-Arab institutions dealing with broadcasting and satellite communications predated the proliferation of Arab-owned satellite channels that took place in the 1990s. These institutions' development reveals how official attitudes and expectations were harmonized.

Members of the Arab Satellite Communications Organization (Arabsat) and the Arab States Broadcasting Union (ASBU) have certain rights and responsibilities which amount to a degree of regulation. The major shareholders in Arabsat have, from the outset, been the Arab world's leading oil exporters, including Saudi Arabia, Kuwait, Libya and Qatar. By the time of the first Arabsat launch, in 1985, Egypt had been suspended from the organization, which was to have a major impact on the size of individual shareholdings. Egypt initially held a 5.2 per cent stake, putting it in sixth place after Saudi Arabia, Kuwait, Libya, Iraq and Qatar (see Table 10), and giving it a place on the nine-member board. By the time it was readmitted to the Arab fold at the end of the 1980s, Egypt had already decided to pursue a satellite project of its own. In 1990, Iraq invaded Kuwait and was itself expelled from Arabsat. Under the reallocation of Arabsat shares that took place in the wake of the 1991 Gulf war, the ownership rested much more decisively with Saudi Arabia (36.66 per cent) and Kuwait (14.59 per cent). Libya's share increased to 11.28 per cent and Qatar's to 9.81 per cent. Egypt's, in contrast, declined to 1.59

per cent, putting it in 12th place. Arabsat member states are represented on the General Assembly, Arabsat's highest authority, by their ministers of telecommunications and others who may be included by 'written authorization'. The proceedings of General Assembly meetings are not released, however. Under Article 7 of Section 7 of the General Assembly's by-laws, all discussion and documentation are classified.[131]

### Table 10: Shares in Arabsat before and after 1990

| Shareholder | Initial number | Initial percentage | Percentage after 1990 |
|---|---|---|---|
| Saudi Arabia | 598 | 29.9 | 36.66 |
| Kuwait | 238 | 11.9 | 14.59 |
| Libya | 184 | 9.2 | 11.28 |
| Iraq | 166 | 8.3 | 1.90[1] |
| Qatar | 160 | 8.0 | 9.81 |
| Egypt | 104 | 5.2 | 1.59 |
| UAE | 76 | 3.8 | 4.66 |
| Jordan | 66 | 3.3 | 4.05 |
| Lebanon | 63 | 3.2 | 3.83 |
| Bahrain | 40 | 2.0 | 2.45 |
| Syria | 34 | 1.7 | 2.08 |
| Algeria | 28 | 1.4 | 1.72 |
| North Yemen | 25 | 1.3 | 1.65[2] |
| Sudan | 21 | 1.1 | 0.27 |
| Oman | 20 | 1.0 | 1.23 |
| Tunisia | 12 | 0.6 | 0.74 |
| Morocco | 10 | 0.5 | 0.61 |
| Somalia | 7 | 0.4 | 0.24 |
| Mauritania | 5 | 0.3 | 0.27 |
| Palestine | 4 | 0.2 | 0.25 |
| South Yemen | 2 | 0.1 | n/a[2] |
| Djibouti | 2 | 0.1 | 0.12 |
| Unsold | 135 | 6.5 | 0.0 |
| **Total** | 2,000 | 100.0 | 100.0 |

[1] Suspended.
[2] Held by unified Yemen.

Sources: Hezab AlSaadon, 'The Role of Arabsat in Television Programme Exchange in the Arab World', PhD thesis (Ohio State University, 1990), p 155; *Middle East Broadcast and Satellite* 1/1 (January 1993); *Arabfile* (newsletter of the Arab League office in London), June 1996, p 17

Arabsat was conceived in the 1970s, at a time when Arab governments were still adjusting to new-found oil wealth. In the early days it was the only satellite to have its footprint precisely over the Middle East and North Africa. Subsequent downturns in oil revenues, combined with the increasing number of satellites serving large parts of the same region, altered Arabsat's operating environment. The new circumstances were acknowledged at the Arabsat General Assembly meeting in May 1998, when it was agreed that internal restructuring was needed and that shares should be sold to a 'strong global partner' that would be able to make the investment necessary to compete.[132] Financial considerations had not entirely taken over, however, as demonstrated by the fact that the Arabsat executive considered the content transmitted by Arabsat users to be more important than the rent they paid when it came to allocating transponder space.

Arabsat is headquartered in the Saudi capital, Riyadh, with a Saudi, Saad bin Abdel-Aziz al-Badna, as its secretary-general. The satellite's primary control facility is also in Riyadh, and Saudi Arabia's PTT Ministry is the administration which notifies Arabsat co-ordination data to the ITU. When Canal France International (CFI) was deprived of its slot on Arabsat in July 1997, after a technical mix-up by France Télécom resulted in ten minutes of sexually explicit material appearing on Gulf television screens instead of an educational programme, French diplomats appealed against the decision not only to Arabsat personnel in Riyadh but also to Saudi government officials.[133] CFI was not reinstated; Mr Badna said it had already been warned about programming that undermined 'Islamic and Arab moral values'.[134] When the slot was transferred to another French satellite broadcaster, TV5, in 1998, Nilesat's chairman, Amin Bassiouny, let his counterparts in CFI know that he was ready to discuss accommodating CFI on Nilesat.[135] With Iraq suspended from Arabsat since its invasion of Kuwait in 1990, Nilesat also leased a whole transponder to Iraq in July 1998.

With Egypt and Saudi Arabia each able to counter any unwelcome attempt at regional regulation by the other, a pattern of control over regional satellite broadcasting emerges that can also be seen in the way broadcasters from these two countries have made selective use of the Tunis-based ASBU. Although ASBU membership was originally limited to state-owned broadcasters, privately owned satellite companies, including those based outside the Arab world, were offered associate membership by the ASBU General Assembly with effect from 1996. These institutions reportedly asked to join in order to benefit from rights negotiated by ASBU to coverage of international sports events.[136] Hassan Hamed, deputy director of the ERTU, told an international conference

in Cairo in February 1999 that the ASBU Satellite Channels Co-
ordinating Committee was convened at the instigation of the Egyptian
minister of information, Safwat al-Sharif.[137] Records show that Sharif
made just such a proposal in a speech entitled 'Egyptian and Arab
Information in the Globalization Era', delivered at the annual Radio and
Television Festival in Cairo in July 1998. In it he proposed a committee
that would co-ordinate Arab satellite channels, to 'preserve the positive
aspects and demolish the negative aspects that can be transmitted in our
Arab media'. Sharif said the media should 'not be an arena to exploit
some negative aspects of our Arab society'.[138] The satellite channels had,
however, already met under ASBU auspices in previous years. In October
1997 they met in Amman. It seems that the Co-ordinating Committee
began to take shape at this point, with Pierre Daher, executive director of
the Lebanese channel, LBC-Sat, starting a two-year term of office as its
chair. After a committee meeting at the end of 1998, it emerged that the
existing members had decided to deny membership to Al-Jazeera, the
controversial news and current affairs channel launched by the Gulf
emirate of Qatar. To qualify for membership, they insisted, Al-Jazeera
had to 'conform to the code of honour of the Arab media'.[139] Al-Jazeera
was told that it could re-apply for membership in six months.[140] The
Committee thus provided a convenient mechanism for outlawing a
certain type of programming, described by one committee member as a
type that 'takes a stance against our culture and background'.[141]

If this sequence of events is considered alongside other examples of
collaboration among Arab governments in matters to do with satellite
television, signs of a rudimentary regional regime come into view.
Chapters 2 and 3 examined evidence of a Saudi–Syrian–Lebanese
triangle of ownership and control of television stations, built on relationships among powerful individuals. When, for example, the Lebanese
government imposed a ban on political news broadcasts by satellite, it
did so at the behest of authorities in the Gulf, as the Lebanese minister
of information, Bassam Sabaa, publicly acknowledged at the time.[142] The
privately owned Syrian channel, ANN, softened its criticism of the Syrian
government of Hafez al-Asad after receiving an injection of funds from
what is believed to have been a Saudi source.[143] The leverage was not all
one way, however, as demonstrated by the rivalry with Saudi Arabia that
was factored into Egyptian government broadcasting decisions. The
element of competition introduced by the arrival of Lebanese satellite
stations was confined within limits determined from Damascus. This
chapter has shown the balance between Nilesat and Arabsat to be an

equally significant element in the regional picture, together with the stance taken by the ASBU Satellite Channels Co-ordinating Committee. In this way, the governments of three key states – Egypt, Syria and Saudi Arabia – steered the expectations and procedures underlying the operation of Arab satellite channels.

## Conclusion

It is clear from the degree of censorship exercised by most of the leading Arab satellite broadcasters that the authorities behind them do not believe they can afford to leave the content of transnational television to chance. Yet households wishing to gain access to satellite television face few serious obstacles in any Arab state. Applying a regime analysis uncovers a regional pattern of governance that helps to explain this apparent anomaly. It shows how shared principles and expectations can make for effective informal regulation. As an informal pan-Arab satellite broadcasting regime evolved, focused on controls over production, restrictions on reception became generally redundant. The regime developed in two phases. During the first half of the 1990s, with the satellite scene dominated jointly by the Egyptian government and the Saudi ruling family, the issue of unwelcome content did not arise. The Saudi expatriate channels, MBC, ART and Orbit, imposed a level of self-censorship that put them under the same constraints as the ERTU. Similar Syrian controls (and indirect Saudi controls) over the Lebanese channels that started in 1996 helped to maintain the status quo. They thereby cemented an informal Egyptian–Saudi–Syrian regime for broadcasting analogous to the embryonic tripartite regime, involving these same countries, that Korany has shown to have dominated and directed pan-Arab affairs at critical junctures in the past.[144]

It was not until the uncensored Qatari channel, Al-Jazeera, became widely available to households with satellite access after November 1997 that a gap appeared in the mesh of shared principles and expectations. It was at this point that steps were taken towards a more explicit collective form of regulation. Thus it was that domestic preoccupations brought about the transformation of unwritten cross-border arrangements, applied by a combination of public and private bodies, into a more formal arrangement structured around the ASBU Satellite Channels Co-ordinating Committee. In order to deny the benefits of membership (such as television rights to sporting events) to broadcasters operating according to different principles, the committee was obliged to institute formal decision-making procedures and rules.

Seen in the global context, the web of inter-Arab broadcasting controls shows yet again the divides that remain between different parts of the world. Despite the growth of global telecommunications networks, the prolonged effort that goes into reaching consensus at ITU conferences and the strategic coalition-building that characterized WRCs in the 1990s, splits over the allocation of orbital slots and spectrum resources persisted. Voting for and against the principle of prior consent to satellite broadcasts, both within UNESCO and the ITU, also exposed enduring disagreement between groups of states. While international human rights instruments exist to promote media pluralism and the free flow of ideas and information across borders, their workings are beset by discontinuities within and between regions. The WTO's global free trade agenda barely hides industrialized countries' mutually incompatible approaches to protection for cultural industries. These in turn underpin developing countries' resistance to unwelcome external interventions in this sector. Put simply, international and regional patterns of governance in transnational broadcasting reflect deep divides.

# CHAPTER SIX

# Global Civil Society? NGO Influence on Transnational Broadcasts

Studies of television frequently foreground the programmes that actually appear on the screen. Yet one of the most compelling reasons for studying television in the first place is the need to discover what material is not shown and why. Censorship in various guises has featured prominently in this book so far, and generally been traced to vested interests of governments and businesses, often interacting with each other across borders. But what of proactive interest groups that are neither governmental nor commercial? What part do they play in broadcasting decisions? Alongside the spread of government-to-government, business-to-business and government-to-business links, a burgeoning has also been perceived in the world at large in mutual, cross-border support systems among non-governmental organizations (NGOs). Accounts of the latter phenomenon often use the term 'civil society' to encompass the assortment of pressure groups and voluntary associations that lend themselves to categorization as NGOs.

It is worth pausing briefly here to consider the insights that might be sacrificed when the concept of civil society is used loosely in this way. In conceptualizing civil society as somehow separate from government and business there is a risk that crucial networks and relationships linking these categories and explaining their behaviour will be overlooked. Antonio Gramsci's understanding of civil society, developed from his reading of Hegel,[1] brings these relationships to the fore in a formulation that implies not only interconnections but a constantly shifting border-line between civil society and the state. Intrinsic to Gramsci's non-reductionist understanding of civil society is his theory of hegemony, whereby he accounts for those situations in which the ruling group is seen to gain the 'spontaneous' consent of the population to the 'general direction' it imposes on social life.[2] The hegemonic social order is sustained by an 'historic bloc' or alliance of economic, political and cultural institutions whose interests it serves. In this way domination is achieved more by consent than coercion, but both forms of domination remain in play. The key passage on civil society in Gramsci's *Prison Notebooks* runs as follows:

> What we can do, for the moment, is to fix two major superstructural 'levels': the one that can be called 'civil society', that is the ensemble of organisms commonly called 'private', and that of 'political society' or 'the State'. These two levels correspond on the one hand to the function of 'hegemony' which the dominant group exercises throughout society, and on the other hand to that of 'direct domination' or rule exercised through the State and the juridical government.[3]

To write about a putative civil society as though it were distinct from state structures is to lose sight of questions about whether dominant groups dominate by coercion or consent. Such questions are particularly apposite in Middle Eastern countries where the majority of so-called private or voluntary organizations generally only survive if they are ultimately sponsored by, or manipulated by, the government, rather than the reverse.[4] Questions about consent, coercion and historic blocs recede even further into the background when the concept of civil society is projected onto a global backdrop. Yet the notion of global civil society has gained such wide circulation that any investigation of transnational media must engage with it, not least because of the hypothesis that, if television can transcend borders and state jurisdictions, its workings must reflect interaction with NGOs and other bodies that transcend them too. Peter Willetts, for example, in urging transnational corporations to meet their obligations to the wider community, states categorically: 'There is now a global civil society. Governments and companies interact with other types of pressure groups both directly and indirectly in international organizations and the media, in a complex global political system.'[5]

In Willetts' model, the media are envisaged as forming yet another category distinct from governments, companies, pressure groups or international organizations. Yet the present study has revealed just how snugly some elements of the media, notably most Middle Eastern satellite channels, fit inside the very same power structures as governments and non-media companies. Setting that detail aside for the moment, the issue remains as to whether and, if so, how pressure groups interact with Middle Eastern satellite television operators. In theory they could do so by contributing directly to the television companies' output. Or they might do so indirectly by influencing producers, regulators, satellite operators, cable companies or audiences.

One way of locating any contribution made by non-governmental and non-commercial groups is to view the production, distribution and appropriation of television programmes as a funnel, where the neck represents the theoretically open-ended potential for devising and making audiovisual material and the nozzle determines the material that is ultimately made available for appropriation. In principle, the neck of the filter might be assumed to be open to input from pressure groups, NGOs, or 'civil society'. As the filter narrows, the opportunities become much reduced. This analogy derives from Nicholas Garnham's argument that, in the production, circulation and appropriation of symbolic forms, the 'hierarchy of determination' is such that the possibilities at each of these levels are 'limited by the resources made available by the logically preceding level'.[6] If it were possible to keep the funnel truly open to all comers – in other words to guarantee access to all citizens – then something akin to Jürgen Habermas's 'public sphere' would exist. Whatever the shortcomings of Habermas's idealized historical account of what he called the public sphere, the public sphere retains validity as a normative concept because it prompts us to ascertain where, how and to whom access to the media is denied. To quote Colin Sparks: '[O]ne might plausibly argue that the fewer and more sporadic the exclusions from the media are, the closer a situation approximates to a public sphere.'[7]

The development of transnational media during the 1990s, and the rise to dominance of a few giant, highly commercialized, transnational media companies, most of them USA-based, drew attention to the question of how much audiovisual space was effectively being closely off to so-called civil society groups. As global media ownership became more concentrated, resistance to the concentration process and the effects of concentration began to coalesce among disaffected media practitioners, communication scholars and community media NGOs. It is important to note that the position adopted by this group directly contradicted any notion that, the wider the reach of a transnational commercial news organization such as CNN, the more effective its contribution to creating a 'global public sphere' and somehow, by extension, a 'global civil society'.[8] Indeed, initiatives such as the People's Communication Charter, launched by the Dutch media scholar, Cees Hamelink, were motivated by concern that the spread of transnational commercial media was endangering the public sphere. Their efforts were directed towards creating a transnational public sphere to ensure provision for the expression of cultural diversity and a plurality of opinions.[9] Members of the alliance feared that, with media ownership concentrated in ever fewer hands, state censorship was giving way to a 'more subtle censorship, through subjection to commercial exigencies and maximizing shareholder gain'.[10] In fact, while Hamelink himself described the People's Communication Charter as a 'civil society initiative',[11] a Gramscian understanding of civil society in terms of hegemony can better situate the Charter and related initiatives vis-à-vis dominant economic and political groups. Essentially, they are counter-hegemonic. The 'civil society' label alone does not indicate this.

However, just as the notion of a global public sphere can be used normatively to denote the kind of transnational audiovisual space campaigners such as Hamelink would like to establish and defend, the notion of global civil society can also perform a useful function as an aspiration rather than a reality,[12] or as an ideal-type. John Keane argues:

> When used carefully as an ideal-type ... global civil society refers to a non-violent, cross-border, social process that is linking and thickening complex chains and loops of non-governmental institutions and actors, whose local effects are felt transnationally, here and there, far and wide, to and from the local, through the regional to the global levels.[13]

According to this definition, global civil society exists when self-governing groups conduct their activities outside the boundaries of governmental structures, with maximum respect for different ways of life, openness and civilized power-sharing.[14] That is to say, the concept of global civil society can be used as an analytical tool that prompts us to assess the interactions of non-governmental bodies against a maximalist checklist such as the one Keane proposes. But when that assessment is complete, the task still remains of determining whether the groups in question are counter-hegemonic.

Armed with these distinctions we can now return to the original question about the part NGOs may or may not play in influencing transnational broadcasting policy in the Middle East. In light of the arguments examined above, and this book's thematic preoccupation with cross-border links that might qualify as evidence of globalization, the question addressed in the present chapter can be rephrased as follows: do local and international NGOs work together to respond to the challenges and opportunities created by the medium of satellite television in the Middle East? With what results?

## World frameworks

At least two practical frameworks for NGO intervention in the governance of global and Middle Eastern transnational communication started to take shape during the late 1990s. The first, envisaged as global in scope, was led by an alliance of communication-oriented NGOs based in both the northern and southern hemispheres. These were united in wanting to develop a 'global framework for democratic media', a project that was forced onto the agenda of world agencies such the International Telecommunication Union and UNESCO in 1998.[15] The project's origins go back much further, however. For example, one of the organizations involved in articulating it was the MacBride Round Table on Communication, an initiative that grew out of UNESCO's 1980 report *Many Voices, One World*, produced by the International Commission for the Study of Communication Problems, headed by Sean MacBride. When UNESCO abandoned its formal commitment to the goals of the New World Information and Communication Order around 1987, a group of individuals came together around the objective of keeping the issue of global communications equality on the international agenda. This time, however, they wanted to do so in a way that would reach beyond intergovernmental and professional communities to grassroots non-governmental bodies. This latter conviction had already long been shared by the World Association for Christian Communication (WACC), which consequently gave its support to the MacBride Round Table. The MacBride Round Table itself, having met for the first time in 1989, constituted itself as an NGO, based in Dublin, in 1994. One of its aims was to try to 'prise open the doors of the ITU for all NGOs'.[16] By 1998 the ITU had established a focus group, with NGO involvement, to make proposals aimed at global communications equality.[17]

Some of the same individuals involved in the MacBride Round Table meetings were simultaneously channelling their efforts in the same direction through other bodies. 1993 saw the first draft text of Cees Hamelink's 'People's Communication Charter', described as an 'effort to mobilize a representative association of information consumers' unable to trust either states or markets to accommodate their information needs. Its aim was to safeguard the endangered 'public sphere' and ensure provision for the expression of cultural diversity and a plurality of opinions.[18] The Charter drew together NGOs based in the West, such as the Centre for Communication and Human Rights in the Netherlands and the Cultural Environment Movement in the USA, and in developing countries, including the Third World Network in Malaysia, and the AMARC World Association of Community Radio Broadcasters, with bases in both Canada and Peru. The preamble to the 1996 version of the Charter, reportedly endorsed by thousands of organizations and individuals, declares that 'All people are entitled to participate in communication and in making decisions about communication within and between societies'. Article 2 states that 'All people have the right of access to communication channels independent of governmental or commercial control'. Backing the Charter was another alliance of likeminded groups called Voices 21, so called because of its aim to build a movement in support of global governance structures for media and communication in the twenty-first century. On the Voices 21 agenda was a proposal for a world congress on media and communication designed to reflect and respond to growing fears that those at the helm of global trends in media and communication are not interested in meeting the needs of the majority of the world's people.

Successes and failures of the NGO campaign for more inclusive global communication governance were documented in 1998, after meetings held at that year's conference of the International Association for Media and Communication Research (IAMCR). Reporting on sessions of the Working Group on Global Media Policy at the conference (in Glasgow, Scotland), Wolfgang Kleinwächter, of the University of Leipzig, compared the campaign of NGOs promoting alternative public media and communication with that of environmental NGOs. He wrote: 'Like Greenpeace working for a healthy natural environment, the communication groups are beginning to unite themselves to build a global platform from which they can work towards a healthy intellectual environment.'[19] Just as many environmental issues necessitate transnational action, Kleinwächter suggested that the activities of media conglomerates warrant a transnational response. He cited moves on Internet governance in 1996–97 on the part of three Geneva-based agencies, the ITU, the World Trade Organization (WTO) and the World Intellectual Property Organization (WIPO), and pointed out that all three had opened their doors, to different degrees, to non-governmental members, mainly from the private sector. But while cyberspace offers an arena with the potential for relatively unfettered communication among individuals and groups, the same cannot be said of transnational television. For this reason, Marc Raboy, a Canadian advocate of public service broadcasting, argued at the IAMCR conference that transnational free-enterprise media would need to be countered with global public service media. Acknowledging that the structural basis of global public service media was not immediately clear, Raboy said this was why existing world bodies such as UNESCO and the ITU had to be opened up. If they would accept participation by a 'broader range of actors than the present assortment of member states', new structures could be developed whereby the media would fulfil their potential as the 'central institutions of an emerging global public sphere'.[20]

Incorporating a broader range of actors in policy design does not automatically lead to implementation of policies that can benefit the same non-governmental, non-business constituency. This was made clear in the Action Plan adopted at the UNESCO-sponsored Intergovernmental Conference on Cultural Policies for Development in Stockholm in the spring of 1998. The Action Plan differed from the original working documents presented to the conference in several ways.[21] These working documents were based on a report of the UN/UNESCO World Commission on Culture and Development. Included in the report was a suggestion that conventional national policy mechanisms for funding public service media could be elevated to the global level to ensure that communication media remained part of the global commons. For example, transnational commercial media activities could be taxed to generate funding for global public service and alternative media. The 140 governments represented in Stockholm did not adopt this idea. Nor did they undertake to do more than consider the provision of public radio and television services. Instead of accepting that legislation should foster competition and prevent excessive concentration of media ownership, they agreed only that legislation should foster freedom of expression. As for holding a world summit on culture and development, this was ruled out by UNESCO's secretary-general at that time, Federico Mayor. He wanted to leave member states and regional organizations to act on the outcome of the Stockholm conference. In other words, a gulf remained between the aspirations of transnationally linked NGOs and the concessions governments, brought together in UNESCO, were prepared to make. Yet the advancement of transnational communication objectives espoused by these NGOs is heavily, if not totally, dependent on financial and legislative structures that only governments can put in place. As Marc Raboy pointed out, time is not on the NGOs' side. He wrote in 1998:

... three or four years from now the member states of UNESCO will have even less implementation power than they do now. Corporate capital, which continues to mobilize and organize on a transnational basis, will have put more institutional structures in place at the global level. And civil society risks being left once again in a role of bridesmaid, watching from the sidelines.[22]

## Euro-Med mechanisms

In contrast to the apparent lack of political will among governments in the global arena, state-backed financial instruments to support media democratization initiatives undertaken by civil society institutions were, in theory, created by the EU under the Euro-Med Partnership pro-gramme. The Euro-Med programme, which dates back to the EU's adoption of a new Mediterranean Policy in 1993, was formally launched under the banner of the 'Barcelona Process' at a conference in Barcelona in November 1995. The EU allocated the equivalent of nearly $5 billion for financial co-operation with 12 country partners on the southern shores of the Mediterranean for the period 1995–99, of which 73 per cent was disbursed under the umbrella of the so-called MEDA Pro-gramme.[23] According to the European Commission, which envisaged the Partnership project as a means of promoting stability, security and more prosperous and dynamic markets on Europe's southern flank, 'respect for human rights and democratic principles are an essential element of co-operation through MEDA'.[24] One-tenth of the MEDA Programme was devoted to regional activities related to the three 'pillars' or dimen-sions of the Euro-Med Partnership, namely the political and security dimension, the economic and financial dimension and the social, cultural and human dimension. The aim of the latter is set out in the Social, Cultural and Human Affairs Chapter of the Barcelona Declara-tion. The chapter specifically refers to civil society in its subtitle, which reads: 'Developing Human Resources, Promoting Understanding between Cultures and Exchanges between Civil Societies'. After a four-line preamble, the partners agree in the very first of the Chapter's 14 clauses that the mass media play an important role in the 'reciprocal recognition and understanding of cultures as a source of mutual enrich-ment'.[25] Four clauses later they 'recognize the essential contribution civil society can make' towards developing the partnership. Thereafter they agree to encourage exchanges among various institutions, including the media, and to encourage support both for 'democratic institutions' and for strengthening the 'rule of law and civil society'. During the 1990s, these aims were reflected in: MEDA funding for the MEDA Democracy programme; financial support for broadcasting Euronews in Arabic; the Euromed Audiovisual programme; and the Med Media programme.

**Table 11: MEDA Democracy grants by purpose and type, 1996–98**

(*Percentage of total*)

| | 1996 | 1997 | 1998[1] |
|---|---|---|---|
| **Objectives** | | | |
| Democracy | 6 | 15 | 1 |
| Rule of law | 1 | 14 | 15 |
| Civil society | 32 | 28 | 17 |
| Fundamental freedoms | 8 | 1 | 29 |
| Trade unions | 6 | 4 | 0 |
| Vulnerable groups | 8 | 19 | 27 |
| Education | 11 | 14 | 20 |
| Conflict resolution | 29 | 5 | 9 |
| **Instruments** | | | |
| Education | 9 | 7 | 6 |
| Training | 16 | 38 | 19 |
| Sensibilization (sic) | 73 | 48 | 74 |
| Networking | 2 | 7 | 19 |

[1] Total adds to more than 100 because of dual purpose grants.

Source: European Commission, DG1B, April 1999

The MEDA Democracy programme was launched in 1996 on the initiative of the European Parliament to give grants to enable non-profit-making associations to promote democracy, the rule of law, freedom of expression, freedom of assembly and association, and protection of vulnerable groups, including women and young people. The relationship between media and democracy was acknowledged in grants such as one for a workshop on parliamentary reporting in Lebanon,[26] and various public education campaigns. During its first three years of operations 151 projects were promised a total of 27 million euros from MEDA Democracy.[27] In both 1996 and 1997, out of eight categories of objectives, strengthening civil society took the biggest sums. In all three years from 1996 to 1998, out of four types of project funded, the raising of awareness (referred to as 'sensibilization' in European Commission documentation), was by far the leading category (see Table 11). But the programme could generally only support existing institutions. Since the number of civil society organizations in existence varies from country to country in the Mediterranean Middle East, depending on the laws governing NGO registration, the level of grants inevitably also varied from country to country in ways unrelated to factors such as population size. Thus, for example, the large number of Palestinian NGOs created before the establishment of the Palestinian Authority was reflected in the fact that Palestinian institutions received by far the highest proportion of country-directed (i.e. non-regional) MEDA Democracy grants. In 1996 they accounted for 27 per cent of the total, while in 1997 and 1998 their share was 12 per cent and 14.4 per cent respectively. In contrast, Egyptian groups, despite their country's size and need, took 3 per cent of total commitments in 1996, 6 per cent in 1997 and 5.3 per cent in 1998. In 1996, no grants at all were channelled to Syria or Tunisia.

As already stated, alongside the MEDA Democracy grants, but under other headings, the European Commission also ran two specifically media-oriented funding programmes for Mediterranean recipients, including civil society groups. One of these, Euromed Audiovisual, only started in 1997 and, as will be related, was still getting under way in 2000. The other, Med Media, predated the Barcelona Process but suffered a lengthy hiatus during the second half of the 1990s. In the interim, however, the European Commission provided a subsidy worth a total of 3 million euros[28] to the loss-making Lyons-based transnational television news channel, Euronews. Since Euronews could reach all Mediterranean and some Gulf countries via Eutelsat, the aim of the subsidy was to finance the addition of news bulletins in Arabic to those already broadcast in five European languages. The subsidy ran for two years, ending on 15 April 1999.[29] Euronews had been launched in 1993 as a service bringing together the output of a consortium of public broadcasters. Reliance on this material, with the addition of voice-overs and on-screen graphics, minimized input from dedicated journalists but did little to boost ratings. In November 1997 the UK news company ITN paid a knockdown price of £5 million[30] to buy a 49 per cent managing stake in the company from Alcatel[31] and indicated its intention of capitalizing on the Arabic newscasts to expand into the Middle East to compete with CNN.[32] While the EU subsidy may have benefited Arabic-speaking NGOs indirectly, by boosting the availability of diverse television news programming by satellite, there was no direct civil society link.

The Euromed Audiovisual programme grew out of an agreement reached by the governments of the 15 EU member states and the 12 Mediterranean partners at a conference at Thessaloniki in November 1997. The conference also suggested the eventual creation of a thematic

Euromed satellite television channel.[33] In the first phase, however, in the interests of 'cultural interpenetration' and developing the audiovisual sector on both sides of the Mediterranean, it was agreed to earmark 20 million euros for up to ten major regional projects lasting three to five years. The money was to encourage regional co-production, training and distribution in the fields of radio, television and cinema. A call for proposals went out in August 1998 and, all together, six projects were chosen in mid-1999. They included schemes of an infrastructural nature, such as creating audiovisual archives, organizing a travelling film festival, supporting training, and encouraging distribution of existing films. In addition, however, were plans for the co-production of series of television cartoons about historic characters and a documentary series about distinguished women, both of which seemed destined eventually to find their way onto satellite channels. Canal Horizons, the Middle Eastern and North African package of the French pay-TV company Canal+, was to play a part in distributing both series, while the Saudi-owned pay-TV company Orbit was to distribute the series on women. The latter, called *Elles ... aux abords de l'an 2000*, was to be produced by the award-winning Egyptian director, Youssef Chahine, through his Cairo-based company, Misr International Films.[34] A second phase of the Euromed Audiovisual programme was launched in September 2000 at a conference in Rabat, with a further 25 projects due to be selected at the end of the year.[35] Through its support to audiovisual media companies operating independently of government structures, this EU programme created a means of expanding civil society input to the transnational television of Middle Eastern origin. However, government-controlled broadcasters, such as Morocco's RTM, were also included.

Before the Euromed Audiovisual programme began, some of its objectives had been pursued by the EU's Med Media programme, which predated the Barcelona Conference of 1995. In the period 1993–95, Med Media financed around 30 projects designed to bring European and Arab media professionals together. Here again, government-controlled organizations were among the beneficiaries, not least because of the extensive nature of government control over media in Arab Mediterranean states. In Egypt, for instance, network partners in Med Media projects included the Ministry of Culture, staff of Egyptian government-run print and broadcast media, and Cairo University,[36] but no Egyptian NGOs. The whole Med Media programme was frozen at the end of 1995 due to alleged misuse of subsidies.[37] It remained frozen until April 1998, at which point the European Commission decided that 'co-operation between civil societies' on both sides of the Mediterranean was important enough to warrant relaunch of its 'decentralized co-operation programmes', of which Med Media was one.[38] The relaunch was then delayed indefinitely, pending reorganization of the administration of all EU external assistance programmes. In the meantime, the Commission stressed the 3.4 million euros of funding provided for two subregional training bodies, Remfoc in the Maghreb and Jemstone in the eastern Mediterranean. Television journalists in southern Mediterranean countries were covered by these training programmes, as noted in Chapter 4. Nevertheless, as shown below, limitations remained on the scope for EU support for television representation of non-governmental and non-commercial groups.

## Local hurdles

In most Middle Eastern countries, non-governmental groups wanting to work towards the aims set out in the EU's MEDA Democracy programme are hamstrung by legal difficulties. These difficulties determine the role civil society can play in the transnational television landscape. Far from easing during the latter part of the 1990s, in several cases the obstacles facing Middle Eastern NGOs increased. The deterioration had negative repercussions not only in terms of NGOs' own solidarity and mutual co-operation but also their freedom to develop relations with external bodies, whether donor agencies or international NGOs. As demonstrated by the case (discussed below) of the Ibn Khaldun Centre for Development Studies in Egypt, heavily penalized in 2000 for receiving EU money to make a documentary film about elections, there is a direct link between constraints on NGO activism in the field of freedom of expression and the filtering process that prevents various forms of television programming ever being made, let alone seen. Conversely, in the unusual situation prevailing in the Palestinian self-rule areas, civil society groups were able to benefit from access to non-governmental broadcast media to counter official moves to subjugate NGOs. Although Egypt has a very large number of voluntary associations, the small minority engaged in advocacy and research into civil rights have to struggle against authority merely to exist. An examination of this struggle shows civil rights are key to the functioning of civil society, and underlines how the 'civil society' label alone fails to distinguish between hegemonic and counter-hegemonic groups.

Various developments in the mid-1990s helped to raise the profile of Egyptian NGOs and gave rise to expectations that the restrictive Law of Associations (Law 32 of 1964), enacted during Nasser's presidency, would finally be relaxed. Law 32, designed to mobilize charitable institutions behind the government's plans for socialist development, limited the field of activities of all private voluntary associations and required them to be registered with the Ministry of Social Affairs. Political changes initiated under Sadat contributed to a big increase in the number of associations in the decade to 1986, so that by 1992 the number registered with the Ministry of Social Affairs had exceeded 15,100, almost exactly double the number in 1976.[39] Many of these were religious organizations providing health and educational services, or community development associations providing jobs. Only associations with aims in accordance with those of the government were officially registered. Thus the Egyptian Organization for Human Rights (EOHR), founded in 1985, was denied formal authorization on the grounds that its political aims violated Law 32. In contrast, various businessmen's associations, which were equally political in their promotion of privatization, were allowed under the same law.[40]

Foreign funding for Egyptian voluntary organizations increased substantially in the wake of the 1994 Cairo International Conference on Population and Development and the 1995 Social Summit in Copenhagen.[41] It is sometimes suggested that the increase in funding helped to splinter the civil society groups. Besides competition in terms of activities and fund-raising, other factors blamed for divisions include a lack of internal democracy or good governance and a tendency towards a go-it-alone culture instead of collaborative enunciation of a common vision.[42] An Egyptian scholar who conducted fieldwork among Egyptian NGOs in the late 1990s found ample evidence to suggest that many so-called civil society groups were not necessarily very civil in the sense of favouring pluralism, freedom of association and freedom of expression for others as well as themselves.[43] Whatever the validity or otherwise of these explanations, one of the most obvious causes of weakness and fragmentation of the NGO community was the legislation subjecting it to almost total government control.[44] A new minister of social affairs, Mervat Tellawi, appointed in 1997, appeared to respond to calls from international donors to liberalize Law 32. She convened a committee to redraft its provisions. However, this process simply culminated at the end of May 1999 in the passing of Law 153, which was more draconian than its predecessor. This outcome was a bitter disappointment but no surprise to the NGOs affected. When the new text surfaced in May 1998, revealing the extent to which the government intended to tighten its grip over NGO activities, including exercising control over foreign funding, they campaigned strongly against it. A paper outlining NGO objections and published in the July 1998 issue of *Civil Society*, the monthly newsletter of the Ibn Khaldun Centre for Development Studies in Cairo, pointed out that the new draft law's prohibition on voluntary associations carrying out activities of a political nature contravened the country's constitution and could even prevent NGOs from inviting members of political parties to seminars.[45]

The paper objected to the provision in the draft law for the Ministry of Social Affairs to approve or refuse an association's request to join any Arab or international gathering. Another restriction on foreign contacts was the insistence that, regardless of whether an association is active locally or regionally, non-Egyptian directors should not account for more than a quarter of the total. The Ministry assumed the right to appoint two representatives to the board of directors of any association, seek the dismissal of any nominee, appoint its own delegate to replace the entire elected board and demand the withdrawal of any decision it deemed to have violated the law. Penalties for breaking the law were set at two years in prison and a fine of £E 10,000 ($2950). Despite strong opposition, the Egyptian parliament, overwhelmingly dominated by the ruling National Democratic Party, passed the law in May 1999, whereupon President Mubarak immediately ratified it.

For some local NGO representatives, Law 153 of 1999 represented the ultimate gag on civil society. It was the 'last link' in a chain that started with marginalization of political parties, went on to paralyse professional syndicates and, in 1995–96, intimidated journalists by imposing jail sentences as the penalty for breaches of a harsh new press law.[46] Their assessment was borne out in September 1999 when the governor of Cairo ordered the closure, under Administrative Decree No. 592, of 14 Cairo-based publications. Among the 14, along with Communist, Wafdist and Nasserist papers, were the newsletter of the Egyptian Organization for Human Rights and the Ibn Khaldun Centre's monthly *Civil Society*.[47] Meanwhile a new minister of social affairs, Amina al-Guindi, was appointed in the October 1999 cabinet reshuffle and NGOs were left to differ among themselves over whether to register under the new law in time for the deadline of 26 May 2000. Hardly had this deadline passed than the Supreme Constitutional Court cancelled

Law 153 on a technicality, saying it had not been presented to the Maglis al-Shura (Consultative Council).[48] Yet uncertainty over the status of the NGO law did not prevent a clampdown on the Ibn Khaldun Centre, its director Saad Eddin Ibrahim, and a dozen of his associates. At dawn on 1 July 2000, Ibrahim was arrested at his home and his files and personal computer confiscated. State Security prosecutors, empowered by Egypt's State of Emergency law, ordered his detention without charge for three renewable periods of 15 days. He was eventually released on £E 10,000 bail on 10 August, but not before State Security prosecutors had arrested 13 people connected with the Ibn Khaldun Centre and the League of Egyptian Women Voters, and closed the offices of both institutions, putting them under police guard.

Lawyers acting for Saad Eddin Ibrahim complained that no detailed charges were raised against him and that they were expected to respond to vague accusations about Ibrahim taking foreign funding without government permission and using it to tarnish Egypt's image. This was not the first time the authorities had taken issue with an NGO for having accepted foreign financial support. Hafez Abu Seada, secretary-general of the EOHR, had been arrested in December 1998 and charged with treason after a local pro-government newspaper, Al-Usboua (The Week), alleged that his organization had received $25,000 from the British embassy in Cairo as payment for fabricating an unfavourable report about police brutality in the Upper Egyptian village of Al-Kosheh.[49] Given its timing, this allegation was widely understood to form part of a government campaign to justify the harsh provisions of its proposed new law on NGOs. Al-Usboua followed up its first round of allegations with a second assault, accusing local human rights groups of betraying their country in return for US, British, Danish, Swedish, German and Dutch money. The paper said the NGOs in question provided the means by which 'the West penetrates and weakens the nation'.[50] A spokesman from the Ministry of Social Affairs agreed with the claim, saying: 'Some irresponsible groups have smeared Egypt ... They are hired. They are in the pay of foreign countries.'[51] Abu Seada spent six days in prison in 1998. He was released just in time to attend celebrations marking the 50th anniversary of the Universal Declaration of Human Rights in Paris; his absence from this event could have been embarrassing for Egyptian–French relations. However, his case was resurrected in February 2000, when he was formally charged with obtaining foreign funds without official permission. Although Abu Seada was later assured that the charges would not be pursued, the case was not immediately closed.[52]

Under the 1992 military decree used to charge Abu Seada, unauthorized receipt of foreign funds carries a penalty of seven to 15 years in prison. This was the possible sentence also facing Saad Eddin Ibrahim. In fact, information from the European Commission reveals that the Ibn Khaldun Centre was awarded a grant of 213,280 euros under the MEDA Democracy programme for a 'Political Education and Electoral Rights' project.[53] According to Egyptian sources, the project was to have included a documentary informing people about their voting rights in the November 2000 elections to Egypt's People's Assembly. It seems to have been prompted by the findings of Ibn Khaldun Centre election monitors in Egypt's parliamentary elections five years earlier, when evidence of irregularities at 80 of the 88 polling stations covered by the centre's staff was passed to the courts.[54] These formed part of a total of approximately 900 complaints lodged against alleged voting irregularities in the 1995 elections, which in turn led Egypt's Court of Cassation to recommend that the election of more than 200 MPs be invalidated.[55] The authorities having ignored this ruling on the previous occasion, the Ibn Khaldun Centre apparently decided to try to raise political awareness ahead of the 2000 polls. An Egyptian company, Video Cairo, owned by Mohammed Gohar, was retained for a fee of £E 30,000 to shoot 30 minutes of film, which was to have been reduced to six minutes after editing.[56] The script was centred on a discussion between a rural couple, who decide that the best way to solve Egypt's problems is to go through the voter registration process in order to cast their vote.[57] In the event, Ibrahim was neither to screen the film nor monitor the 2000 elections. On 24 September, six weeks after his release, the prosecutor-general, Maher Abdel-Wahed, formally charged him with raising funds illegally and broadcasting false statements that could damage Egypt's reputation. At the same time 27 staff of the Ibn Khaldun Centre were charged with aiding and abetting embezzlement, bribery and fraud.[58]

Given the Ibn Khaldun Centre's explicit campaigning on behalf of civil society, not least through its monthly journal *Civil Society*, published in both Arabic and English, the prosecution and harassment of its director, staff and associates provides a highly illuminating case study. It exposes the extent of limitations on NGO influence over the making and dissemination of audiovisual material a whole decade after satellite television broadcasts were launched by the Egyptian state broadcaster in the name of the Egyptian people. But it also reveals the nature and depth of splits within the NGO community itself, both in Egypt and further afield. For, while the incarceration of Saad Eddin Ibrahim and the seizure of Ibn Khaldun Centre resources galvanized some local human rights organizations to protest, it gave sections of the press and assorted commentators an opportunity to distance themselves from the kind of activism that uses foreign money to research potentially contentious local affairs. Newspapers published by the political opposition parties readily joined the smear campaign that was to accuse Ibrahim of spying for NATO, meeting Israelis, forging ballot papers, downloading secret voting lists and stealing money. Academics, journalists, entrepreneurs and others, who might otherwise be regarded as stalwarts of civil society, could be heard not merely questioning Ibrahim's integrity but tossing around words like 'crook' and 'traitor' even though his case had not been heard in court.[59] Nor was the condemnation limited to Egypt. Prominent Jordanian newspaper columnists joined in to support the charges against Ibrahim, seeing parallels with Jordanians whom they were eager to pillory for using foreign funding to foster civil rights. The Jordanian journalist and political commentator Rami Khouri denounced these attacks. He described them as a form of 'neo-McCarthyism' against 'modern, enlightened, cosmopolitan Arab citizen[s]' – people who, he said, were 'deeply rooted in local cultural values' but 'equally comfortable in the pluralistic, liberal modernity of the West'. Khouri noted that independent civil society activists and institutions now faced a powerful double threat, from heavy-handed states on the one hand and 'confused and insecure political forces and personalities' on the other.[60]

In Khouri's analysis, such resistance to pluralism was all part of the same situation in which independent, credible civil society institutions in the Arab world had been able to emerge only in 'Morocco, Lebanon, Jordan, Palestine and Egypt'.[61] Now, even here, they were being squeezed from all sides. Meanwhile the identity crisis fuelled by their need to struggle on multiple fronts was highlighted in a study of Lebanese civil society and, specifically, Lebanese women's NGOs. The author, Dalal al-Bizri, identified a 'modernization and imitation crisis' in which advocacy groups became locked in conflict with each other 'at the expense of society itself'. She found that local power equations and hierarchical structures led to organizations being divided along political and interest group lines, when in principle they should be united by their common aspirations and objectives.[62] In the view of many involved in the struggle, the media's role was paramount. Restrictive press laws and broadcasting monopolies put activists under siege, giving governments free rein to project their own image of advocacy groups nationally and internationally.[63] In contrast, a diversity of media outlets would have allowed activists to put their case in their own words to the wider public, at home and abroad. Palestinian NGOs, for example, benefited from internal and external alliances when the Palestinian Authority under Yasser Arafat tried in 1998 to introduce legislation to tame the NGO movement. The number of private Palestinian television and radio stations in operation, combined with a high concentration of international media representatives in Jerusalem, meant that activists had at least some opportunity to speak for themselves.

## Cross-border co-operation

The animosity generated by foreign funding for civil society groups in the Middle East provides a salutary reminder that these groups' primary source of external support in the second half of the 1990s lay not with other NGOs but with states. This in itself raises doubts about whether non-governmental institutions and actors inside and outside this region are linked in the 'complex' and 'thickening' 'chains and loops' that John Keane sees as constituting *idealtypisch* global civil society.[64] However, international NGOs were not absent from the scene. While the mid- to late 1990s was an eventful period in the life of regional NGOs, it was also an eventful time in the development of satellite television and the coincidence aroused the interest of several Western groups. They saw the satellite broadcasting phenomenon as possibly heralding a new era of free speech and vibrant civil society in the Middle East. The experiences of four such organizations, which deliberately set out to explore new possibilities for audiovisual communication to, from and within the region, afford a useful opportunity to compare NGO–NGO and NGO–state links across Middle Eastern borders. The interventions by four Western civil society actors reviewed here were not unusual during this period, either in their format or subject matter.[65] They are mentioned not because they 'prove' anything, but because they provide a small window onto forms of interaction involving local NGOs, foreign NGOs and people with the knowledge or power to influence the content of satellite broadcasts. They involve events planned in Cairo by Germany's Friedrich Naumann Foundation, London-based Amnesty International, the New York-based Lawyers' Committee for Human Rights and the London-based freedom of expression group, ARTICLE 19. Each example illustrates the range of possibilities encompassed by the single term 'non-governmental'.

The Friedrich Naumann Foundation is, in effect, a state-funded NGO. Germany has five foundations (*Stiftungen*) aligned with political parties represented in the federal parliament and funded by German tax payers via the federal government and the European Union. Their stated aim in the developing world is to promote socio-political education in order to assist the democratic process.[66] The Friedrich Naumann Foundation (FNF), linked with the Free Democratic Party, was created in 1958 and named after the man who introduced civic education in Germany after the First World War.[67] It has been active internationally since starting a training project for journalists in Tunisia in 1964 and now has projects and partners in more than 60 countries. The Foundation says of itself that it 'believes in the importance of dialogue between actors of civil societies' and it has contributed directly to programmes to build NGO capacity and networks in Jordan, Palestine, Syria, Lebanon and Egypt.[68] The FNF is not the only *Stiftung* currently active in the Middle East. The Friedrich Ebert Foundation, aligned with the Social Democratic Party and dating back to 1925, has funded development work with women and children. The Konrad Adenauer Foundation, set up as an offshoot of the Christian Democratic Union in 1964, has, among other projects, funded research by the Ibn Khaldun Centre.[69] The work of the FNF, however, is especially relevant to the present study because it has included workshops devoted to the subject of satellite television. Two such workshops were held in Egypt in 1998.

When the FNF arrived in Egypt it began with a ten-year programme (1976–86) to train students of radio and television journalism at Cairo University, followed by a ten-year programme to train journalists at the government-controlled Egyptian Radio and Television Union (ERTU) to make development-oriented programming for local radio stations and local television channels.[70] From 1980 to 1997 it also co-operated with the Ministry of Agriculture to help agricultural co-operatives around Ismailiya. When the agricultural programme ended, the foundation renewed its collaboration with the Faculty of Mass Communication of Cairo University, this time helping to organize a series of seminars on media freedom, satellite television, the Nile Thematic Channels and media privatization. The rationale for its choice was the recent rapid development of electronic media and a recognition on the part of Egyptian decision makers that changing circumstances called for new journalistic approaches and qualifications.[71] The FNF budget was sufficient to convene six seminars in this series in 1998. However, reportedly due to a sudden influx of students and consequent increase in the workload of staff at the Cairo University Faculty of Mass Communication,[72] only three took place during the year, followed by a fourth in April 1999. It should perhaps be noted here that the president of Cairo University at the time was a direct appointee of the Egyptian president.[73] Put another way, Cairo University was no NGO. Significantly, in view of the vociferous attacks on foreign grants to Egyptian NGOs described above, no voices were raised in protest at Cairo University's acceptance of German funds.

As far as the German foundation was concerned, the purpose of the seminars was to encourage media practitioners and analysts to exchange opinions and experience with government-appointed officials in the relevant departments of the ERTU. The first seminar dealing explicitly with transnational broadcasting, entitled 'Satellite Channels and the Future of Television', was held in February 1998. The second, dealing with 'Challenges Facing the Specialized Channels in Egypt', took place in November the same year. Both were attended by senior figures, including the minister of information, Safwat al-Sharif, and the ERTU director and deputy director, Abdel-Rahman Hafez and Hassan Hamed.[74] Other participants included the dean and staff of Cairo University's Faculty of Mass Communication, editors of government-controlled newspapers and university professors with seats on the ERTU Board of Trustees. That is to say, the people attending these seminars represented a fairly small circle with close links to government and no obvious links to local civil rights NGOs. This was a case of a non-governmental German organization deliberately interacting with a governmental Egyptian one, prompted by a common interest in satellite television.

The second example concerns another seminar in Egypt, convened under the auspices of Amnesty International (AI). Amnesty International's name is recognized over large parts of the globe. Founded in the UK in 1961, the organization had more than a million members worldwide by the end of the 1990s, at which point it was receiving funding from subscribers and regular donors in over 100 countries.[75] As a 'knowledge-based' NGO,[76] it is involved in gathering data from all over the world for campaigns against individual cases of detention and torture and campaigns on transnational human rights issues. In this way it clearly fosters cross-border non-governmental links. To understand the reality of these links, however, it is important to note the Amnesty rule, adopted in the late 1960s, that people in the organization work only on cases outside their own countries.[77] The rule was adopted for reasons of impartiality, as it had been demonstrated that researchers would be less careful to cross-check information about abuses on their home ground, and because few governments could be relied on to let internal human rights activists get on with their work without interference or threats to their freedom and safety.

Thus, at the point in 1994 when AI held its seminar in Egypt, its operations in that country had mainly consisted of non-Egyptians addressing concerns about detentions and torture directly to the Egyptian government. AI representatives met President Mubarak and other officials in May 1992. The organization also held a press conference in Cairo in June 1993 to coincide with the Organization of African Unity summit taking place in the city at the same time. Speaking at the press conference, AI Secretary-General Pierre Sané called on the Egyptians chairing the OAU summit and the African Commission on Human and People's Rights to 'take the lead and press for enlightened action' (by governments).[78] In contrast, the AI media workshop held in Cairo on 26-27 May 1994, which brought together government representatives, media practitioners and human rights campaigners, had a regional rather than an exclusively Egyptian agenda. The title was 'Developing an Effective Role for the Media in Promoting Human Rights',[79] and it was apparently prompted by the rapid development of satellite television in the region at the time.[80] This was reflected in the participation of delegates from Middle Eastern satellite channels, including the Saudi-owned, London-based broadcaster MBC, and Egyptian state television. Hassan Hamed, who was later to become executive director of the Nile Thematic Channels, attended as head of television programming within the ERTU. The encounter may well have familiarized participants with Amnesty International's work and facilitated future networking, but the media it targeted for human rights promotion had primarily to be those owned by, or allied to, Middle East governments. In any event, the AI media seminar itself was a one-off exercise.

A year later, the Lawyers' Committee for Human Rights tried to engage with Middle Eastern NGOs in Cairo, to train their representatives to use video cameras. It failed. The training session eventually took place outside the Middle East. This was a case of a New York-based NGO making contact with counterpart groups from the region but not on their home ground. The Lawyers' Committee for Human Rights (LCHR), formed in 1978, works on the assumption that, when governments are 'made aware that their actions are being scrutinized by an international audience' they 'tend to open prison doors, commute sentences or stop torture'.[81] The Committee therefore acts at both the local and international levels. It seeks to influence the US government to promote the rule of law in both its foreign and domestic policy, and presses for greater integration of human rights into the work of the UN and World Bank. Outside the USA it aims to help build the legal institutions and structures that will guarantee human rights in the long term. To this end the group fosters cross-border lawyers' networks and aims to equip those in need with the tools of mass communication so that they can 'alert the world to the abuses they witness'. In other words, 'global partnerships'[82] and transnational media are key features of the Committee's rationale and activities.

In practice, however, an attempt to strengthen links with NGOs in Egypt and to train them to use audiovisual technology to promote and protect human rights was thwarted by the Egyptian government. The LCHR Witness programme and the EOHR arranged to hold a training session in May 1995 for representatives of seven Cairo-based human rights NGOs and visitors from Kuwait, Morocco and Turkey.[83] An LCHR representative obtained permission for the event from the Egyptian Ministry of the Interior in March 1995. A few weeks later, however, the Committee was informed through the Egyptian embassy in Washington and in meetings with Ministry of Foreign Affairs officials in Cairo that, if it persisted with the training session for organizations 'with no legal status', it would be jeopardizing the safety of members of the EOHR and the other Egyptian NGOs.[84] Security agents deployed at the venue on the day of the proposed event made it impossible for the training session to proceed as planned and it was reconvened elsewhere.[85]

The last of the four examples relates to a conference on satellite television organized by ARTICLE 19 in Cairo in February 1999. ARTICLE 19, the Global Campaign for Free Expression, was formed in London in 1987. It takes its name and purpose from Article 19 of the Universal Declaration of Human Rights. The article itself has a distinctly cross-border focus, guaranteeing the right to freedom of opinion and expression and the right to receive and impart information and ideas 'through any media and regardless of frontiers'. ARTICLE 19, the NGO, has a monitoring and campaigning remit which requires it to collaborate with an international network of individuals and organizations to promote awareness of censorship issues and take action on individual cases. In

August 2000 it co-ordinated an appeal by seven international human rights bodies to EU institutions to break their silence and condemn the arrest and detention of Saad Eddin Ibrahim.[86] This research and advocacy work is funded from a range of sources, including European governments, which pay through their own aid agencies or foreign ministries or through the European Commission. For example, ARTICLE 19 worked with an Egyptian NGO, the Legal Research and Resource Centre for Human Rights, to produce a report on censorship in Egypt[87] with funding from the European Commission.

Financial support for ARTICLE 19's satellite broadcasting conference came from Reuters and the Ford Foundation. The three main themes of the conference were regulation, access and impact, with presenters and participants drawn from the Maghreb, the Gulf, Lebanon, Arab East Jerusalem, Egypt, the UK and USA. The fact that it was held in Cairo boosted the number of Egyptian participants and produced a particularly strong showing from the American University in Cairo, where Hussein Amin, in his dual capacity as professor at the Adham Center for Television Journalism and member of the ERTU Board of Trustees, used his good offices to arrange presentations from staff, students and associates of the Adham Center and from staff and advisers of the ERTU. Thus Hassan Hamed, who had previously attended both the Friedrich Naumann Foundation seminars and the Amnesty International seminar, also played an important part in the conference arranged by ARTICLE 19. Meanwhile non-Egyptian satellite channels reportedly declined invitations to attend[88] and the presence of Egyptian civil rights NGOs was discreet, with none holding the floor. Discussions centred around distinctions between censorship and regulation, around barriers to incoming television channels in both Europe and the Middle East, and around the quality of programming carried by Arab satellite television channels. Aspects of the debate were reported in Al-Ahram Weekly (in English) and on the electronic journal edited by Hussein Amin, tbsjournal.com. This coverage demonstrated that public discussion of potentially sensitive matters of broadcasting policy could take place in Cairo. It provided yet another indication of Cairo's prominence as an international conference centre. It did not indicate that local civil rights groups had any influence on satellite television policy.

## Conclusion

In 1997 Jan Aart Scholte, reviewing *The New Realism: Perspectives on Multilateralism and World Order*, edited by Robert Cox, wrote: 'I wonder ... whether several contributors do not overestimate the anti-systemic quality of much that currently goes under the umbrella of "global civil society".'[89] The evidence presented here bears out Scholte's scepticism. It confirms that global civil society may exist as an idea but not as a reality. Ten years after cross-border television took off in the Middle East, independent local pressure groups working in the field of civil rights could still be found only in a minority of Middle Eastern states and even there they were effectively denied access to leading satellite channels by the same raft of laws that prevented them from operating autonomously or accepting funding from overseas. In this environment, the 'complex global political system' envisaged by Peter Willetts remained a distant prospect. Instead of governments and pressure groups interacting directly and indirectly in international organizations and the media,[90] pressure groups in most of the Middle East faced measures specifically designed to block their interaction with foreign governments, while the local mass media continued to provide a mouthpiece for the governments responsible for those measures. In Egypt, at least, it was as if the spectre of transnational broadcasts about political and civil rights spurred the authorities to clamp down on local advocacy groups. Given that Egypt at this stage was unusual in the region in having both extensive state-owned satellite broadcasting capability and a clutch of (barely tolerated) human rights NGOs, its reaction to the Ibn Khaldun Centre's proposed film about voter registration assumed considerable significance vis-à-vis the region as a whole.

Globalization was thus still 'work in progress', not only in terms of the geographical areas covered by complex cross-border relationships but also in terms of the interest groups incorporated into these relationships. The Egyptian government, though prepared to do business with the global media conglomerates that own CNN and MTV (see Chapter 3), was much less hospitable to the Witness Programme of the Lawyers' Committee for Human Rights. When international NGOs sought to emulate big business in 'pris[ing] open the doors'[91] of bodies such as the ITU and UNESCO, with the aim of achieving equitable 'access to communication channels independent of governmental or commercial control',[92] they faced an uphill struggle. Yet, as demonstrated by the rejection of NGO proposals submitted to the UNESCO conference in

Stockholm, transnational civil society needs the backing of states if it is to undertake effective action. Without the money that could be raised through taxation and without the legislation that could curb acquisitions by transnational media corporations, NGO campaigns against ownership concentration and media commercialization stood limited chance of success.

Media pluralism and freedom of expression across frontiers could legitimately qualify as criteria of globalization. Unlike economic liberalization, however, they seem rarely to have had the benefit of governments' political will. The rhetoric of the 'global public sphere' therefore needs to be used as cautiously as that of 'global civil society'. Substituting the word 'transnational' for 'global' may give a more accurate description of cross-border links among civil society actors that exist in some cases, in some parts of the world. But this chapter has shown how even the simple term 'civil society' can be problematic if questions about the media representation of counter-hegemonic groups are ignored.

# CHAPTER SEVEN

# Text and Context: Satellite Channels in a Changing Environment

Transnational interaction has been an underlying preoccupation of this book, because that is what globalization is supposed to be about. From the mutual impact of Middle Eastern satellite television ventures on each other, to business links among their owners, to collective cross-border collusion against unwelcome intruders in the field: individuals and institutions with established power bases were seen to collaborate and compete transnationally, operating through networks, striking bargains and exchanging favours. In contrast, the unfolding story revealed aspects of the region's transnational television phenomenon where interaction was conspicuously absent. Productive exchanges with a whole range of local non-government bodies, whether aspiring media entrepreneurs or advertisers in the private sector, were found to be in short supply. The same applied to both local and international NGOs working to promote basic freedoms and civil rights. In other words, certain interest groups and cultural practices were found to have made much more headway in expanding and interlinking across the globe than others.

A further strand of interaction, namely that between Middle Eastern satellite channels and their audiences, represents a major field of research which is well beyond the scope of this book. Chapter 4 drew attention to difficulties attending the collection of quantitative audience data in the region. As for qualitative studies, a few examples were cited in the notes to Chapter 1. Detailed ethnographic work on how viewers receive and appropriate transnational television material has started, but, where the Middle East is concerned, it has a long way to go. In the meantime, it is proposed to end the present study by singling out some relevant changes under way in the wider environment in which the senders and receivers of television messages are destined to interact. The analysis that follows makes no claim to be comprehensive. It focuses on

the issues of age and gender, highlighting the exceptionally high proportion of children in the region's viewing public and the media-related
concerns of its re-emerging women's movement. Members of both
population groups have demonstrated by their actions that satellite
television can be a force to be reckoned with in the raising of political
awareness, sometimes in unforeseen ways. The chapter goes on to
consider pressures for and against the use of digital technology to
promote diversity in regional satellite television. Reviewing these issues
helps to develop the discussion of civil rights advocacy contained in
Chapter 6. It leads on to the wider issue of human rights and whether
transnational television broadcasting has expanded in a way that bodes
well or ill for the dissemination of information about human rights
observance and abuse. It ends by summarizing conclusions gathered
throughout the book.

## Viewer age and gender

The second Palestinian *intifada* (uprising) that erupted in September
2000, almost 13 years after the start of the first, provided a powerful
indicator of the impact of transnational television among young people
in the Middle East. When the first *intifada* broke out in December 1987,
there were no Middle Eastern satellite channels broadcasting far and
wide to show scenes of Israeli troops shooting at Palestinian children
throwing stones. Indeed, Palestinians at that time found it hard to get
any accurate or balanced reporting about their revolt out of the Israeli-
occupied territories and onto foreign television screens. It was especially
hard to get television coverage of crucial non-violent aspects of the
campaign. Only later, when local people who had worked as 'guides and
fixers' for foreign television crews inside the Occupied Territories
acquired the equipment and expertise to start compiling their own video
footage, did Palestinians gradually find limited ways and means to
represent themselves and their struggle to the outside world.[1]

By the start of the second *intifada*, the regional media landscape had
changed dramatically. Camera crews working for pan-Arab and Western
channels captured scenes of mayhem in the West Bank and Gaza for
instant transmission around the world. But the way the scenes were
presented and explained differed markedly between Arab stations, which
attributed the situation to Israeli aggression, and their Western counterparts. Stations such as CNN, ABC (of the USA) and RAI (of Italy)
seemed to have great difficulty using words like 'illegal', 'occupation', or

'settlement' in relation to Israeli actions in the West Bank and Gaza Strip.[2] Such polarization of interpretations underlined the role played by Arabic-language channels that had only come into being since the last *intifada* and the 1991 Gulf war. These channels captured the carnage in the Occupied Territories, which was made all the more horrific by the number of Palestinian children killed and injured by bullets to the head and upper body. In October and November 2000 alone, over 80 Palestinian children were killed.[3] Television pictures of stone-throwing children challenging Israeli troops and of wounded children had a galvanizing effect on young people throughout the Arab world. One abiding image symbolizing the mounting Palestinian death toll was that of the shooting of a 12-year-old boy, Mohammed al-Durrah, killed by Israeli gunfire as he crouched in terror with his father behind a water barrel at a crossroads in the Gaza Strip. It was a Palestinian cameraman, Talal Abu Rameh, working for French television, who recorded the boy's last moments. The relaying of those pictures to every Arabic-speaking home with satellite access caused an outpouring of anger far greater than had occurred in 1987. In Egypt, thousands joined angry demonstrations at the universities of Cairo and Ain Shams, and school students stoned Cairo branches of the Sainsbury supermarket chain, suspecting it of links with Israel. News quickly spread of an Egyptian youngster, the same age as Mohammed al-Durrah, taking a bus towards Gaza, a stone in his hand, determined to fight shoulder to shoulder with Palestinians. In Saudi Arabia and Kuwait, despite years of official acrimony towards the Palestinians for their stance during the 1991 Gulf war, youths led spontaneous street protests in solidarity with the Palestinian *intifada*. A demonstration by Saudi women in Jeddah on behalf of Palestinian children broke with local traditions in several ways.[4]

These protests were prompted in no small part by the news broadcasts of the Doha-based satellite channel, Al-Jazeera. Whereas television channels controlled by governments dependent on US economic or military support, such as those of Egypt and Saudi Arabia, might have hesitated to show what US backing for Israel had led to, Al-Jazeera had no such qualms. By juxtaposing news of Israeli bombardments of Palestinian homes and offices with news that Arab leaders were having difficulty arranging an emergency summit, the channel could not help but highlight what many young people perceived to be their governments' failure to take independent action commensurate with the scale of the crisis. One caller from Cairo told a phone-in programme on Al-

Jazeera, 'We have a generation of paralysed rulers who cannot respond to the demands of the furious masses and who are trying to subdue this awakening nation.'[5] By seizing on an issue – the plight of the Palestinians – that no Arab leader could publicly afford to downplay, school and university students responding to televised scenes of the *intifada* found a platform from which to vent pent-up frustrations and discontent.

## Table 12: Children as a proportion of the population, 1998

(*Percentage of total*)

| Country | Under 18s | Under 5s |
|---|---|---|
| Algeria | 44.5 | 13.4 |
| Bahrain | 35.6 | 10.6 |
| Egypt | 43.3 | 12.2 |
| Iran | 46.2 | 11.1 |
| Iraq | 48.6 | 15.3 |
| Israel | 33.6 | 9.7 |
| Jordan | 49.0 | 15.8 |
| Kuwait | 43.0 | 10.8 |
| Lebanon | 39.1 | 11.7 |
| Libya | 46.6 | 13.1 |
| Morocco | 40.2 | 11.4 |
| Oman | 51.6 | 16.3 |
| Qatar | 31.1 | 8.6 |
| Saudi Arabia | 47.4 | 15.5 |
| Sudan | 47.6 | 14.5 |
| Syria | 50.0 | 14.0 |
| Tunisia | 38.4 | 9.9 |
| UAE | 34.1 | 9.0 |
| Yemen | 54.4 | 19.9 |
| *Mean* | 45.5 | 13.1 |
| Developing countries | 39.2 | 11.4 |
| World | 35.9 | 10.3 |

Source: UNICEF, *State of the World's Children 2000* (*www.unicef.org*)

Young people's personal and collective experiences of satellite television will be an important factor in the future of the medium in the Middle East, if only because of the extraordinarily high proportion of under-18s in populations across the region. In the world as a whole,

UNICEF data published in 2000 showed that people aged under 18 accounted for just under 36 per cent of the total population. In developing countries the equivalent proportion was just over 39 per cent. In the Middle East and North Africa, including Iran and Israel, it was 45.5 per cent. In some Arab countries, notably Oman, Syria and Yemen, over 50 per cent of the population was under 18 in 1998 (see Table 12).

These statistics, however, are not the only ones that matter in a discussion of the composition of television audiences by age group. The leisure time available to unemployed school-leavers and university graduates with satellite access has also to be taken into account. In Saudi Arabia, where Ministry of Planning figures showed that 84 per cent of Saudis were aged under 40 in 1999, as many as one-fifth of all Saudi males in the 20–30 age range were without a job. Brad Bourland, chief economist at Saudi American Bank, predicted in mid-2000 that unemployment among this group would persist at 20 per cent in the short term.[6] Yet the malaise experienced by young Saudis as a result of watching satellite television has been documented. Mai Yamani, recounting her interviews with Saudis from various backgrounds, all aged in their teens and twenties, paints a vivid picture of satellite television's impact in accentuating differences between generations in the kingdom. Alongside the Internet and a more secular education system, it has reportedly led to a perception that 'externally driven change is becoming faster and more uncontrolled'.[7] Stark contrasts between the 'drab presentation' and 'limited scope' of Saudi Arabia's terrestrial television channels and their transnational competitors not only caused young people to reject the state-run media but also had the effect of drawing attention to the issue of censorship.[8] Yamani's young interviewees were by no means unanimous in rejecting all forms of censorship. But they were clearly troubled and unsettled by the cultural contradictions played out daily on their television screens.

In the absence of transnational standards regarding the quantity and content of television programming aimed at young people in the region, it was left to advertising-funded commercial companies to respond to this potential audience according to their own priorities. In 2000, four years after the start-up of its satellite channel, Future TV of Lebanon teamed up with Dubai's Technology, E-Commerce and Media Free Zone Authority to prepare the launch of the first pan-Arab station aimed specifically at viewers aged 12 and up. Based in Dubai's Internet City and broadcasting for 14 hours a day, the channel was given the name Zen TV ('zen' being an Arabic word for 'good') and was promoted as an all-round

attempt to address the 'aspirations and problems of youth'.[9] The advertisements attracted by its fashion and entertainment component,
together with the screening of dubbed or subtitled imported programming, were expected to help make the venture economically viable in
three years. Around half the programmes were to be made in Lebanon.[10]
With start-up set for 2001, it remained to be seen what contribution this
highly commercial operation, launched from within the business empire
of Lebanon's prime minister, Rafiq Hariri, would make to standards of
children's programming across the Arabic-language satellite channels. As
had happened with many previous new arrivals in the sector, the
addition of another channel created an illusion of more choice while
effectively reinforcing ownership concentration.

Bound up with the match, or mismatch, between channel owners'
and young viewers' responses to the medium of transnational television
is the question of whether satellite channels will improve or detract from
the status of women in different countries of the Middle East. Negative
stereotyping of women in television programmes, as well as obstacles
facing female professionals seeking to work in the television sector, are
problems experienced worldwide. It was for this reason that the UN's
Fourth World Conference for Women, held in Beijing, China, in 1995,
included women's access to the media as one of the 12 critical areas of
concern addressed in the Beijing Platform for Action. Thus Section J (of
Sections A to L of the Beijing Platform for Action) established two
strategic media-related objectives: to increase the participation and access
of women to expression and decision-making in and through the media
and new technologies of communication; and to promote balanced and
non-stereotyped media portrayal of women. Good practice, positive
actions and lessons learned in each of the 12 areas of concern were
reviewed at a Special Session of the UN General Assembly in New York
in June 2000.

Reports of good practice and positive actions in Arabic-language satellite television were not exactly plentiful in the material gathered for
review in New York. On the contrary, the report prepared by Arab
regional NGOs in readiness for the Special Session could do little more
with regard to Section J of the Beijing Platform for Action than note a
sprinkling of national responses. Typical examples were the airing of
programmes deemed to be of special interest to women, and the appointment of one or two women to senior positions in information
ministries or state television networks in Egypt, Jordan, Yemen and
Kuwait.[11] The most proactive policies identified were those of the

Palestinian Women's Affairs Technical Committee (WATC), which had managed to deploy press and broadcasting, including Palestinian state television, in a bid to demolish stereotypes and combat sexual discrimination.[12] Despite these few positive examples, the Arab NGOs' report stated that the majority of media institutions in the Arab world were still failing to reflect realistic images of women in their diverse roles. It called for the formation of 'media watch' groups to monitor programmes and raise their concerns with editors and producers. This should be done, the report said, by creating networks to facilitate women's access to the relevant people and institutions.[13]

Arab scholars researching the representation of women on Arab satellite channels at the end of the 1990s found high visibility for women featuring in advertisements or as glamorous presenters. In contrast, there was very low visibility for the weighty contributions made by women in other fields or their struggles in the face of everyday discrimination. With the proliferation of satellite channels, and parallel explosion in the volume of television advertising, the opportunities increased for women to be portrayed as impressionable consumers of the products advertised or as mindless decorative objects essential to the visual content of any television advertisement, regardless of its relevance to women's needs. As the number of television dramas multiplied, the stereotyping of women's roles was reinforced. One researcher found that dramas showing women combining the roles of housewife and employee typically pictured them failing at both.[14] Another noted the number of contemporary Egyptian films with titles such as *A Dangerous Woman, The Devil is a Woman, Torture is a Woman, The Curse of a Woman*, and so on.[15] Nevertheless, a survey conducted in Lebanon in 1995 found that women there accounted for an astonishing 80 per cent of students enrolled in journalism and mass communication courses, whereas women students on equivalent courses in Europe represented just 52 per cent of the total.[16] The researcher who set out to investigate this statistic found it doubly surprising since real power within the Lebanese media remained what she called a 'male monopoly'. Some of her respondents attributed the high percentage of female students to the proliferation of audiovisual media and their glamorous image.[17] Data presented at a seminar on gender and communication policy in Beirut in November 1999[18] gave some indication as to the role models exerting this attraction. May Elian, a reporter with *Nahar al-Shabab*, told the seminar that LBC had twice as many women as men on its news desk while Future TV had three times as many. But in the editorial departments of *Al-Nahar* newspaper these ratios were reversed. According to information collated by Elian, the discrepancy was linked to a widely held view that television journalism is superficial. She quoted Gebran Tueini, editor of *Al-Nahar*, as follows:

> Unfortunately the difference between the representation of women in the televised media and print media is that the visual media are superficial and appearance conscious – filled with 'just-one-question' reporters. TV works according to the 'star' system, empowering women through their beauty. But press journalism depends on research and hard work and needs to be cultivated and taken seriously.[19]

It seems apparent from these anomalies that two divergent trends could be associated with the Arab-owned satellite channels. On the one hand, the channels appeared to raise women's profiles, by giving prominence to female presenters and celebrities on screen. On the other, activists became ever more acutely aware that this prominence reflected no fundamental change in approach to the representation of women. On the contrary they perceived a deterioration, amounting to what some described as 'symbolic violence' against women.[20] In the run-up to the 1995 Fourth World Conference for Women in Beijing, media professionals and academics in Egypt worked to document and analyse media portrayals of women. Their efforts confirmed the prevalence of negative stereotypes but also revealed that many female television viewers were generally unaware of this situation. However, attempts to form a media watch group to combat unacceptable images and ideas about women, and promote positive initiatives, failed because of disagreements over priorities and frames of reference for action.[21] Since then women's groups from different countries in the Middle East have taken advantage of easier communication via the Internet to share their experience in this field. From this perspective, it could be argued that satellite channels, in conjunction with other stimuli, acted as an unwitting catalyst for raising awareness about questions of access and representation in relation to women and television. Simply by being transnational, satellite television was liable to give women in different parts of the region a sense of common cause.

## Digital technology

Whatever their potential, information and communication technologies cannot in themselves produce results. It is the way people adopt them, develop them and regulate them that determines their impact. Brian

Winston has demonstrated that, throughout the history of electrical and electronic communication systems, significant changes have always been accommodated by pre-existing social formations.[22] Any radical potential that might disrupt these formations has usually been suppressed, subject only to certain 'supervening necessities' perceived by power-holders and policy-makers.[23] The present research has largely borne out Winston's thesis with regard to satellite transmission of analogue channels. Despite the unusual dynamic created by the interplay of so many different interest groups in a region where some 270 million people speak the same language and can share in the same communication systems, it is fair to say that most activity in the field of transnational television was aimed at containing its radical potential rather than exploiting it. But ten years on from the first channel's launch, the process of adopting and absorbing digital television technology in the Middle East was still far from over. With digital compression, the number of television channels broadcast from a single satellite could be multiplied by a factor of seven or eight. In theory, therefore, it offered renewed potential to promote democracy by extending choice and diversity and enabling interactivity. In practice, however, this potential could only be fulfilled in circumstances where television owners were equipped not only with a satellite dish but also with the right set-top box to receive the digital signals of their choice. In the Middle East the arrival of locally owned broadcasting satellites with digital technology outpaced the spread of set-top boxes capable of receiving free-to-air digital signals. At the same time new broadcasters without the backing of governments or powerful political figures found themselves restricted to digital transmission when they would have preferred the analogue route as a better means of reaching a wider audience. During this period, digitalization meant that, while new broadcasters could be accommodated at relatively low cost, they would remain marginalized pending widespread penetration of digital receiving equipment.

Although pay-TV channels, led by Orbit and ART, started offering bouquets of multiple digital channels in the region from 1994, the most decisive moves towards digital compression of satellite channels for Middle East consumption came in 1998–2000. Nilesat 101 and Nilesat 102, both equipped with digital technology, were launched in 1998 and 2000 respectively. Arabsat 3A, the first of the third generation of Arabsat craft, was launched in 1999. The increase in broadcasting capacity was sudden and enormous, with an additional 44 transponders (including 20 on Arabsat 3A alone) providing potential for more than 300 additional television channels. Such a major change, in an environment where other operators serving the region were also increasing their capacity, inevitably lowered the cost of leasing satellite capacity. In 1998, while the standard rate for leasing a whole transponder on Nilesat was $3 million per year, the price of a single slot on a shared transponder was $500,000 per year, payable in four quarterly instalments in advance.[24] While the lower entry thresholds opened the way for newcomers, they also encouraged established broadcasters to hedge their bets by transmitting from both Arabsat and Nilesat at the same time. Analogue channels already being broadcast from Arabsat 2A were simply digitally compressed and rebroadcast as digital channels on Arabsat 3A.[25] Meanwhile companies established on Arabsat 2A, such as MBC, Future International and Al-Jazeera, decided during the course of 1999 to operate from the Nilesat platform as well. While Nilesat 101 afforded ample space for the Egyptian Ministries of Education, Higher Education, Health and Science and Research to broadcast up to a dozen different free-to-air educational channels, the majority of other free-to-air services from the satellite one year after its launch were either established commercial stations with influential backing or were linked directly to Arab governments, notably Iraq, Libya, Oman, Bahrain, Kuwait and the Palestinian Authority.

However, the economics of Nilesat were such that some peripheral developments were permitted to take place. One was the leasing of capacity to Nilesat's first private sector user, Video Cairo Sat, a provider of satellite news footage to other regional broadcasters. By feeding only pictorial content by satellite and relegating the accompanying words to transmission by Internet, Video Cairo could circumvent censorship obstacles and leave tricky editorial judgements up to its customers. Meanwhile Video Cairo's participation in the Nilesat project was beneficial to the Egyptian Radio and Television Union (ERTU), part-owner of Nilesat, because it helped draw the attention of other regional broadcasters to the benefits of digital transmission via Nilesat. When Video Cairo's clients said they were unable to receive Nilesat transmissions, Video Cairo took responsibility for obtaining the necessary receivers from the manufacturer and distributing them.[26]

With the arrival of Nilesat 102 more private broadcasting projects began to emerge. Nilesat's chief engineer, Saleh Hamza, told an interviewer that he thought 'demand for new TV from the private sector' was not yet fully met.[27] He mentioned possible deals between Nilesat and the Lebanese terrestrial broadcaster NBN (owned by the speaker of the Lebanese parliament, Nabih Berri) as well as an unnamed group seeking to start a women's channel. Other prospective private users included the Egyptian investors behind a new venture called Al-Mehwar. And there was Al-Mustakillah (The Independent), a television project owned by a London-based company named Nova TV. Al-Mustakillah was started by Mohammed El-Hachimi Hamdi, a Tunisian, who had previously worked for *Asharq al-Awsat*, the London-based, Saudi-owned newspaper, and launched his own newspaper in 1993. Also called *Al-Mustakillah*, the newspaper progressed from being a monthly to a fortnightly to a weekly. The television channel of the same name began in February 1999, broadcasting for just one hour a day and expanding gradually to eight hours per day by mid-2000. Instead of uplinking from the UK, Al-Mustakillah arranged transmissions from Nilesat by sending its daily output on tape by courier to Egypt.[28] This arrangement meant all its material had to be pre-recorded. While broadcasts from Nilesat were paid for, transmission in digital from Arabsat 3A was also agreed on a complimentary trial basis.

It is significant, given its reliance on these satellite platforms and on pre-recorded material, that Al-Mustakillah managed to air programmes that were politically sensitive in both Egypt and Saudi Arabia. In July 2000, after Saad Eddin Ibrahim, director of the Ibn Khaldun Centre in Cairo, was arrested and detained without charge under Egypt's State of Emergency laws, the channel taped a panel debate in which Hussein Shaaban, president of the UK branch of the Arab Organization of Human Rights, took part. It had earlier screened a programme in which representatives of Amnesty International in London discussed their organization's campaign to focus international attention on Saudi Arabia's human rights record. Al-Mustakillah staff had evidence from faxes and other audience feedback that this programme was seen in Saudi Arabia.[29] However, three aims expressed by Al-Mustakillah representatives at this time highlighted the disadvantages experienced by their broadcasting operation as compared with the mainstream channels. They wanted to broadcast in analogue to make their free-to-air material available to television households without digital receivers; they also wanted to air live shows and increase their broadcasting time. For Al-Mustakillah's income from advertising to diversify and grow, progress on all three fronts was essential.

Take-up of set-top boxes for reception of free-to-air digital channels was a relatively slow process after Nilesat's launch. It was not helped by the fact that all the leading Arabic-language free-to-air channels could still be received on existing equipment. Digital receivers already in use inside Egypt were unsuited to Nilesat's free-to-air broadcasts as they had been intended exclusively for pay TV. The motivation for distributing new set-top boxes able to receive both encrypted and non-encrypted signals was consequently limited to the ERTU, the ministries broadcasting educational and medical information from Nilesat, and the two pay-TV broadcasters with transponders on Nilesat, namely Showtime and ART. The state-owned Arab Organization for Industrialization, holder of a 10 per cent stake in Nilesat, announced that it would invest in making decoders with the right specifications. Meanwhile the ERTU subsidiary, CNE, and the National Bank of Egypt put together a financing package to stretch payments for the decoders out over five years.[30] The package was to involve a £E 200 down-payment and monthly instalments of £E 50. But it was not until a year after Nilesat's April 1998 launch that the various components of this package started to come together and the ERTU, ART and Showtime could embark on a joint promotional campaign. The Ministry of Education played its part with a plan to distribute free satellite dishes and decoders to 16,000 Egyptian schools by the end of 1999.[31] Even then, the new decoders were not compatible with those of the region's other main pay-TV provider, Orbit. Orbit at that stage was still using its own digital compression ratio of MPEG 1.5 instead of the standard MPEG-2 agreed by the majority of stations represented on the Satellite Channels Co-ordinating Committee of the Arab States Broadcasting Union. Orbit's encryption system was also different. Technology specialists looked forward to a time when multi-purpose digital set-top boxes would be able to receive signals from a range of different broadcast platforms, handle several different encryption systems and combine this with Internet access and the ability to store intelligently material obtained from all these sources.[32] Pending the ready availability of such hardware throughout the Middle East, it seemed likely that most ordinary households would delay investing in anything more than the basic equipment needed to receive the best-known free-to-air analogue channels. Viewing of new types of programming accommodated on the margins of the digital revolution would remain a minority activity.

## Screening human rights

The new information and communication technologies that took off during the 1990s are often regarded as having facilitated the spread of information about human rights abuses and ways of eliminating them. As the software needed to navigate the World Wide Web was developed in the early part of the decade, governments, business and pressure groups all took advantage of it to share information nationally and internationally. The convergence of media, information technology and telecommunications enabled broadcasters to make their presence felt transnationally via the web to users with sufficient bandwidth. At the same time it enabled activists of all kinds, including those working in the field of human rights, to share their information and expertise in new, instantly available, low-cost formats much less subject to the limitations of distance and national censorship constraints. Chapter 6 related how the mid-1990s saw the spawning of numerous human rights advocacy groups in the Middle East and North Africa as funding became available through such channels as the EU's MEDA Democracy programme, which went into operation in 1996. Internet communication may also have played a part in the proliferation process. Difficulties over the national registration of these groups, noted in Chapter 6, make it hard to generalize about their emergence and expansion. What is important is the fact that their growth coincided with the rise of both satellite broadcasting and Internet across the region. In the social sciences the trend spawned terms like 'global civil society' and the 'global public sphere'. Among human rights activists it generated a perception that human rights activism globally was about to enter a new age. As Sir Geoffrey Chandler, Chair of Amnesty International's UK Business Group, pointed out in 1998, the year of the 50th anniversary of the Universal Declaration of Human Rights, support for human rights organizations grew 'hugely' from the late 1980s onwards, in part as a result of the 'discrediting of politics and politicians as potential instruments of desired change'.[33] Having seen how environmental issues had been forced onto the public agenda over the previous 20 years, people began to feel that, thanks in part to new communication technologies, the same would happen to flagrant human rights violations over the coming 10–20 years.

Although the Universal Declaration of Human Rights, the UN's flagship statement, dates from 1948, the international human rights treaties which grew out of it are of more recent vintage. The six principal human rights instruments deal with political and civil rights, economic, social and cultural rights, the elimination of racial discrimination and discrimination against women, the prohibition of torture and the rights of the child. These were adopted in stages between the 1960s and the late

1980s, with the most recent, the Convention on the Rights of the Child, entering into force in 1990. In fact the 1990s, the first decade of transnational television in the Middle East, marked a particularly important period in the history of human rights treaties. Whereas only 10 per cent of all countries in the world had ratified all six major human rights instruments by 1990, that proportion increased to nearly 50 per cent by February 2000.[34] With these benchmarks and monitoring mechanisms in place, human rights advocates had reason to believe that human rights concerns would be forced onto the agendas of governments, intergovernmental organizations and transnational corporations to an extent not seen hitherto. Despite the assumptions often made about cross-border communications, however, it was not a foregone conclusion that the medium of television would make a net positive contribution to any such advance.

Two trends emerging in 1999–2000 suggested that, in the Middle East at least, the contrary might even be the case. One of these hinged on the role of television images in times of conflict. As the geographical reach of these images spread and competition among media organizations increased the use of television for instantaneous communication of breaking news, the stakes grew ever higher in the media wars arising from political conflicts. In these circumstances, instead of being viewed as instruments of free expression about human rights denial, television stations and personnel were seen in two instances (discussed below) as military targets. The second trend, linked to digitalization and the proliferation of television channels, is sometimes described as 'nichification'. In this process, the availability of additional channels for international news and current affairs coverage can result in information ultimately reaching fewer people. This is because subjects such as human rights are increasingly squeezed into broadcasting niches where, instead of being brought to the attention of the general public, they are seen only by specialists who know what they are looking for and where to look.

The notion of television images being regarded as weapons of war is contrary to the 1949 Geneva Convention protocol that specifically recognizes the civilian status of journalists engaged in a professional mission in areas of armed conflict. The protocol draws no dubious distinctions between professionalism and propaganda in this context. NATO therefore set a highly dangerous precedent during its air campaign against Yugoslavia when, on 23 April 1999, it deliberately bombed Radio Television Serbia (RTS), the main Serbian government-controlled television service, killing 16 people.[35] Based on this event, subsequent attacks on media facilities and personnel could be dressed up as legitimate defence against propaganda. Two weeks into the second Palestinian uprising, on 12 October 2000, Israeli forces launched a deliberate rocket attack against two transmission towers and other facilities of the Palestinian radio station, Voice of Palestine, in Ramallah. The Israeli authorities justified the attack by claiming that Palestinian television had incited Palestinians to commit acts of violence against Israelis. They alleged that scenes of Palestinians dragging an effigy of an Israeli soldier, shown on Palestinian TV, were to blame for the murder of two Israeli soldiers by a mob who invaded a police station in Ramallah.[36] Israeli government press officers used a similar argument for refusing to renew the press accreditation of Palestinian journalists working for foreign news agencies. They said that doing so would facilitate a Palestinian propaganda war. In other words, the very potency of photographs and video footage in struggles over human rights has caused them, on occasion, to be seen as tantamount to weapons. The Committee to Protect Journalists, based in New York, predicted in October 2000 that both sides in the Israeli–Palestinian conflict would continue to regard television images as weapons of war.[37]

As the military targeting of broadcasting illustrates, television narratives – whether in news programmes, documentaries or drama – can draw attention to human rights issues on a scale far greater than anything achieved by radio or the printed press. It is ironic, therefore, that the increase in television broadcasting capacity arising from digitalization seemed to provide an opportunity for international or public affairs reporting to be pigeonholed as a specialist or minority interest. The advantages and disadvantages of this development for human rights NGOs in most of the Middle East were brought out at the Second International Conference of the Human Rights Movement in the Arab World.[38] Held in Cairo in October 2000, this event devoted two whole sessions to the role of the media in the dissemination of human rights culture and human rights education. These sessions included a paper on the possibilities of benefiting from existing satellite channels and another exploring the viability of establishing a new satellite television channel, radio station or newspaper specializing in human rights. Both brought home the lack in Middle Eastern television of stations based on any principle other than commercialism or government control. Whereas independently regulated and publicly funded public service broadcasting would have a remit to facilitate broad debate on human rights issues, this is not the case with other broadcasting models. In the absence of a precedent for, or understanding of, public service television in the region, and with the Internet still not accessible to all, some participants in the Cairo conference saw the creation of a new satellite television channel as the most cost-effective means of getting a human rights message across to the biggest possible audience.

The deliberations in Cairo included the presentation of a business plan, drawn up by Kamal Batal, director of the Lebanese group MIRSAD (Multi-Initiative on Rights: Search, Assist and Defend). This envisaged a new channel transmitting from Eutelsat and seeking to attract advertising revenue at a rate of some $500 per 30 seconds of airtime. Its board of directors, expected to take six months to assemble, would be composed of non-politicians. Its programming, disseminated in Arabic, Farsi, Turkish, Hebrew and occasionally English, would be forthcoming from the archives of organizations such as Globalvision in the USA, Amnesty International, Human Rights Watch and the International Monitor Institute (IMI). The latter, based in Los Angeles, holds thousands of hours of video material on human rights violations in the Balkans, Rwanda, Sierra Leone, Myanmar and Cambodia, as well as the Middle East, catalogued in a way that allows footage to be retrieved on the basis of name, place, date and incident.[39] Other means of communication, including telephone hotlines and an Internet website, would be exploited as back-up to publicize schedules and build a loyal community of viewers who would spread news of the channel by word of mouth. The project was not, according to Kamal Batal, intended as a substitute for existing channels that might cover human rights issues from time to time. Its raison d'être arose, he said, because 'our experience tells us we want to be in control'.[40]

Some of those listening to this presentation had reservations about any attempt to use television to preach about human rights. They preferred to think first about making good-quality films and documentaries on human rights issues and having these interspersed with sports and ordinary entertainment programming, or shown on a channel such as Al-Jazeera, with an established reputation for breaking with regional taboos. With Al-Jazeera planning in 2000 to add a second channel of its own, specifically for documentaries and short films, there was a feeling among conference participants that human rights advocates would do better to concentrate on creating new material for screening on an existing channel rather than starting a whole new television venture of their own. Yet enduring suspicion of Al-Jazeera, even among self-proclaimed human rights defenders in the Middle East, demonstrated continued confusion surrounding the right to freedom of opinion, expression and information and its pluralistic implications. In these circumstances, the region's proliferation of both human rights NGOs and satellite television channels did not seem to herald a comparable proliferation of television programmes about human rights.

## Concluding overview

It was argued at the beginning of this book that, in order to assess the likely political impact of Middle Eastern satellite television channels, it was essential first to understand their origins and characteristics. Given the apparent erosion of jurisdictional boundaries inherent in the spread of transnational television, it was proposed in turn to examine the channels' background from one or more of the diverse perspectives offered by theories of globalization. Models of global cultural flow, of the 'stretching and deepening' of interaction among states and societies, of 'hybridization', and of 'global civil society' were deployed as templates against which to examine the dimensions and contours of the transnational television phenomenon in the Middle East.[41] Where necessary – as, for example, in assessing the role of cross-border broadcasting in socio-economic development, or determining whether external regulation of broadcasting undermines national sovereignty – additional insights were drawn from current thinking on freedom of expression in the so-called globalization era and from regime analysis. From whichever angle and in whichever light it was viewed, however, the regional satellite television phenomenon seemed to demonstrate the shallow, selective and often illusory nature of many developments that might, a priori, be taken for evidence of globalization.

The most that can be said about the leading private Middle East satellite channels' contribution to globalization is that the billionaires who founded them simultaneously expanded their connections with other members of a super-rich elite whose business interests stretched far and wide. For these owners, television ventures could be seen to oil the wheels of business as television programmes provided an additional medium of exchange with investment partners and allies worldwide. It is true that deregulatory policies in some Western countries removed barriers to private investment by foreign media moguls. These enabled broadcasting companies to be established in environments where not only laws on content but also labour laws were more favourable to company owners than they were in their countries of origin, notably Saudi Arabia and Syria. But the question of whether deregulation in this context led inexorably to globalization in the form of freely flowing information must be answered with reference to the political objectives of the émigré broadcasters. In fact it was not until the end of 1996, five years after MBC became the first Middle East satellite television operation to be based outside the region, that uncensored satellite television programmes in Arabic became a hot issue. This happened only with the arrival of the Qatari channel, Al-Jazeera. Al-Jazeera carried contentious programming because the Qatari government gave it licence to do so, and it beamed this programming from inside the Middle East, from the Gulf city of Doha. The Qatari emir engaged in deregulation when he abolished the Ministry of Information that might otherwise have censored Al-Jazeera. He attracted attention to the tiny state of Qatar by exploiting the technology of satellite broadcasting via Al-Jazeera. This and other examples demonstrated that, when Middle Eastern interest groups both inside and outside the region decided to take advantage of this technology, their choice could be explained more clearly in terms of locally grounded politics than in terms of a concept taken from the lexicon of globalization theorists, such as deterritorialization.

Concepts like 'global civil society' and the 'global public sphere' were also exposed as unsuited to the tasks of describing or explaining the status of pressure groups vis-à-vis transnational television in the Middle East. Terms like these represent aspirations, not reality. This was revealed by an examination of NGO efforts to communicate information about civil rights. Even in those few Middle East countries where they were tolerated, civil rights NGOs faced increasing suppression and marginalization in 1999–2000, not only by governments but also by other so-called civil society groups. Such attempts showed globalization to be a process that favours some interest groups more than others. As media corporations owned by private companies or controlled by governments expanded transnationally during the 1990s, they left no space for independently regulated public service media at the transnational level. In the absence of the necessary institutional arrangements, NGOs were no more guaranteed access to transnational media outlets than they were to national ones.

Meanwhile Middle Eastern governments still had the upper hand in the evolution of regional satellite television a decade after it took off. The institution of free zones for media enterprises at the start of 2000 testified to this most eloquently. Had national policies been more conducive to media pluralism and freedom of expression, the idea of the media free zone would have been redundant. The purpose of free zones was to contain transnational broadcasting and print media within enclaves where they would first and foremost create jobs and stimulate transfer of technology. In most cases, calls for free expression in these 'free' zones were countered by reference to a pan-Arab code of ethics reflecting penal code restrictions on both terrestrial and satellite media enforced across the Arab world. Indeed, the Satellite Channels Co-ordinating Committee of the Arab States Broadcasting Union played a part in formalizing a code of conduct for transnational broadcasters and making compliance with it a pre-condition of benefiting from member-ship of the committee. Such perpetuation and reinforcement of media taboos highlighted disparities between those inside and outside this broadcasting club. Here the impact of the satellite television phenome-non was to expose the different levels and types of regulation applied in different countries and regions. Of itself, satellite technology could not alter those regulatory codes.

Thus it was change in the political environment that surfaced via the transnational television landscape, rather than television content which triggered change. In a society where opinions are divided both within and among countries over the urgency and direction of change, these divisions will be as visible in the workings of the media as they are in the workings of other national and regional institutions. Media doors are, sometimes literally, sometimes metaphorically, open to some people and closed to others. It is inside media structures and media policy-making, not public appearances, that conflicting orientations emerge. In the case of the Middle East, where satellite channels enabled expatriate commu-nities to bridge the divide between their country of residence and country of origin, it was often these communities who used phone-in programmes and talkshows to add intensity and new dimensions to debates. Broadcasting entities are generally implicated in the working-out of currents and counter-currents in the political, economic, social and cultural spheres all at the same time. As such they provide a particularly rich source of insights into both cleavages and alliances among key interest groups. But, as demonstrated in these pages, this is as much because of what they fail to broadcast, and why, as what they actually show.

# Notes

## Chapter 1: The Potential of Satellite Television in the Middle East

1. The Palestinian producer, Daoud Kuttab, took part in the meeting and wrote about it in the *Jordan Times* of 25 February 2000, under the headline 'Democracy through television'.

2. The meeting was sponsored by the American actor, Richard Dreyfuss, and organized by Donna Bojarsky of Dreyfuss Productions in association with the Columbia University Middle East Institute and School of Journalism.

3. In his article 'Structural transformations of the public sphere' (*The Communication Review* 1/1 (1995), pp 1–22), Keane refers to the contemporary erosion and fragmentation of 'anything resembling a single, spatially integrated public sphere within a nation state framework' (p 1).

4. H.A. Innis, *Empire and Communications* (Oxford, 1950). Innis argued that complex writing systems were the 'basis' of large-scale political organization and administration in the East (p 100).

5. The author was told that the minister used this phrase in private conversations.

6. Author's interview with the Egyptian sociology professor and civil rights campaigner, Saad Eddin Ibrahim, Cairo, 6 September 1998.

7. Edward Herman and Robert McChesney, *The Global Media: The New Missionaries of Corporate Capitalism* (London, 1997), p 15.

8. *Ibid.*, p 16.

9. Michael Nelson, *War of the Black Heavens: The Battles of Western Broadcasting in the Cold War* (Syracuse, 1997), pp 182–3.

10. The difficulties of researching the relationship between media power and the making of government policies in the West are cogently discussed by Piers Robinson in 'World politics and media power: problems of research design', *Media, Culture & Society* 22 (2000), pp 227–32.

11. David Harvey, *The Condition of Postmodernity* (Oxford, 1990), p 233.

12. *www.arabicnews.com*, 24 March 2000.

13. Saudi Press Agency report from Riyadh, 15 February 2000.

14. Lila Abu Lughod, 'Finding a place for Islam: Egyptian television serials and the national interest', *Public Culture* 11 (1993), p 494.

15   See for example the Fortune Promoseven study quoted in *Gulf Marketing Review*, October 1997, and Atef Adli al-Abd and Fawzia Abdullah al-Ali, *Dirassat fi'l Ilam al-Fada'i* [Studies in Space Media] (Cairo, 1995), pp 113 and 143.

16   Robin Cohen, *Global Diasporas: An Introduction* (London, 1997), pp 174–5.

17   Benedict Anderson, *Imagined Communities* (London, 1991), p 46.

18   John Sinclair, Elizabeth Jacka and Stuart Cunningham, *New Patterns in Global Television: Peripheral Vision* (Oxford, 1996), p 24.

19   Arjun Appadurai, 'Disjuncture and difference in the global cultural economy', in M. Featherstone (ed), *Global Culture: Nationalism, Globalization and Modernity* (London, 1990), pp 297–9.

20   Data from the Central Agency for Public Mobilization and Statistics (CAPMAS) reported in the BBC, *Summary of World Broadcasts*, 10 June 1997. The total population resident inside Egypt numbered 59.72 million.

21   Data from the September 1992 Saudi census, quoted in Jean-Michel Foulquier, *Arabie Séoudite: La Dictature Protégée* (Paris, 1995), Annex 1. A list published by the Saudi-owned daily *Asharq al-Awsat* on 12 December 1995 put the number of Egyptians in Saudi Arabia at 1,195,189.

22   Mohamed Khachani, 'Migration from Arab Maghreb countries to Europe: present situation and prospects', *Forum: Newsletter of the Economic Research Forum in Cairo* 5/1 (1998), pp 23–4.

23   Associated Press report of August 1995, reproduced in MED TV, *The International Impact of MED TV* (London, 1996).

24   Homa Hoodfar, 'Women at the intersection of citizenship and the family code', in S. Joseh (ed), *Gender and Citizenship in the Middle East* (New York, 2000), p 305.

25   See Andrew Gamble, 'The new political economy', *Political Studies* XLIII (September), pp 516–30. Gamble states that markets have to be 'politically constructed and politically maintained' (p 523).

26   Anthony Giddens, *The Constitution of Society: Outline of the Theory of Structuration* (Cambridge, 1984); John B. Thompson, 'The theory of structuration', in D. Held and J.B. Thompson (eds), *Social Theory of Modern Societies: Anthony Giddens and His Critics* (Cambridge, 1989), p 60.

27   Douglas Boyd recounts the history in *Broadcasting in the Arab World*, 3rd edn (Ames: Iowa, 1999), pp 152–3.

28   Hezab AlSaadon, 'The Role of Arabsat in Television Programme Exchange in the Arab World', PhD thesis (Ohio State University, 1990), p 155.

29   See, for example: Julian Clover, 'Updating Bernard Shaw', *Cable and Satellite Europe*, July 1998; Raymond Snoddy, 'CNN digs its claws in', *Financial Times*, 9 December 1996.

30   Douglas Boyd, 'Saudi Arabia's international media strategy: influence through multinational ownership'. Paper presented at the Annual Meeting of the Association for Education in Journalism and Mass Communication (Baltimore, Maryland, August 1998), p 10.

[31]  Hussein Amin, 'The development of Spacenet and its impact', in R. Weisenborn (ed), *Media in the Midst of War: The Gulf War from Cairo to the Global Village* (Cairo, 1992), p 18.

[32]  Hussein Amin and Douglas Boyd, 'The development of direct broadcast television to and within the Middle East', *Journal of South Asian and Middle East Studies* XVIII/2 (Winter 1994), p 42.

[33]  Belkacem Mostefaoui gives the background in *La Télévision Française au Maghreb* (Paris, 1995), pp 59–60 and 67–9.

[34]  Measures undertaken by France in 1989 included: creating the Conseil de l'audiovisuel extérieur de la France; charging the state holding company Sofirad with promoting and supporting television initiatives; and establishing Canal France International as a 'programme bank' (Mostefaoui: *La Télévision Française*, p 68).

[35]  Naomi Sakr, 'Frontiers of freedom: diverse responses to satellite television in the Middle East and North Africa', *Javnost/The Public* 6/1 (1999), p 96.

[36]  BBC, *Summary of World Broadcasts*, 1 January 1996. The Yemeni Space Channel later switched to Arabsat 2A (*Middle East Broadcast & Satellite* 4/6 (November 1996), p 10).

[37]  BBC, *Summary of World Broadcasts*, 2 September 1996.

[38]  Author's telephone interview with Mohammed Jassem al-Ali, director of Al-Jazeera Satellite Channel, 27 May 1998.

[39]  The story of this ban, along with many other aspects of individual governments' satellite broadcasting policies, is dealt with in Chapters 2 and 5.

[40]  *Eutelsat News* 36 (December 1998), pp 1–2.

[41]  *Middle East Satellite Today* 3/4 (August 1997), p 3.

[42]  BBC, *World Media*, 12 December 1997.

[43]  John Sinclair, 'Mexico, Brazil and the Latin world', in J. Sinclair et al: *New Patterns*, p 62.

[44]  Raymond Snoddy, 'Satellite's small world', *Financial Times*, 7 July 1997.

[45]  Tony Camp, chairman of CSS & Grey, quoted in *Gulf Marketing Review*, July 1997.

[46]  e.g. 96 per cent in Algeria (according to Algeria's Conseil national de l'audiovisuel, pre-1992), 93 per cent in Egypt (according to BBC International Broadcasting Audience Research, *Media Survey in Egypt, October–November 1996: Main Findings* (London, May 1997); 99 per cent of urban homes in Syria (1994 BBC research); 90 per cent in Morocco (Naji Jamaleddine, 'Structure du paysage médiatique national', unpublished monograph, 1995); and 95 per cent in Lebanon (Stat-IPSOS). An estimated 99 per cent of UAE and Saudi households owned televisions in the mid-1990s, and at least half of these had more than one set, according to Pan-Arab Research Centre data reproduced in the 1996 edition of Zenith Media's *Middle East and Africa Market and Mediafact*. Statistical tables in the annual *World Telecommunication Development Report* of the International Telecommunication Union are designed to show the proportion of households owning televisions and the number of domestic satellite antennas, but these

columns are empty for the overwhelming majority of Middle East and North African states. See for example the 1999 edition, pp A-72-4.

47  Law No. 95-71 of 24 July 1995, Articles 3 and 5.

48  ARTICLE 19, *Surveillance and Repression: Freedom of Expression in Tunisia* (London, 1998), pp 47-51.

49  This numerical data was compiled by Canal France International in 1995/96 for a presentation entitled 'Measurement of satellite TV access'.

50  Mostefaoui: *La Télévision Française*, p 61.

51  Jamaleddine: 'Structure du paysage'.

52  BBC International Broadcasting Audience Research: *Media Survey in Egypt*, p 8. The research involved interviews with 3077 people aged 15 years and representing 89 per cent of the population The troubled southern governorates of Assiut and Sohag were excluded, along with desert border areas.

53  BBC, *Summary of World Broadcasts*, 21 November 1994.

54  Data shared with the author by media industry analysts in Beirut, 25 March 1998.

55  Author's interview with Mohammed Khair al-Wadi, Editor-in-Chief of the Syrian daily *Tishrin*, London, 17 March 1998.

56  Eutelsat survey for mid-1998.

57  The text of Shaikh Abdullah's speech was reproduced in *ArabAd* 8/4 (April 1998), pp 36-7.

58  Al-Abd and Al-Ali: *Dirassat f'il Ilam*, p 112.

59  BBC, *Summary of World Broadcasts*, 13 July 1995.

60  Gholamreza Arjomandi, 'The impacts of direct broadcasting satellite on the Iranian media sphere'. Paper submitted to an ARTICLE 19 conference on 'Satellite Broadcasting in the Middle East and North Africa: Regulation, Access and Impact', Cairo, February 1999, p 8. (Unfortunately Dr Arjomandi was unable to deliver his paper to the Cairo conference in person.)

61  *Ibid.*, pp 4-6.

62  *The Economist*, 17 December 1994.

63  BBC, *Summary of World Broadcasts*, 26 August 1997.

64  *The Guardian*, 16 August 2000.

65  See Note 3.

66  UNDP, *Human Development Report 1999* (New York, 1999), pp 33-4.

67  Marjorie Ferguson, 'The mythology about globalization', *European Journal of Communication* 7 (1992), pp 70 and 87.

68  See, for example, Jan Aart Scholte, 'Global capitalism and the state', *International Affairs* 73/3 (1997), p 431. An international investor speaking on the record at the Royal Institute of International Affairs on 7 July 1998, used a similar expression, asserting that profits are maximized when business can treat the world as 'one country'.

69  Immanuel Wallerstein expounded world-system 'unicity' in *The Capitalist World Economy* (Cambridge, 1979), e.g. pp 67-73. Leslie Sklair argues for a more differentiated approach identifying transnational practices in the economic, political

and cultural-ideological spheres, in *Sociology of the Global System*, 2nd edn (London, 1995).

[70] Roland Robertson speaks of the 'intensification of consciousness of the world as a whole', in *Globalization: Social Theory and Global Culture* (London, 1992), p 8; Joseph Camilleri and Jim Falk, in *The End of Sovereignty?* (Aldershot, 1992), suggest that globalization processes are prompting individuals to map their 'actions and understanding within a perspective of the world as a whole' (p 65).

[71] Peter Feuilherade, 'Clandestine broadcasters come and go', *Middle East International*, 8 August 1997, and author's telephone interview with Nuri Comez of Med TV, 3 August 1998.

[72] Jon Alterman, *New Media, New Politics?* (Washington, 1998), pp 76-7.

[73] Andrew Hurrell and Ngaire Woods, 'Globalization and inequality', *Millennium: Journal of International Studies* 24/3 (Winter 1995), p 447.

[74] Hurrell and Woods point to the possibility that promoting particular sets of values will in fact reinforce divisions within international society ('Globalization and inequality', p 464).

[75] Lotfi Madani, 'Les télévisions étrangères par satellite en Algérie: formation des audiences et des usages', *Revue Tiers Monde* 37/146 (April-June 1996), pp 315-30; Alec Hargreaves and Dalila Mahdjoub, 'Satellite viewing among ethnic minorities in France', *European Journal of Communication* 12/4 (1997), pp 459-77; Susannah Kennedy, 'Navigating the satellite sky: watching Arabic-language television in Europe'. Paper presented at the ARTICLE 19 conference on satellite broadcasting (Cairo, February 1999).

## Chapter 2: Whys and Wherefores of Satellite Channel Ownership

[1] Arjun Appadurai, 'Disjuncture and difference in the global cultural economy', in M. Featherstone (ed), *Global Culture: Nationalism, Globalization and Modernity* (London, 1990), pp 301-2.

[2] *Ibid.*, pp 296 and 306.

[3] David Held and Anthony McGrew, 'Globalization and the liberal democratic state', *Government and Opposition* 28/2 (1993), p 278. Examples of such interpenetration in a Middle East context can be seen in the private family business interests of some people holding government office and in the conditions attached by foreign governments to aid and arms deals.

[4] Susan Strange, *The Retreat of the State* (Cambridge, 1996), p 38.

[5] *Ibid.*, p 42.

[6] *Ibid.*, p 99.

[7] The 'co-operative norms, habits and practices' that form the 'essential structures of a state' are 'endlessly fluctuating in response to internal dynamics and external challenges', according to James Rosenau, 'The state in an era of cascading politics', in J. Caporaso (ed), *The Elusive State: International and Comparative Perspectives* (London, 1989), p 37. For Andrew Kirby, state formation involves a permanently unfinished displacement of power, since 'large vestiges of power

remain outside the state' ('State, local state, context and spatiality: a reappraisal of state theory', in Caporaso (ed): *The Elusive State*, pp 205-6).

[8] Philip Abrams, 'Notes on the difficulty of studying the state, 1977', *Journal of Historical Sociology* 1/1 (March 1988), pp 67-71.

[9] *Ibid.*, pp 77-81.

[10] I owe this formulation to Roger Owen, who included it in his presentation to the seminar on 'The Changing Role of the State in the Middle East and North Africa' at the School of Oriental and African Studies, University of London, May 1998.

[11] Mohammed Gohar, quoted by Diana Digges, 'On the verge ... of convergence', *Middle East Times*, 28 January 1996.

[12] See the section 'Struggles for diversity' in Chapter 4 for more detail.

[13] *Middle East Economic Survey*, 4 October 1999.

[14] The increase in NDP seats between 1990 and 1995, and objections raised by the Egyptian judiciary to the (mis)conduct of general elections, are documented by Eberhard Kienle, 'More than a response to Islamism: the political deliberalization of Egypt in the 1990s', *Middle East Journal* 52/2 (Spring 1998), pp 224-7.

[15] See Kienle: 'More than a response', p 228; Economist Intelligence Unit, *Egypt Country Profile 1995-96* (London, 1995), p 6; Richard Engel, 'State shakes up press houses', *Middle East Times*, 4 May 1998.

[16] Author's interviews in Egypt, 1998-99.

[17] Author's interview with the ERTU's deputy director Hassan Hamed, 15 August 1998.

[18] Personal communications from Professor Magda Bagnied (American University in Cairo) and Dr Sami al-Sharif (Cairo University), members of two advisory committees, Cairo, 21 February 1999.

[19] Hussein Amin, 'The development of Spacenet and its impact', in R. Weisenborn (ed), *Media in the Midst of War: The Gulf War from Cairo to the Global Village* (Cairo, 1992), p 17.

[20] Hussein Amin and Douglas Boyd, 'The development of direct broadcast television to and within the Middle East', *Journal of South Asian and Middle East Studies* XVIII/2 (Winter 1994), p 42.

[21] Author's interview with Amin Bassiouny, chairman of Nilesat, Cairo, 15 August 1998. Background information covered in this section on Egypt is also discussed in Naomi Sakr, 'Contested blueprints for Egypt's satellite channels', *Gazette* 63/2-3 (May 2001), pp 149-67.

[22] ERTU, *External Services of Radio Cairo* (Cairo, 1991).

[23] Karen Finlon Dajani, 'Egypt's Role as a Major Media Producer, Supplier and Distributor to the Arab World: An Historical Descriptive Study', PhD thesis (University of Michigan, Ann Arbor, 1980), pp 106-9.

[24] Inshirah El Shal, 'Introduction á la télévision égyptienne: quelques repères chronologiques', *Revue Tiers Monde* 37/146 (April-June 1996), p 249; Sonia Dabous, 'Egypt', in Y. Kamalipour and H. Mowlana, *Mass Media in the Middle East* (Westport: CT, 1994), p 67.

[25] Naglaa El-Emary, 'L'industrie du feuilleton télévision égyptien à l'ère des télévisions transfrontières', *Revue Tiers Monde* 37/146 (April–June 1996), p 260-1.

[26] State Information Service, *Arab Republic of Egypt Yearbook 1994* (Cairo, 1995), p 238.

[27] Author's interview with Sana Mansour, head of the ERTU Satellite Sector, Cairo, 15 August 1998.

[28] *Majallat al-Izaa w'al telefiziyun* 3015 (26 December 1992), quoted in El-Emary: 'L'industrie du feuilleton', p 262.

[29] Raymond Baker, 'Combative cultural politics: film, art and political spaces in Egypt', *Alif Journal of Comparative Poetics* 15 (1995), pp 19–32; Nicole Khouri, 'La politique antiterroriste de l'état égyptien à la télévision en 1994', *Revue Tiers Monde* 37/146 (April–June 1996), pp 263–83.

[30] Information minister Safwat al-Sharif said in July 1997 that President Mubarak was keen to 'spread the Egyptian media worldwide, displaying the Egyptian people's civilization and culture as well as expressing the Arab nation as a whole' (*www.sis.gov.eg*, 9 July 1997). Amin Bassiouny, chairman of Nilesat, told an interviewer in 1998: 'We want to be up to date with technology and science, while keeping the cultural identity of the Arab world for future generations' (*Middle East Economic Digest*, 19 June 1998, p 2).

[31] Author's transcript of Sharif's speech, delivered to the Arab–US Association of Communication Educators (AUSACE), Cairo, 7 September 1998.

[32] Some cases of human rights abuse against Egyptians in Saudi Arabia have attracted international attention. For example, the case of Mohammed Ali al-Sayyid, who was sentenced to 4000 lashes in 1990, was reported by Amnesty International USA in a 1996 report on human rights violations in countries receiving US security assistance. The Egyptian Organization for Human Rights lodged an appeal on 10 October 1994, against the sentence of 200 lashes and 45 days' imprisonment passed against Dr Mohammed Kamel Mohammed Khalifa after he complained that his son had been abused at a Saudi school.

[33] One floor of the Ramses Hilton in Cairo has long been occupied by a Saudi prince and his entourage, who have regularly attracted negative comment in the Egyptian press.

[34] Miral Fahmy, 'Farming Toshka is no pipe dream for Saudi prince', *Middle East Times*, 5 December 1997.

[35] A particularly strong denunciation is contained in Moheb Zaki's *Civil Society and Democratization in Egypt, 1981–1994* (Cairo, 1995), pp 191–2.

[36] Saudi Television Censorship Guidelines are reproduced in Hezab AlSaadon, 'The Role of Arabsat in Television Programme Exchange in the Arab World', PhD thesis (Ohio State University, 1990), pp 110–11. Shaikh Saleh's guidelines are summarized in ARTICLE 19, *The Egyptian Predicament: Islamists, the State and Censorship* (London, 1997), p 84. An Egyptian producer joked to this author that, hypothetically, Saudi Television would not allow him to run a news item about a singing dog.

[37]  ERTU: *External Services*, p 7.
[38]  State Information Service, *Egypt Yearbook 1995* (Cairo, 1996), p 168; 'Executive Plan of the Egyptian Satellite Sector for 1997-98' (internal document supplied by the Egyptian Press Office in London).
[39]  Eutelsat II-F3 at 16°E was replaced by W2, the first in a new generation of Eutelsat craft, on 5 October 1998 (Eutelsat press release, 5 October 1998).
[40]  Economist Intelligence Unit, *Egypt Country Profile 1998–99* (London, 1998), p 30.
[41]  State Information Service, *Arab Republic of Egypt Yearbook* (Cairo, 1994), pp 238-9.
[42]  State Information Service: *Egypt Yearbook 1995*, p 242; *Egypt Yearbook 1997*, p 168.
[43]  Rebecca Hawkes, 'Egyptian TV adapting to change', *Middle East Broadcast & Satellite*, September 1996, p 45.
[44]  *Middle East Broadcast & Satellite*, November 1996, p 10.
[45]  BBC, *World Media*, 5 September 1997.
[46]  BBC, *Summary of World Broadcasts*, 17 May 1995.
[47]  BBC, *Summary of World Broadcasts*, 23 June 1997.
[48]  BBC, *Summary of World Broadcasts*, 21 June 1997.
[49]  Author's interview, Cairo, 15 August 1998. Aspects of the allocation of geostationary orbital slots are discussed in Chapter 5.
[50]  Amin and Boyd: 'The development of direct broadcast television', p 44.
[51]  ERTU director Abdel-Rahman Hafez told a Cairo University seminar on satellite television in March 1998: 'Even though we hired some channels from Arabsat after the end of the boycott, Egyptian officials once again started to think about manufacturing an Egyptian satellite in view of the fact that Arabsat had a relatively short lifespan' (*TV Dish*, March 1998).
[52]  Matra Marconi won the contract in competition with Hughes and Lockheed Martin Astrospace of the USA, British Aerospace, and a Franco-German consortium of Aerospatiale and Daimler Benz (James Exelby, 'Egypt's first satellite to be built by French', *Middle East Times*, 1 October 1995).
[53]  *Financial Times*, 16 October 1995.
[54]  Author's interview with Amin Bassiouny, chairman of Nilesat, Cairo, 15 August 1998.
[55]  BBC, *Summary of World Broadcasts*, 24 October 1995.
[56]  *Ibid.*
[57]  *Al-Ahram Weekly*, 23 July 1997, quoted on *www.sis.gov.eg*.
[58]  Hamdi Abdel-Halim, head of transmission projects at ERTU, quoted in *Al-Ahram Weekly*, 23 July 1997.
[59]  Julian Clover, 'Jewel of the Nile', *Cable & Satellite Europe*, February 1998, p 23.
[60]  Author's interview with Amin Bassiouny, Cairo, 15 August 1998.
[61]  Quoted on *www.sis.gov.eg*, 1 June 1998.
[62]  *www.ssi.gov.eg*, 1 June 1998.
[63]  Chris Forrester, 'Nilesat 2 gets seal of approval', *Middle East Broadcast & Satellite*, January 1999, p 3.

[64] Author's interview with Amin Bassiouny, Cairo, 15 August 1998.

[65] Author's interview, Cairo, 21 February 1999.

[66] By Hamdi Abdel-Halim, head of transmission projects at ERTU, quoted in Al-Ahram Weekly, 23 July 1997.

[67] Author's interviews, August 1998, February 1999.

[68] James Napoli, Hussein Amin and Luanne Napoli, 'Privatization of the Egyptian media', Journal of South Asian and Middle Eastern Studies 18/4 (Summer 1995), p 56.

[69] See Table 9 in Chapter 4.

[70] Author's interview with Sana Mansour, Cairo, 15 August 1998.

[71] Information in this paragraph is drawn from interviews with private advertising agency personnel, Cairo, 18 August 1998.

[72] This is the phrase used in an article entitled 'Egypt in the 21st century – transition to an information-based community', on the official website run by the State Information Service.

[73] www.arabicnews.com, 20 June 2000.

[74] This translation of the article in Al-Riyadh of 9 November 1997, is taken from the BBC weekly World Media of 21 November 1997.

[75] According to Burke's Royal Families of the World, vol 2, quoted in David Holden and Richard Johns, The House of Saud (London, 1982), p 552.

[76] King Fahd's proclamations of affection for 'Azouz' (Abdel-Aziz's pet name) are recorded by Saïd Aburish in The Rise, Corruption and Coming Fall of the House of Saud (London, 1995), p 60.

[77] A translation of the full Basic Law can be found in Anders Jerichow, The Saudi File: People, Power, Politics (Richmond, 1998), pp 10–19.

[78] Jon Alterman, New Media, New Politics? (Washington, 1998), p 21.

[79] According to Edwin Hart, director of MBC News and International Operations until 1999, news was the 'primary product' of MBC during his tenure (Cable and Satellite Europe, February 1998, p 25).

[80] Muhammad Ayish, 'Arab television goes commercial', Gazette 59 (December 1997), p 482.

[81] ARTICLE 19: The Egyptian Predicament, p 84.

[82] Gulf Marketing Review Supplement, May 1997, p 10.

[83] See a shortened Saudi family tree in Michael Field, The Merchants: The Big Business Families of Arabia (London, 1984), Appendix 4.

[84] Gulf Marketing Review, June 1994, p 6.

[85] James Hansen, 'Relaunching a bid for Arab viewers', International Herald Tribune, 26 April 1995.

[86] Mai Yamani, Changed Identities: The Challenge of the New Generation in Saudi Arabia (London, 2000), pp 39–41.

[87] Author's interview with Sami Raffoul, general manager of the Pan-Arab Research Centre in Dubai, 20 October 1997.

[88] Amin and Boyd: 'The development of direct broadcast television', p 46.

[89] L. Marlow, 'The new Saudi press barons', Time, 22 June 1992.

[90]  MBC press release, 15 February 1999.

[91]  MBC press release, 28 October 1999.

[92]  Interview with Chris Forrester in *Gulf Marketing Review*, October 1999, p 32.

[93]  *Middle East Economic Digest*, 23 January 1998, p 6.

[94]  Sherin Moody, 'Pay television in the Middle East'. Paper presented to the ARTICLE 19 conference on satellite broadcasting in the Middle East and North Africa (Cairo, February 1998), p 5.

[95]  *ArabAd* 9/1 (January 1999), pp 14–15.

[96]  Author's interviews, Cairo, 21 and 24 February 1999.

[97]  *Gulf Marketing Review Special Report on Saudi Arabia*, May 1997, p 10.

[98]  *Ibid.*

[99]  Interviews with ART personnel in Cairo, 24 February 1999.

[100] *TV Dish* (in Arabic), 56 (August 1998), p 22.

[101] Personal communication from an ART source, 7 July 1999.

[102] Douglas Boyd, 'Saudi Arabia's international media strategy: influence through multinational ownership'. Paper presented at the Annual Meeting of the Association for Education in Journalism and Mass Communication (Baltimore, Maryland, August 1998), pp 13–14.

[103] *Newsweek*, 6 June 1994.

[104] Personal communication from Raya Alcadi on behalf of Orbit, 30 July 1998.

[105] Madawi Al-Rashid. 'State building in Saudi Arabia: the forgotten mutawwa'. Paper presented at the School of Oriental and African Studies, University of London, 30 November 1999.

[106] *Mideast Mirror*, 8 January 1996.

[107] Raymond Snoddy and David Gardner, 'BBC–Saudi TV row reveals raw spot', *Financial Times*, 10 April 1996.

[108] Nabil Dajani, *Disoriented Media is a Fragmented Society: The Lebanese Experience* (Beirut, 1992), and Nabil Dajani, 'The confessional scene in Lebanese television'. Paper presented at the Carsten Niehbuhr Institute workshop on 'Islam on TV', Copenhagen, December 1999, p 2.

[109] Dajani: *Disoriented Media*, pp 175–7.

[110] The French–Moroccan channel 2M, launched as a private subscriber service in Morocco in 1989, is not comparable as it was not available unencrypted until after it was taken over by the state in 1997.

[111] Author's interview with Maître Touma Arida, Member of the Conseil national de l'audiovisuel, Beirut, 28 March 1998.

[112] Human Rights Watch/Middle East, *Lebanon, Restrictions on Broadcasting: In Whose Interest?* (New York, 1997), p 10.

[113] *ArabAd* 9/1 (January 1999), p 14.

[114] *Middle East Economic Digest*, 2 October 1998.

[115] Human Rights Watch/Middle East: *Lebanon, Restrictions*, p 9.

[116] Dajani: *Disoriented Media*, p 105.

[117] Author's interview with Pierre Daher, Beirut, 26 March 1998.

[118] Interview in *www.tbsjournal.com* 1 (August 1998).

119 *Daily Star*, Beirut, 7 August 1998.
120 Interview with Future TV's managing director, Ali Jaber, by Chris Forrester in *Gulf Marketing Review*, December 1997, p 31. Author's interview with Nadim Munla, Future TV's president, Beirut, 26 March 1998.
121 BBC, *Summary of World Broadcasts*, 15 December 1997.
122 Author's interview, 26 March 1998.
123 Author's interview with Nadim Munla, 26 March 1998.
124 *Daily Star*, Beirut, 30 October 1999.
125 ARTICLE 19, *Walls of Silence: Media and Censorship in Syria* (London, 1998).
126 Translation carried in *Middle East International* 607 (3 September 1999), p 25.
127 *Daily Star*, Beirut, 2 November 1999.
128 Interview with *Al-Hayat*, 11 February 1996.
129 BBC World Service press release, London, 4 November 1996.
130 Economist Intelligence Unit, *Bahrain/Qatar Country Profile 1999–2000*, (London, 1999), p 46.
131 *Ibid.*, p 9.
132 BBC, *Summary of World Broadcasts*, 26 January 1996.
133 BBC, *Summary of World Broadcasts*, 31 October 1996.
134 Author's telephone interview with Mohammed Jassem al-Ali, 27 May 1998.
135 *Ibid.*
136 *Al-Hayat* website, 2 October 1999.
137 Associated Press report from Doha, 19 June 1999.
138 *Arabies*, September 1997, p 56.
139 Muqabel's arrest was publicized by Amnesty International in an Urgent Action Alert of 24 July 1997. Her release during the last week of February 1998 was reported to the author by a member of ANN management during an interview in London on 28 February 1998.
140 *Asharq al-Awsat*, 10 February 1998.
141 Economist Intelligence Unit, *Syria Country Report*, 4th quarter 1999.
142 Author's interview with Qassem Mazraani, ANN Editor-in-Chief, London, 7 February 1998.
143 *Ibid.*
144 Author's interview with Paul Hitti, ANN executive director, London, 28 February 1998.
145 *ArabAd* 8/10 (October 1998), p 38.
146 *www.arabicnews.com*, 16 November 1999.
147 Ann Zimmerman, 'Kurdish broadcasting in Iraq', *Middle East Report* No 189, 24/4 (July–August 1994), p 20.
148 Peter Feuilherade, 'Med-TV: "Kurdistan in the sky"', *http://news.bbc.co.uk*, 23 March 1999.
149 Part of the letter is reproduced in a MED TV booklet, entitled *The International Impact of MED TV*, published in 1996.
150 According to eye-witness reports by Western visitors.

[151] 'Court rules in favour of Kurdish TV channel', *Cable and Satellite Europe*, September 1998, p 8.

[152] ITC press release, 23 April 1999.

[153] Reuters report, 22 March 1999.

[154] Independent Television Commission, *Factfile 1998* (London, 1998), p 35.

[155] Ian Black, 'Turks want "pro-Kurd" TV censored by Britain', *The Guardian*, 21 June 1999.

[156] *The Guardian*, 29 November 2000.

[157] Appadurai: 'Disjuncture and difference in the global cultural economy', p 301.

[158] Strange: *The Retreat of the State*, p 42.

[159] Appadurai: 'Disjuncture and difference in the global cultural economy', p 296.

## Chapter 3: Points of Contact between Regional Channels and the Rest

[1] David Held and Anthony McGrew, 'Globalization and the liberal democratic state', *Government and Opposition* 28/2 (1993), p 262.

[2] Robert O. Keohane and Joseph S. Nye, *Power and Interdependence*, 2nd edn (Glenview: IL, 1989), pp 24–5.

[3] Robert O. Keohane and Joseph S. Nye, 'Power and interdependence in the information age', *Foreign Affairs*, September/October 1998, pp 83–4.

[4] *Ibid.*

[5] Robert Cooper, *The Post-Modern State and the World Order* (London, 1996), p 19.

[6] *Ibid.*, p 42.

[7] *Ibid.*, p 35.

[8] *Ibid.*, pp 17–19.

[9] Held and McGrew: 'Globalization', p 262.

[10] Keohane and Nye: *Power and Interdependence*', p 25.

[11] e.g. Jeremy Tunstall and Michael Palmer, *Media Moguls* (London, 1991); Leo Bogart et al, 'Media Moguls & Megalomania', *Index on Censorship* 23/4–5 (1994), pp 14–62.

[12] Edward S. Herman and Robert W. McChesney, *The Global Media: The New Missionaries of Corporate Capitalism* (London, 1997), pp 68–70.

[13] Graham Murdock, 'Redrawing the map of the communications industries: concentration and ownership in the era of privatization', in M. Ferguson (ed), *Public Communication: The New Imperatives* (London, 1990), p 6.

[14] Jane Martinson, 'Divorce fear for Viacom deal', *The Guardian*, 20 September 1999.

[15] Christopher Parkes, 'A deal too far for Sumner's wife', *Financial Times*, 21 September 1999.

[16] For examples, see Hilary Curtis, 'The mouth of the south', *The Guardian*, 17 May 1999.

[17] *Middle East Economic Digest*, 26 May 2000, p 5.

[18] David Holden and Richard Johns, *The House of Saud* (London, 1982), pp 209–21.

19  Saïd Aburish, *The Rise, Corruption and Coming Fall of the House of Saud* (London, 1995), p 107.
20  *Mideast Mirror*, 23 June 1999 and other press reports.
21  Reuters report from Dubai, as carried by the *Jordan Times*, 6 June 2000.
22  Interview in *ArabAd* 9/1 (January 1999), p 15.
23  Interview with AFP, 6 December 1999.
24  Vernon Silver, 'Saudi prince raises profile as succession looms', *International Herald Tribune*, 5 October 1999.
25  Mark Nicholson, 'Mythic hero's princely sum', *Financial Times*, 4–5 June 1994.
26  *Financial Times*, 2 June 1994.
27  *Middle East Economic Survey*, 18 September 1995.
28  *La Repubblica*, quoted in *Mideast Mirror*, 1 June 1995, p 21.
29  *Financial Times* 21 July 1995; *Le Monde*, 20 July 1995; *Middle East Economic Digest*, 28 June 1996.
30  Naomi Sakr, 'The Making and Implementation of Egyptian Policy towards Satellite Television Broadcasting', PhD thesis (University of Westminster, 1999), pp 187 and 242.
31  Interview with *Money Magazine*, October 1998, quoted in *ArabAd* 9/1 (January 1999), p 16.
32  Quoted in *Middle East Economic Digest*, 5 December 1997, p 22.
33  Paul Betts, 'Murdoch extends European TV plans', *Financial Times*, 29 December 1998; *Middle East Economic Digest*, 2 April 1999, p 30.
34  *Middle East Economic Digest*, 2 April 1999, p 30.
35  *Middle East Economic Digest*, 5 June 1998, p 5; 16 April 1999, p 13.
36  *The Guardian*, 31 October 2000.
37  *Middle East Economic Digest*, 23 January 1998, p 14; 30 January 1998, p 15.
38  Silver: 'Saudi prince'.
39  *Middle East Economic Digest*, 5 June 1998, p 5.
40  *Financial Times*, 19 October 1999.
41  *Middle East Economic Digest*, 2 October 1998, p 22.
42  *Middle East Economic Digest*, 5 June 1998, p 5.
43  *Middle East Economic Digest*, 31 March 2000, p 5.
44  Silver: 'Saudi prince'.
45  *Saudi Economic Survey*, 17 November 1999, p 3.
46  *ArabAd* 9/1 (January 1999), p 14.
47  *Daily Star*, Beirut, 22 November 1999.
48  *Middle East Economic Digest*, 2 October 1998, p 4.
49  Jean-Michel Foulquier, *Arabie Séoudite: La Dictature Protégée* (Paris, 1995), pp 37–8; *Middle East Economic Digest*, 4 August 1995, p 3.
50  *Middle East Economic Digest*, 4 August 1995, p 3.
51  Bassem El Hachem, *Radio Orient* (Paris, 1998), p 42.
52  Khaled Yacoub Oweis, 'Arab consortium invests in Syria's new leadership', *Middle East Times*, 21 July 2000.
53  Sulaiman al-Firzli, *Al-Hadath al-Dawli*, 27 August 1999.

54   *Daily Star*, Beirut, 3 July 2000.
55   Author's interview, Beirut, 26 March 1998.
56   El Hachem: *Radio Orient*, pp 42–3.
57   *Ibid.*, pp 42–6.
58   Author's interview, Beirut, 27 March 1998.
59   Author's interviews, Beirut, 26–27 March 1998.
60   *Ibid.*
61   *Daily Star*, Beirut, 13 April 1999.
62   *ArabAd* 10/1 (January 2000), pp 28–9.
63   *Daily Star*, Beirut, 29 January 2000.
64   El Emary: 'L'industrie du feuilleton', p 258.
65   *Middle East Economic Digest*, 4 August 1995, p 3; 23 January 1998, p 6.
66   *Middle East Economic Digest*, 16 February 1996, p 18.
67   *Arabies*, December 1997, p 57.
68   *ArabAd* 9/3 (March 1999), p 127.
69   Author's interview with ART representatives, Cairo, 24 February 1999.
70   ARTICLE 19, *The Egyptian Predicament: Islamists, the State and Censorship* (London, 1997), p 84.
71   Information from ART, Cairo, February 1999.
72   Author's interview with ART staff, Cairo, 24 February 1999.
73   Author's interview with Egyptian showbusiness reporter, Cairo, 24 February 1999.
74   Steve Negus, 'TV wars', *Middle East International*, 10 January 1997, p 9.
75   Including Radi al-Khas and Fares Lubbadeh.
76   Yomna Kamel, 'Arab satellite TV returns home', *Middle East Times*, 27 November 1999.
77   *In Focus* (Adham Center Newsletter), Spring 1998, p 1.
78   *Arabies*, May 1997, pp 52–3.
79   Jacques Bertoin, 'Qui a peur de la chaîne arabe?', *Le Monde* (Media Supplement), 31 March–1 April 1996.
80   *Arabies*, May 1997, p 53.
81   *Gulf Marketing Review*, September 1998, p 14; Dana Zureikat, 'ART puts together first ever Arab global telethon', *tbsjournal.com* 2 (Spring 1999).
82   Point made by ART consultant, Abdullah Schleifer, interviewed for Zureikat: 'ART puts together'.
83   *Forbes*' 1999 list; http://news.bbc.co.uk, 21 June 1999.
84   Douglas Boyd, 'Saudi Arabia's international media strategy: influence through multinational ownership'. Paper presented at the Annual Meeting of the Association for Education in Journalism and Mass Communication (Baltimore, Maryland, August 1998), p 13.
85   MBC press release, 18 June 1999.
86   Albert Moran, *Copycat TV: Globalisation, Program Formats and Cultural Identity* (Luton, 1998), pp 32–3.
87   MBC press release, 19 October 1998.

88 MBC press release, 7 November 2000.

89 John Tomlinson, 'Internationalism, globalization and cultural imperialism', in K. Thompson (ed), *Media and Cultural Regulation* (London, 1997), p 138.

90 Francis Wheen, 'Murdoch's cultural revolution', *The Guardian*, 20 October 1999.

91 Christopher Parkes, 'Disney hints at better ties with Beijing', *Financial Times*, 14 December 1998.

92 John Tomlinson, *Cultural Imperialism* (London, 1991), p 34.

93 That is not to say they necessarily endorse any hyperbole about it, e.g. Piers Robinson, 'World politics and media power: problems of research design', *Media, Culture & Society* 22 (2000), p 228; Dwayne Winseck, 'Gulf war in the global village: CNN, democracy and the information age', in J. Wasko and V. Mosco (eds), *Democratic Communications in the Information Age* (Toronto, 1992), pp 60-74.

94 Philip M. Taylor, *War and the Media: Propaganda and Persuasion in the Gulf War* (Manchester, 1992), p 7.

95 Raymond Snoddy, 'CNN digs its claws in', *Financial Times*, 9 December 1996.

96 Hussein Amin and Douglas Boyd, 'The development of direct broadcast television to and within the Middle East', *Journal of South Asian and Middle East Studies* XVIII/2 (Winter 1994), p 46.

97 Author's interview, Dubai, 20 October 1997.

98 Author's interview with Jihad al-Sibai, deputy vice-president for media, Fortune Promoseven, Dubai, 19 October 1997.

99 Advertisement in *Asharq al-Awsat*, 18 September 1991, quoted in El Emary: 'L'industrie du feuilleton', p 257.

100 Curtis: 'The mouth of the south'.

101 Chris Forrester, 'Middle East TV in '98: reaching maturity?', *Middle East Satellite Today* 3/6 (December 1997), p 7.

102 Al-Quds al-Arabi, quoted in *Mideast Mirror*, 8 January 1996, p 15.

103 *Gulf Marketing Review*, July 1998, p 35.

104 Private communication to the author, 12 October 1998.

105 Quoted in Ray Weisenborn, 'Cool media, the Gulf war and then – CNN', in R. Weisenborn (ed), *Media in the Midst of War: The Gulf War from Cairo to the Global Village* (Cairo, 1992), p 9.

106 Author's interview, Dubai, 20 October 1997.

107 Adeeb called for an end to censorship at a conference in Bahrain (*Gulf Marketing Review*, April 1997, p 14).

108 *Gulf Marketing Review*, June 1997, p 22.

109 Interview conducted by Rebecca Hawkes in *Middle East Broadcast & Satellite*, May 1997, p 28.

110 Author's interview, Beirut, 26 March 1998.

111 ARTICLE 19, *Surveillance and Repression: Freedom of Expression in Tunisia* (London, 1998), pp 48-9.

112 *Gulf Marketing Review*, July 1997, p 12.

[113] Author's interview with Saad Eddin Ibrahim, head of the Ibn Khaldun Centre for Development, Cairo, 6 September 1998.

[114] Private communication from Video Cairo Sat, 23 February 1999.

[115] Joe Foote, 'CNE in Egypt: some light at the end of an arduous tunnel', *tbsjournal.com* 1 (August 1998).

[116] James Napoli, Hussein Amin and Richard Boylan, 'Assessment of the Egyptian print and electronic media'. Report submitted to the US Agency for International Development, 1995, p 55.

[117] Weisenborn: 'Cool Media', p 7; Napoli, Amin and Boylan: 'Assessment', p 26.

[118] James Napoli, Hussein Amin and Luanne Napoli, 'Privatization of the Egyptian media', *Journal of South Asian and Middle Eastern Studies* 18/4 (Summer 1995), p 54.

[119] Personal communication from Abdullah Schleifer, 9 July 1999.

[120] Economist Intelligence Unit, *Egypt Country Profile 1995–96* (London, 1995), pp 22 and 60.

[121] Foote: 'CNE in Egypt'.

[122] *Ibid.*

[123] *Ibid.*

[124] Rasha Abdullah, 'The impact of Music Television (MTV) on music broadcasting in Egypt and the region'. Paper delivered to ARTICLE 19 conference on satellite broadcasting in the Middle East and North Africa (Cairo, February 1999).

[125] *Ibid.*

[126] According to MultiChoice CEO Hans Hawinkels, speaking at the launch of MultiChoice Egypt (*Middle East Satellite Today*, March 1995, p 3).

[127] *Ibid.*

[128] ART staff (interviewed in Cairo, 24 February 1999) explained the move by saying that ART, being a 'conservative' station, needed to dissociate itself from the kind of material broadcast by Showtime, which is 'not conservative at all'.

[129] Letter to the Editor in *tbsjournal.com* 2 (Spring 1999).

[130] Egyptian radio report from Cairo on 17 July 1995, reported in BBC, *Summary of World Broadcasts*, 19 July 1995.

[131] Baskerville Communications Corporation, *Middle East Television* (Shrub Oak: NY, 1996), p 42.

[132] James Whittington, 'Egypt seeks to lead Arab media world', *Financial Times*, 22 November 1995.

[133] Napoli, Amin and Napoli: 'Privatization of the Egyptian media', p 56.

[134] Private communication from a participant in the conference, 17 November 1997.

[135] *Arabies*, February 1996, p 76; *Middle East Times*, 21 January 1996, 14 July 1996, 15 August 1997.

[136] *Middle East Satellite Today* 3/6 (December 1997), p 1.

[137] Tariq Hassan-Gordon, 'MTV selects new Egyptian stars', *Middle East Times*, 18 August 2000.

[138] Boyd: 'Saudi Arabia's international media strategy', p 14.

[139] *Middle East Economic Digest*, 2 February 1996; *Middle East Satellite Today*, June 1997, p 6.

[140] *Middle East Broadcast and Satellite* 4/2 (March 1996), p 23; 6/4 (July 1998), p 8.

[141] According to Disney Channel's Middle East managing director, Scott Hicks, interviewed by Rahul Goswami in *Gulf Marketing Review*, May 1999, p 39.

[142] *Ibid.*

[143] For an overview of Disney's holdings see Robert McChesney, 'Media convergence and globalisation', in Daya Kishan Thussu (ed), *Electronic Empires: Global Media and Local Resistance* (London, 1998), pp 34-5.

[144] *Gulf Marketing Review*, October 1999, p 9.

[145] Economist Intelligence Unit, *Saudi Arabia Country Report*, 4th quarter 1999, p 14.

[146] *Middle East Satellite Today* 3/1 (February 1997), p 1.

[147] Silver: 'Saudi prince raises profile'.

[148] *Middle East Satellite Today* 3/2 (April 1997), p 1.

[149] *Daily Star*, Beirut, 8 January 2000.

[150] Keohane and Nye: *Power and Interdependence*, p 25.

## Chapter 4: Missing Links: Transnational Television and Development

[1] UNDP, *Human Development Report 1994* (New York, 1994), p 4.

[2] According to Richard Jolly, Human Development Report Co-ordinator, introducing the 2000 report at a seminar in London on 30 June 2000.

[3] UNDP, *Human Development Report 2000* (New York, 2000), pp 1 and 38-43.

[4] e.g. Cees Hamelink, *The Politics of World Communication* (London, 1994), p 33.

[5] Robert O. Keohane and Joseph S. Nye, 'Power and interdependence in the information age', *Foreign Affairs*, September/October 1998, pp 89-90.

[6] *Ibid.*, p 90.

[7] Naomi Sakr, 'Satellite television and development in the Middle East', *Middle East Report* 210 (Spring 1999), p 6.

[8] Abdel-Rahman Rashed, *Asharq al-Awsat*, 20 October 1999 (translated in *Mideast Mirror*, 20 October 1999).

[9] Interview posted on *Al-Hayat* website, 2 October 1999, and translated by the BBC, *Summary of World Broadcasts*, 5 October 1999.

[10] Resolution 59 (I), 14 December 1946.

[11] By late 2000, the non-signatories were Bahrain, Oman, Qatar, Saudi Arabia and the United Arab Emirates.

[12] *The Guardian*, 4 July 2000; *Financial Times*, 13 September 2000.

[13] *Middle East Economic Digest*, 25 September 1998; *www.worldbank.org/mdf/mdf2*.

[14] Author's transcript.

[15] Quoted by *Time* magazine in an article on Al-Jazeera, 'Kicking up a sandstorm', on 15 March 1999.

[16] UNDP: *Human Development Report 2000*, p 39.

[17] *Al-Ra'i*, 30 May 1996.

18  Raouf Basti, *Radiodiffusion dans le monde arabe: quelles voies à emprunter?* (ASBU, no date), p 11 (author's translation).

19  *Business Middle East*, 1-15 June 1996, p 3.

20  The phrases quoted are from the address by Hanan Ashrawi, then head of the Palestinian Independent Commission on Citizens' Rights, to the conference on 'Palestinian Broadcasting: Promises and Challenges', held in Jerusalem in January 1994. The conference proceedings were published by the Jerusalem Film Institute and Internews.

21  Annex 1 of the Declaration of Principles, which elaborated on arrangements for 'direct, free and general political elections' to the Palestinian Interim Self-Government Authority, specified that agreement should be reached on organizing the mass media, including the 'possibility of licensing a radio and television station'. It took several more years for Palestinian rights vis-à-vis the frequency spectrum to be asserted within the International Telecommunication Union (see Chapter 5).

22  Naomi Sakr, 'Media Concerns in an Emerging State: A Case Study of Developing Palestinian Media Structures in the West Bank and Gaza Strip, 1993-94', MA thesis (Institute of Education, University of London, 1994).

23  BBC, *Summary of World Broadcasts*, 14 February 1996.

24  BBC, *Summary of World Broadcasts*, 14 September 1996.

25  *Middle East Economic Digest*, 23 June 2000, p 21.

26  BBC, *Summary of World Broadcasts*, 25 February 2000.

27  *www.arabicnews.com*, 2 June 2000. The conference adopted the Rabat Declaration, calling for media pluralism and independence.

28  *www.arabicnews.com*, 3 July 2000.

29  *Middle East Times*, 9 December 2000.

30  *Jordan Times*, 4 July 2000.

31  *Ibid*.

32  *Jordan Times*, 6 July 2000.

33  ARTICLE 19, *The Egyptian Predicament: Islamists, the State and Censorship* (London, 1997), p 29.

34  Naomi Sakr, 'Contested blueprints for Egypt's satellite channels', *Gazette* 63/2-3 (May 2001), pp 158-9.

35  e.g. Marcelo Giugale and Hamed Mobarak (eds), *Private Sector Development in Egypt* (Cairo, 1996), p 44; James Napoli, Hussein Amin and Richard Boylan, 'Assessment of the Egyptian print and electronic media'. Report submitted to the US Agency for International Development, 1995, p 90.

36  *www.arabicnews.com*, 27 January 2000.

37  The author was told of this plan during interviews in Cairo in August 1998 and February 1999.

38  *www.arabicnews.com*, 27 January 2000.

39  Abdullah Schleifer, 'Video Cairo Sat: breaking new ground as usual, but this time on Nilesat', *tbsjournal.com* 3 (Fall 1999).

40  Heba Kandil, 'ERTU, investors at odds over media privatization', *tbsjournal.com* 4 (Spring 2000).

41  *Al-Ahram Hebdo*, 20–26 September 2000.

42  *Middle East International*, 30 May 1997, p 9.

43  *Palestine Report*, 30 May 1997, p 6.

44  See, for example: *Palestine Report*, 25 October 1996, p 9; *Middle East International*, 23 February 2000, p 11; press release by LAW, the Palestinian legal and human rights group, 30 May 2000.

45  *Middle East Times*, 6 February 2000.

46  Economist Intelligence Unit, *Jordan Country Profile 1999–2000* (London, 1999), p 15.

47  Alia Shukri Hamzeh, 'Cabinet puts media free zone in final form', *Jordan Times*, 18 January 2000.

48  *Ibid.*

49  Alia Hamzeh and Amy Henderson, 'Potential users of "media free zone" demand guarantee of total freedom', *Jordan Times*, 3 November 1999.

50  *www.arabicnews.com*, 19 January 2000.

51  *Middle East Economic Survey*, 14 February 2000.

52  Author's interview, 18 August 1998.

53  Author's interview, Cairo, 24 February 1999.

54  Jon Alterman, *New Media, New Politics?* (Washington, 1998), pp 15 and 32.

55  Eutelsat, *Cable and Satellite Penetration Results* (Paris, 1997 and 1998).

56  ARTICLE 19, *Walls of Silence: Media and Censorship in Syria* (London, 1998), p 68.

57  Author's interview with an Al-Jazeera representative, Cairo, 16 September 2000.

58  *ArabAd* 9/4 (1999), p 36.

59  *Middle East Broadcast & Satellite* 6/8 (November 1999), p 3.

60  PARC's annual conference in Dubai, which in 1997 was entitled 'Future tense'. A transcript of Munla's talk was published in *ArabAd* 8/2 (February 1998), pp 18–19, under the heading 'Can the Arab economy sustain the boom of media expenditure?'

61  *ArabAd* 9/2 (1999), p 48.

62  Author's interview, Beirut, 26 March 1998.

63  Interview with Chris Forrester, *Gulf Marketing Review*, May 1998, p 25.

64  Peter Golding, 'Media professionalism in the Third World: the transfer of an ideology', in James Curran, Michael Gurevitch and Janet Woollacott (eds), *Mass Communication and Society* (London, 1977), p 301.

65  John Keane, *The Media and Democracy* (Oxford, 1991), pp 35–50.

66  Author's interview, Cairo, 15 August 1998.

67  Author's interview, Beirut, 26 March 1998.

68  The film-maker was Joanna Head. Reem Saad's own work has concentrated on Egyptian village and peasant communities affected by agrarian reform.

69  Reem Saad, 'Shame, reputation and Egypt's lovers: a controversy over the nation's image', *Visual Anthropology* 10 (1997), p 406.

70  *Ibid.*

71 Author's interview by telephone to Doha, 27 May 1998.

72 Author's discussions in Amman, 23 November 1998.

73 BBC, *Summary of World Broadcasts*, 6 November 1998.

74 *Jordan Times*, 5 November 1998.

75 Jordanian TV, 4 November 1998, as reported in BBC, *Summary of World Broadcasts*, 6 November 1998.

76 Abdullah Hasanat, 'Impediments to freedom of expression in Jordan'. Paper delivered to a conference on 'Culture and Communication: A Global Information Society' (Amman, November 1998).

77 *Middle East Times*, 22 November 1998.

78 *Middle East Times*, 26 October 2000.

79 As reported in *Mideast Mirror*, 21 June 1999, p 16.

80 *Mideast Mirror*, 10 February 2000, p 19.

81 *Mideast Mirror*, 21 June 1999, p 15.

82 BBC, *Summary of World Broadcasts*, 6 May 1998, quoting a report in the Amman daily *Al-Majd* of 4 May 1998.

83 Reuters report from Rabat, 17 May 1998.

84 *Middle East International*, 28 July 2000, p 18.

85 Chris Forrester, 'Broadcasting censorship: it's a question of culture', *Middle East Broadcast & Satellite* 6/7 (October 1999), p 15. Similar observations were contained in a personal communication to the author from Saudi Arabia, 28 July 1999.

86 Quoted in *Time* magazine, 15 March 1999.

87 *Mideast Mirror*, 21 June 1999, p 16.

88 Forrester: 'Broadcasting censorship', p 15.

89 *Al-Ahram Weekly*, quoted in *Middle East Times*, 22 November 1998.

90 *ArabAd* 8/11 (December 1998), p 187.

91 *Ibid.*, p 186.

92 Author's interview, Cairo, 15 August 1998.

93 Author's transcript of speech given on 7 September to the Association of US-Arab Communication Educators (AUSACE) in Cairo.

94 See July 1998 issues of *Majallat al-Izaa w'al Telefiziyun* (Radio and Television Magazine).

95 Including a seminar on 'Challenges Facing the Thematic Channels in Egypt', organized in Cairo in November 1998 by Cairo University's Faculty of Mass Communication and the Friedrich Naumann Foundation.

96 *Gulf News*, 10 November 1999.

97 *Gulf News*, 2 February 2000.

98 *Ibid.*

99 *Gulf News*, 1 April 2000.

100 *Daily Star*, Beirut, 22 January 2000; Jemstone Network, *A Practical Handbook on Independent and Investigative Journalism* (Amman, November 1999), p 4.

## Chapter 5: International and Regional Regulation of Satellite Broadcasting

[1] According to John Ruggie, quoted in Robert O. Keohane and Joseph S. Nye, *Power and Interdependence*, 2nd edn (Glenview: IL, 1989), p 250.

[2] Robert O. Keohane, *After Hegemony: Co-operation and Discord in the World Political Economy* (Princeton: NJ, 1984), p 89.

[3] Stephen D. Krasner, *Structural Conflict: The Third World Against Global Liberalism* (Berkeley and Los Angeles, 1985), p 4.

[4] *Ibid.*, p 4.

[5] Sandra Braman, 'Trade and information policy', *Media, Culture & Society* 12/3 (1990), p 378.

[6] e.g. Guy de Jonquières and Louise Kehoe, 'Regulators @odds', *Financial Times*, 8 October 1998.

[7] Gist of a survey on the European Union in *The Economist* (23 October 1999), quoted approvingly by Roger Morgan, 'A European "society of states" - but only states of mind?', *International Affairs* 76/3 (July 2000), p 560.

[8] Susan Strange, 'Cave! Hic dragones: a critique of regime analysis', *International Organization* 36/2 (Spring 1982), pp 490–5.

[9] John Vogler, *The Global Commons: A Regime Analysis* (Chichester, 1995), p 19.

[10] *Ibid.*, p 18.

[11] As in Cooper's 'modern' and 'post-modern' worlds, and Keohane and Nye's 'complex interdependence', used as a basis for analysis in Chapter 3.

[12] ITU, *WRC-97: Information Note to the Press 4* (21 November), p 1.

[13] OTA (US Congress Office of Technology Assessment), *The 1992 World Administrative Radio Conference: Issues for US International Spectrum Policy – Background Paper* (Washington, 1991), p 11.

[14] Gareth Thomas, George Hupis, Richard Kupisz and David Cantor, 'Allocation of geostationary orbit and frequency resources for Europe', *Telecommunications Policy* 18/9 (1994), p 718.

[15] In the USA the Federal Communications Commission imposes a two-degree spacing rule (Thomas et al: 'Allocation of geostationary orbit and frequency resources', p 718).

[16] Krasner: *Structural Conflict*, p 81.

[17] James Savage, *The Politics of International Telecommunications Regulation* (Boulder: CO, 1989), p 109; George Codding Jr, *The Future of Satellite Communications* (Boulder: CO, 1990), pp 101–2.

[18] Savage: *The Politics of International Telecommunications Regulation*, pp 71 and 106; Mark W. Zacker and Brent A. Sutton, *Governing Global Networks: International Regimes for Transportation and Communications* (Cambridge, 1996), p 145.

[19] Vogler: *The Global Commons*, p 112.

[20] Jill Hills, *The Democracy Gap: The Policies of Information and Communication Technologies in the United States and Europe* (New York, 1991), p 94; Philippe

Achilleas, 'Satellite broadcasting and international law'. Paper delivered to the ARTICLE 19 conference on satellite broadcasting in the Middle East and North Africa (Cairo, February 1999), p 1.

21  Codding: *The Future of Satellite Communications*, p 112.

22  Interview with Nilesat chairman, Amin Bassiouny, Cairo, 15 August 1998.

23  ITU, *WARC-92: Press Release* (ITU/92-2 (rev)), 3 March 1992, pp 1-6.

24  ITU, *WRC-95: Press Release* (ITU/95-34), 18 November 1995, p 3.

25  According to Don MacLean, head of the ITU Strategic Planning Unit, addressing the Royal Institute of International Affairs Conference on Global Policy and Multimedia Telecommunications (London, November 1994); W.H. Bellchambers, 'Kyoto is an opportunity to revitalise an old and honoured organisation', *Intermedia* 22/4 (August–September 1994), p 34.

26  ITU, *WRC-97: Information Note to the Press 4* (21 November 1997), p 5.

27  ITU, *WRC-97: Information Note to the Press 3* (14 November 1997), p 10.

28  The list of reserved slots is contained in the ITU's quarterly Space Network List. The UAE's first priority at that time was to launch its telecommunications satellite, Thurayya.

29  Julian Clover, 'Hostilities resumed in SES–Eutelsat Star Wars', in *Cable and Satellite Europe*, April 1998, p 12.

30  Eutelsat press release, 15 July 1998, which also said the Radio Regulations Board's decision did not seem to be the result of a 'fully objective analysis'.

31  Bellchambers: 'Kyoto is an opportunity', p 35.

32  ITU, *Extract from the Summary Record of the 4th Meeting of Committee 4, WRC-97*.

33  *Ibid.*

34  Author's interview with Nilesat chairman, Amin Bassiouny, Cairo, 15 August 1998.

35  ITU, *WARC-92: Press Release* (ITU/92-1), 21 January 1992, p 4.

36  ITU, *WARC-92, Press Release* (ITU/92-2 (rev)), 3 March 1992, p 1.

37  Liching Sung, 'WARC-92: setting the agenda for the future', *Telecommunications Policy* 16/8 (1992), p 624.

38  OTA, *The 1992 World Administrative Radio Conference: Technology and Policy Implications* (Washington, 1993), p 9.

39  *Ibid.*; Sung: 'WARC-92'.

40  OTA: *The 1992 World Administrative Radio Conference*, p 15.

41  Sung: 'WARC-92', pp 630-1.

42  OTA: *The 1992 World Administrative Radio Conference*, p 17.

43  ITU, *WARC-92: Press Release* (ITU/92-1), 21 January 1992, p 4.

44  Mike Mills, 'Ready to launch a global radio network', *Washington Post*, 23 March 1998; Sung: 'WARC-92', p 630.

45  Giovanni Verlini, 'It's a wide world', *Middle East Broadcast & Satellite* 6/5 (September 1998), p 51.

46  Richard Ernsberger, 'Sky-high dream', *Newsweek*, 16 March 1998.

47  AfriStar was launched in October 1998, to be brought into operation in early 1999.

[48] Author's interview with Noah Samara, London, 24 June 1998.

[49] Verlini: 'It's a wide world'.

[50] OTA: *The 1992 World Administrative Radio Conference*, p 26.

[51] Donald MacLean, 'So you have reorganized. So what?'. Presentation to the Royal Institute of International Affairs Conference on Global Policy and Multimedia Telecommunications (London, November 1994).

[52] Author's interview with Mohamed Fakhr el Din, Senior Adviser, ITU Regional Office for Arab States, Cairo, 16 August 1998.

[53] ITU, *WRC-97: Information Note to the Press 2* (7 November), p 5. This entitlement, equivalent to half that agreed for full ITU members at WRC-97, recognized the transitional status of the Palestinian self-rule areas under the terms of the Declaration of Principles agreed by Israel and the Palestinians in 1993.

[54] ITU, *Final Report of the WTDC-98*, Resolution 18 (Plen-7).

[55] Robert Cox and Harold Jacobson (eds), *The Anatomy of Influence* (New Haven and London, 1973), p 5.

[56] James P. Sewell, 'UNESCO: pluralism rampant', in Cox and Jacobson (eds): *The Anatomy of Influence*, p 151.

[57] This summary of treaty body functions is based on the list set out in the UNDP's *Human Development Report 2000* (New York, 2000), p 45.

[58] Andrew Hurrell, 'International society and the study of regimes: a reflective approach', in V. Rittberger (ed), *Regime Theory and International Relations* (Oxford, 1993), p 52.

[59] Stephen D. Krasner, 'Global communications and national power', *World Politics* 43/3 (April 1991), p 349.

[60] Savage: *The Politics of International Telecommunications Regulation*, p 148.

[61] *Ibid.*, pp 5–6.

[62] Marika Natasha Taishoff, *State Responsibility and the Direct Broadcast Satellite* (London, 1987), p 147.

[63] Leo Gross, 'Some international law aspects of the freedom of information and the right to communicate', in K. Nordenstreng and H. Schiller (eds), *National Sovereignty and International Communication* (Norwood: NJ, 1979).

[64] Sara Fletcher Luther, *The United States and the Direct Broadcast Satellite: The Politics of International Broadcasting in Space* (Oxford, 1988), p 143.

[65] ITU, *WRC-97: Information Note to the Press 4* (21 November 1997), p 6.

[66] Information from a source inside the ITU. The same source also pointed out that, since the ITU's reorganization in 1993, WRCs and standardization conferences are no longer synchronized, the former taking place every two years and the latter every four years. Because this means waiting such a long time for WRC decisions to be followed through, the practice has developed whereby the Radio-communications Bureau prints out co-ordination data and circulates it to administrations in advance of the standardization conference.

[67] Author's interview with Nilesat chairman, Amin Bassiouny, Cairo, 15 August 1998.

[68] *Ibid.*

69   *Ibid.*
70   Personal communication from an ITU source, 16 August 1998.
71   Kuwait News Agency report carried in BBC, *Summary of World Broadcasts*, 20 July 1998. p 14.
72   Stephen D. Krasner, 'Sovereignty, regimes and human rights', in V. Rittberger (ed), *Regime Theory and International Relations* (Oxford, 1993), p 165.
73   Robert Cooper, *The Post-Modern State and the World Order* (London, 1996), pp 19 and 42.
74   The article is quoted in full in Chapter 4.
75   Jack Donnelly, 'International human rights: a regime analysis', *International Organization* 40/3 (Summer 1986), p 633.
76   UNDP: *Human Development Report 2000*, p 47.
77   Howard Frederick, 'Communication, peace and international law', in C. Roach (ed), *Communication and Culture in War and Peace* (London, 1993), p 225.
78   Nathan Brown, 'The Supreme Constitutional Court and the meaning of liberal legality in Egypt'. Paper presented at the 29th Annual Meeting of the Middle East Studies Association of North America (Washington, December 1995), p 17.
79   See, for example, the HRC's observations on Tunisia's media policy (UN Doc. CCPR/C/79/Add.43 (1994), paragraphs 7-9, quoted in ARTICLE 19, *Surveillance and Repression: Freedom of Expression in Tunisia* (London, 1998), pp 14-15.
80   ARTICLE 19, *Walls of Silence: Media and Censorship in Syria* (London, 1998), p 10.
81   UN Human Rights Committee, *Consideration of Reports Submitted by States Parties under Article 40 of the Covenant: Comments of the HRC on the Second Periodic Report of Egypt* (CCPR/C/51/Add. 71), adopted on 20 July 1993.
82   ICCPR, States parties reporting status entry form, *www.unhchr.ch*, July 1999.
83   European Commission, DG1B (External Relations), *The Euro-Mediterranean Parnership: Barcelona Declaration and Working Programme, Brussels, 1995*, Appendix 2.
84   ARTICLE 19: *Surveillance and Repression*, p 19.
85   European Parliament Resolution on Tunisia, B5-0508, 0509, 0510, 0525 and 0527/2000.
86   Appeal circulated by ARTICLE 19, 3 August 2000. Details of the case are discussed in Chapter 6.
87   MacBride Commission, 'Many Voices, One World', in O. Boyd-Barrett and P. Braham (eds), *Media, Knowledge and Power* (London, 1987), pp 19-34.
88   UNESCO, *Basic Texts in Communication 89-95* (CII-96/WS/2) (Paris, 1996), p 13.
89   *Ibid.*, p 87.
90   UNESCO, *Final Report of the Seminar on Promoting Independent and Pluralistic Arab Media* (CII-96/CONF.702/LD.1) (Paris, 1996), pp 60-1.
91   Decision No. 150 ex 3.1, Part 3, November 1997.
92   Author's interview with Gervasio Kaliwo, Programme Officer for Arab States, Communication Division, UNESCO, Paris, 25 June 1997.
93   Sewell: 'Pluralism Rampant', p 151.
94   Economist Intelligence Unit, *World Trade Report*, 1st quarter 1998, p 5.

95    *Ibid.*
96    Fawaz Alamy, addressing the IBC 'Investing in Saudi Arabia' conference in London, June 2000.
97    Toby Miller, 'National policy and the traded image', in P. Drummond, R. Paterson and J. Willis (eds), *National Identity and Europe: The Television Revolution* (London, 1993), p 98.
98    Mario Kakabadse, 'The WTO and the commodification of cultural products: implications for Asia', *Media Asia* 22/2 (1995), p 71.
99    Miller: 'National policy and the traded image', p 97.
100   Kakabadse: 'The WTO', p 74.
101   The *Financial Times* reported in a news item and a leader article on 15 December 1993, that the audiovisual sector had been 'excluded' from the Uruguay Round.
102   Economist Intelligence Unit, *The EIU Guide to World Trade under the WTO* (London, 1995), p 109.
103   Economist Intelligence Unit, *The EIU Guide to the New GATT* (London, 1994), p 29.
104   Kakabadse: The WTO', p 74.
105   Economist Intelligence Unit: *The EIU Guide to World Trade under the WTO*, p 110.
106   Kakabadse: 'The WTO', p 75.
107   *Ibid.*
108   Vincent Mosco, 'Free trade in communication: building a world business order', in K. Nordenstreng and H. Schiller (eds). *Beyond National Sovereignty: International Communication in the 1990s* (Norwood: NJ, 1993), p 196.
109   The significance of this clause was emphasized by Edward Alden, 'Canada faces $4bn sanctions', *Financial Times*, 19 January 1999.
110   Mosco: 'Free trade in communication', p 198.
111   Economist Intelligence Unit, *World Trade Report*, 2nd quarter 1997, pp 22-3, and 1st quarter 1998, p 19.
112   *Financial Times*, 30 July 1998.
113   *Financial Times*, 28 August 1995.
114   Economist Intelligence Unit, *World Trade Report*, 2nd quarter 1997, p 6.
115   Economist Intelligence Unit: *The EIU Guide to the New GATT*, p 31.
116   Economist Intelligence Unit, *World Trade Report*, 2nd quarter 1997, p 13.
117   *Ibid.* and Economist Intelligence Unit, *World Trade Report*, 1st quarter 1998, p 11.
118   Economist Intelligence Unit, *World Trade Report*, 1st quarter 1998, p 19.
119   Mark W. Zacker and Brent A. Sutton, *Governing Global Networks: International Regimes for Transportation and Communications* (Cambridge, 1996), p 151.
120   *Ibid.*
121   Rasha El-Ibiary, 'Film pirates run industry aground', *Middle East Times*, 15 August 1997.
122   Author's interview, Cairo, 15 August 1998.
123   Economist Intelligence Unit, 'Distribution, sales and marketing', *Egypt Business Report*, 1st quarter 1996, p 49.

124 Economist Intelligence Unit, 'Intellectual property protection', *Egypt Business Report*, 2nd quarter 1997, p 11.

125 Jan Millichip, 'Lebanon pulls plug on rampant "coat-hanger" piracy', *The Independent*, 2 October 1996.

126 Forum discussion transcribed in the first issue of the online journal, *tbsjournal.com*, in August 1998.

127 *Daily Star*, Beirut, 16 November 1999.

128 Gillian Doyle, 'Towards a pan-European directive? From "concentration and pluralism" to "media ownership"', *Communications Law* 3/1 (1998), pp 11–15.

129 Bahgat Korany, 'The old/new Middle East', in L. Guazzone (ed), *The Middle East in Global Change: The Politics and Economics of Interdependence versus Fragmentation* (London, 1997), p 146.

130 Korany: 'The old/new Middle East', pp 147–8.

131 Hezab AlSaadon, 'The Role of Arabsat in Television Programme Exchange in the Arab World', PhD thesis (Ohio State University, 1990), p 147.

132 *Middle East Economic Digest*, 5 June 1998.

133 *Arabies*, October 1997, p 57.

134 BBC, *Summary of World Broadcasts*, 21 July 1997.

135 Author's interview, Cairo, 15 August 1998.

136 Author's interview with ASBU director-general, Amin al-Buni, Tunis, 9 June 1995.

137 Author's transcript of the remark, on 20 February 1999, to the ARTICLE 19 conference on satellite broadcasting in the Middle East and North Africa.

138 *TV Dish* 56 (August 1998), p 20.

139 Peter Feuilherade, 'Qatar's Al-Jazeera livens up Arab TV scene', *http://news.bbc.co.uk*, 7 January 1999.

140 Roula Khalaf, 'Qatar: satellite TV breaks mould', *Financial Times*, 13 March 1999.

141 Hassan Hamed; see Note 137.

142 BBC, *Summary of World Broadasts*, 15 December 1997.

143 Information collated from sources inside and outside ANN during February and March 1998.

144 Korany: 'The old/new Middle East', pp 147–8.

## Chapter 6: Global Civil Society? NGO Influence on Transnational Broadcasts

1 Hegel presented civil society as pre-political or pre-state society in need of regulation by the state. For a comparison of Gramsci's innovations with those of his predecessors see Norberto Bobbio, 'Gramsci and the concept of civil society', in J. Keane (ed), *Civil Society and the State* (London, 1988), pp 73–99.

2 Quintin Hoare and Geoffrey Nowell Smith (eds and trans), *Selections from the Prison Notebooks of Antonio Gramsci* (London, 1971), p 12.

3 *Ibid.*

4   See Bruce Stanley's helpful alternative focus on networks in his 'Review of "Civil Society in the Middle East, Vol 1", edited by Augustus Richard Norton', *Middle East Policy* 3/4 (April 1995), pp 129–30. See also Bruce Stanley, 'NGO–PNA relations in Palestine'. Paper presented to the annual conference of the British Society for Middle Eastern Studies (Oxford, July 1997).

5   Peter Willetts, 'Political globalization and the impact of NGOs upon transnational companies', in J. Mitchell (ed), *Companies in a World of Conflict: NGOs, Sanctions and Corporate Responsibility* (London, 1998), p 196.

6   Nicholas Garnham, *Capitalism and Communication*, (London, 1990), p 10.

7   Colin Sparks, 'Is there a global public sphere?', in Daya Kishan Thussu (ed), *Electronic Empires: Global Media and Local Resistance* (London, 1998), p 112.

8   This is the argument of Ingrid Volkmer in her book on CNN, *News in the Global Sphere* (Luton, 1999).

9   This terminology is drawn from the text of the People's Communication Charter, and Cees Hamelink's introduction to it in *tbsjournal.com* 2 (Spring 1999).

10  Sean O'Siochru, 'Voices 21: a global movement for people's media and communications in the 21st century', *tbsjournal.com* 2 (Spring 1999).

11  *tbsjournal.com* 2 (Spring 1999).

12  Cees Hamelink, *The Politics of World Communication* (London, 1994), p 4. Hamelink explains in a footnote that the word 'global' is problematic because it suggests a condition that has already been achieved.

13  John Keane, 'Global civil society?', draft paper, August 2000, p 4. Quoted with permission.

14  *Ibid.*

15  Marc Raboy, 'Challenges for the global regulation of communication', *Javnost/The Public* V/4 (1998), p 67.

16  'MacBride Round Table: a brief description'. Leaflet circulated by the MacBride Round Table in 1998.

17  *Ibid.*

18  'People's Communication Charter' (text and introduction), *tbsjournal.com* 2 (Spring 1999).

19  Wolfgang Kleinwächter, 'A new trilateralism in global communication negotiations? How governments, industry and citizens try to create a new "Global Communications Charter"', *Javnost/The Public* V/4 (1998), p 79.

20  Raboy: 'Challenges', p 67.

21  *Ibid.*, pp 70–1.

22  *Ibid.*, p 71.

23  Algeria, Egypt, Jordan, Lebanon, Morocco, Syria, Tunisia, Turkey and the Palestinian Authority are the principal beneficiaries of MEDA funding but Israel, Malta and Cyprus are also included in the Partnership.

24  See the introductory section (pages un-numbered) of *Euro-Mediterranean Partnership: Information Notes*, April 1999. The section was compiled by Unit IB/A.4 of the European Commission.

25 Text from *www.euromed.net* (1 June 1999).

26 e.g. in October 1998 a group of Arab reporters held discussions on this subject with parliamentarians in Beirut, Lisbon and London (Zeina Abu Rizk, 'Beydoun highlights role of parliament at media debate', *Daily Star*, Beirut, 6 October 1998).

27 Statistics are drawn from the MEDA Democracy section of *Euro-Mediterranean Partnership: Information Notes*, (April 1999), compiled by Unit 1B/A.2 of the European Commission.

28 'Assessment of activities carried out within the framework of the cultural chapter of the Euro-Mediterranean Partnership since the Barcelona Conference', Annex to *Euro-Mediterranean Partnership: Information Notes* (European Commission, April 1999).

29 'Grève à Euronews sans interruption des émissions', Agence France Presse report from Lyons, 8 April 1999.

30 The amount paid by ITN was almost half Alcatel's asking price, which was in turn about 20 per cent lower than the latter had paid for the stake it bought in March 1995 ('Les chains publiques acceptent l'arrivée d'ITN dans Euronews', *Le Monde*, 28 October 1997).

31 'ITN takes over Euronews in £5 m deal', *Cable & Satellite Europe*, January 1998, p 7.

32 According to ITN chief executive Stewart Purvis, interviewed in *Middle East Broadcast & Satellite*, January 1998, p 8.

33 'Conclusions de la conférence de Thessalonique sur la coopération audiovisuelle et sur la télévision', 15 November 1997, reproduced on *www.euromed.net*.

34 Details of all the projects were posted on *www.euromed.net*.

35 *Euromed Synopsis* 107–8 (20 July 2000) and 112 (22 September 2000).

36 *Med Media Programme of the European Union* 2 (1994), pp 23–35.

37 Section on 'Co-operation between Civil Societies', compiled by Unit IB/A.4 of the European Commission, in *Euro-Mediterranean Partnership: Information Notes*, April 1999.

38 *Euro-Mediterranean Partnership: Information Notes*, April 1999.

39 Moheb Zaki, *Civil Society and Democratization in Egypt, 1981–94* (Cairo, 1995), pp 57–9.

40 *Ibid.*, p 62.

41 Otavio Peixoto, 'Grassroots associations, non-governmental organizations and the growth of civil society in Egypt', *Forum: Newsletter of the Economic Research Forum for the Arab States, Turkey and Iran* 3/1 (1996), p 14.

42 Jean Dib Hajj, 'NGO networking in the Arab world'. Paper presented to the Third Mediterranean Development Forum, Cairo, March 2000.

43 Maha Abdel-Rahman, 'Civil Society against Itself: Egyptian NGOs in the Neo-Liberal Era'. Paper presented to the conference of the European Association for Middle East Studies (Ghent, September 1999).

44 Zaki: *Civil Society*, p 65.

45 'NGOs fight new draft law', *Civil Society* 79 (July 1998), pp 2–4.

46  Bahey El Din Hassan, 'The dilemma of the Arab human rights movement'. Paper presented to the 33rd Annual Meeting of the Middle East Studies Association (Washington: DC, November 1999), p 4.

47  The full list appeared in *Civil Society* 98 (February 2000), p 15.

48  AFP report from Cairo, 8 June 2000.

49  Ed Webb of the British embassy said the cheque was for the EOHR Women's Legal Aid Project, which had been funded by the Dutch government until 1996 (Simon Apiku, 'Government jails human rights leader over cash', *Middle East Times*, 7 December 1998; Mark Huband, 'Egypt's human rights group leader arrested', *Financial Times*, 3 December 1998).

50  Paul Schemm, 'EOHR leader gets out with a haircut', *Middle East Times*, 13 December 1998.

51  *Ibid*.

52  Nicola Pratt, 'Egypt harasses human rights activists', MERIP Press Information Note 28, 17 August 2000.

53  Personal communication from Sophie Huet, European Commission DG1B, 9 June 1999.

54  Tariq Hassan-Gordon, 'Ibrahim finally charged', *Middle East Times*, 29 September 2000.

55  Eberhard Kienle, 'More than a response to Islamism: the political deliberalization of Egypt in the 1990s', *Middle East Journal* 52/2 (Spring 1998), p 227.

56  Simon Apiku, 'Gagging Egypt's Mr. Civil Society', *Middle East Times*, 7 July 2000.

57  Steve Negus, 'Who's smearing whom?', *Middle East International* 629 (14 July 2000).

58  *www.arabicnews.com*, 25 September 2000.

59  The author heard these comments during visits to Cairo in September and October 2000.

60  Rami Khouri, 'Ibrahim and the confused Arab state', *Jordan Times*, 5 July 2000.

61  *Ibid*.

62  Dalal Al-Bizri, 'Al-Mujtamaa al-Madani: Al-Jamiayyat al-Nisa'iyya al-Lubnaniya' [Civil Society: women's organizations in Lebanon] in Fatima Azrawil and Dalal Al-Bizri (eds), *Al-Mar'a al-Arabiyya: al-Waqia wa al-Tasawur* [Arab Women: Reality and Perception] (Cairo, 1995), pp 151 and 154. The relevant extract from Al-Bizri's work is translated by Fadia Faqir in 'The Price of Honour: Violence against Women in Jordan', draft paper, March 2000. Faqir finds Al-Bizri's explanation equally applicable to Jordan. Quoted with permission.

63  Hassan: 'The dilemma of the Arab human rights movement', p 5.

64  Keane: 'Global civil society', p 4.

65  e.g. the US-based Freedom Forum held a seminar entitled 'Free Media, Fair Media' in Cairo in September 1998, involving speakers from all over the Arab world ('Conference admits Egyptian and Arab press flawed', *Middle East Times*, 20 September 1998).

[66] Veronica Forrester, 'The German political foundations', in C. Stevens and J. Verloren van Themaat (eds), *Pressure Groups, Policies and Development: The Private Sector and EEC Third World Policy* (London, 1985), p 40.

[67] FNF brochure, *Friedrich Naumann Foundation: Freedom and Responsibility Worldwide*, p 1.

[68] *The Friedrich Naumann Foundation*, leaflet produced by the foundation's Amman office, pp 2-3.

[69] In his foreword to Moheb Zaki's book on *Civil Society and Democratization in Egypt, 1981-94*, which was funded by the Konrad Adenauer Foundation, Olaf Köndgen mentions that the Foundation 'traditionally' co-operated with the Faculty of Law at Ain Shams University and the Centre for Political Research and Studies at Cairo University. Köndgen implies that he does not consider these to be 'non-governmental' institutions.

[70] Author's interview with Hani Abdel-Malak, assistant to the regional director, Friedrich Naumann Foundation, Cairo, 22 February 1999.

[71] *Ibid.*

[72] Author's interview with Professor Farag Elkamel, head of the Centre for Communication Training, Documentation and Production, Faculty of Mass Communication, Cairo University, 24 February 1999.

[73] Kienle: 'More than a response to Islamism', p 228.

[74] The *Seminar Report* produced by the FNF does not attribute statements or questions to individuals. Participants and points made are listed separately.

[75] 'Facts and figures about Amnesty International and its work for human rights', www.amnesty.org.

[76] David Sogge, 'Northern lights', in D. Sogge (ed), *Compassion and Calculation: The Business of Private Foreign Aid* (London, 1996), p 145.

[77] 'Amnesty International: a brief history', www.amnesty.org.

[78] Amnesty International, *Weekly Update Service*, 25 June 1993.

[79] Amnesty International press release, ref. NWS 11/113/94, 26 May 1994.

[80] According to a close observer from another NGO.

[81] 'About the Lawyers' Committee for Human Rights', www.lchr.org.

[82] A paragraph of 'Support the Lawyers' Committee for Human Rights', www.lchr.org, states: 'Help make the rule of law and global partnerships the defining human rights strategies of the 21st century'.

[83] Neil Hicks, 'Escalating attacks on human rights protection in Egypt', in *Report of the Lawyers Committee for Human Rights* (New York, September 1995), pp 8-9.

[84] *Ibid.*

[85] *Ibid.*

[86] ARTICLE 19 press release, 3 August 2000. The six other groups joining the appeal were the International Human Rights Federation, the Euro-Mediterranean Human Rights Network, Human Rights Watch, the World Organization against Torture, the Observatory for the Protection of Human Rights Defenders and Amnesty International.

87  ARTICLE 19, *The Egyptian Predicament: Islamists, the State and Censorship* (London, August 1997).
88  According to Saïd Essoulami, former head of ARTICLE 19's Middle East and North Africa Programme, who organized the conference.
89  Jan Aart Scholte, 'Review of "The New Realism: Perspectives on Multilateralism and World Order", edited by Robert Cox', *International Affairs* 73/4 (1997), p 771.
90  Willetts: 'Political globalization', p 196.
91  *MacBride Round Table: A Brief Description.*
92  The right to such access is claimed in Article 2 of the People's Communication Charter.

## Chapter 7: Text and Context: Satellite Channels in a Changing Environment

1   Daoud Kuttab, 'Palestinian diaries: grass roots TV production in the Occupied Territories', in T. Dowmunt (ed), *Channels of Resistance: Global Television and Local Empowerment* (London 1993), pp 138–45.
2   For a detailed analysis of the language used by Western journalists about the *intifada*, see the article 'Chasing media shadows' in the Jerusalem Media and Communication Centre's *Palestine Report* of 1 November 2000.
3   Jerusalem Media and Communication Centre website (*www.jmcc.org*), 29 November 2000.
4   Mai Yamani, 'Awakening',. *The World Today* 56/12 (December 2000), p 22.
5   *Daily Telegraph*, 16 October 2000.
6   *Saudi Economic Survey*, 27 September 2000, p 17.
7   Mai Yamani, *Changed Identities: The Challenge of the New Generation in Saudi Arabia* (London, 2000), p 57.
8   *Ibid.*, p 19.
9   *Gulf News*, 9 March 2000.
10  *Ibid.*
11  *Arab Regional NGOs' Alternative Report for 2000*, submitted to the Conference of NGOs in Consultative Status with ECOSOC by the NGO Co-ordinating Committee of the Jordanian National Commission for Women, February 2000. I am indebted to Christine Arab of UNIFEM for supplying a copy of the report.
12  For detailed examples see Naomi Sakr/Centre for Media Freedom - Middle East and North Africa, *Women's Rights and the Arab Media* (London, November 2000), pp 43–5.
13  *The Arab NGOs' Alternative Report for 2000*, Section J.
14  Amina Dhaheri, 'The image of women in Arab media'. Paper presented to a seminar on 'Media Realities and Horizons in the Arab World' at the Ajman University for Science and Technology (UAE, 10 May 2000).
15  *Al-Ahram Weekly*, 25 November–1 December 1999.
16  Irene Lorfing, *Women, Media and Sustainable Development* (Beirut, 1997), p 30.

[17] *Ibid.*, pp 88–9.

[18] Organized by the Institute for Women's Studies in the Arab World and the World Association for Christian Communication.

[19] Quotation from May Elian's paper published in the *Daily Star*, Beirut, 13 November 1999.

[20] This is implicit in the title of the 1998–99 report of the Collectif 95 Maghreb Egalité, *Les Maghrébines entre violences symboliques et violences physiques*. The report takes a detailed look at Moroccan terrestrial television, but many of its comments have a more general application.

[21] The sequence of events is recounted in Nadje Al-Ali, *Secularism, Gender and the State in the Middle East: The Egyptian Women's Movement* (Cambridge, 2000), pp 178–81.

[22] Brian Winston, *Media Technology and Society: A History, from the Telegraph to the Internet* (London, 1998), p 2.

[23] *Ibid.*, pp 336–42.

[24] Author's interview with Nilesat chairman, Amin Bassiouny, Cairo, 15 August 1998.

[25] *Middle East Broadcast & Satellite* 6/3 (April 1999), p 29.

[26] Private communication from a Video Cairo source, 23 February 1999.

[27] The interviewer was Chris Forrester, reporting for *Middle East Broadcast & Satellite* 7/2 (2000), p 32.

[28] Author's interview with Adel Hamdi, Al-Mustakillah journalist, London, 18 July 2000.

[29] *Ibid.*

[30] *Middle East Economic Digest*, 12 June 1998, p 13.

[31] *Al-Ahram Hebdo*, 9–15 September 1998.

[32] See, for example, Chris Forrester's comments in *Middle East Broadcast & Satellite* 6/5 (July/August 1999), p 13.

[33] Speech to a conference on multinational investment and human rights, organized by the Royal Institute of International Affairs in London on 20 April 1998.

[34] UNDP, *Human Development Report 2000* (New York, 2000), p 3.

[35] According to the International Federation of Journalists. See Aidan White's letter to *The Guardian*, 27 October 2000.

[36] According to a report by the Committee to Protect Journalists on threats against Palestinian journalists in the Occupied Territories. The report, *Bloodied and Beleaguered*, by Joel Campagna, was released in New York on 20 October 2000.

[37] CPJ/Campagna: *Bloodied and Beleaguered*, p 14.

[38] The conference was organized by the Cairo Institute for Human Rights Studies with support from the Office of the UN High Commissioner for Human Rights and the Euro-Mediterranean Human Rights Network.

[39] See *www.imisite.org*.

[40] Author's transcript of conference proceedings, Cairo, 16 October 2000.

41   The authors in question include Appadurai (discussed in Chapter 2), Held and
     McGrew and Tomlinson (Chapter 3) and Willetts, Keane and others (Chapter 6).

# Bibliography

Abdel-Rahman, Maha, 'Civil society against itself: Egyptian NGOs in the neo-liberal era'. Paper presented to the conference of the European Association for Middle East Studies (Ghent, September 1999)

Abdulla, Rasha, 'The impact of Music Television (MTV) on music broadcasting in Egypt and the region'. Paper delivered to ARTICLE 19 conference on 'Satellite Broadcasting in the Middle East and North Africa' (Cairo, February 1999)

Abrams, Philip, 1988, 'Notes on the difficulty of studying the state (1977)', *Journal of Historical Sociology* 1/1 (March 1988), pp 58-89

Abu Lughod, Lila, 'Finding a place for Islam: Egyptian television serials and the national interest', *Public Culture* 11 (1993), pp 493-513

Aburish, Saïd K., *The Rise, Corruption and Coming Fall of the House of Saud* (London, 1995)

Achilleas, Philippe, 'Satellite broadcasting and international law'. Paper presented to ARTICLE 19 conference on 'Satellite Broadcasting in the Middle East and North Africa' (Cairo, February 1999)

Al-Abd, Atef Adli and Al-Ali, Fawzia Abdullah, *Dirassat fi'l Ilam al-Fada'i* [Studies in Space Media] (Cairo, 1995)

Al-Ali, Nadje, *Secularism, Gender and the State in the Middle East: The Egyptian Women's Movement* (Cambridge, 2000)

Al-Bizri, Dalal, 'Al-Mujtamaa al-Madani: Al-Jamiayyat al-Nisa'iyya al-Lubnaniya' [Civil Society: women's organizations in Lebanon] in Azrawil, Fatima and Al-Bizri, Dalal (eds), *Al-Mar'a al-Arabiyya: al-Waqia wa al-Tasawur* [Arab Women: Reality and Perception] (Cairo, 1995)

Al-Rashid, Madawi, 'State building in Saudi Arabia: the forgotten mutawwa'. Paper presented at the School of Oriental and African Studies, University of London (November 1999)

AlSaadon, Hezab, 'The Role of Arabsat in Television Program Exchange in the Arab World', PhD thesis (Ohio State University, 1990)

Alterman, Jon B., *New Media, New Politics? From Satellite Television to the Internet in the Arab World*, Washington Institute for Near East Policy: Policy Paper 49 (Washington: DC, 1999)

Amin, Hussein, 'The development of SpaceNet and its impact', in Weisenborn, R. (ed), *Media in the Midst of War: The Gulf War from Cairo to the Global Village* (Cairo, 1992), pp 15-20

Amin, Hussein and Boyd, Douglas, 'The development of direct broadcast television to and within the Middle East', *Journal of South Asian and Middle East Studies* XVIII/2 (Winter 1994), pp 37-50

Anderson, Benedict, *Imagined Communities*, 2nd edn (London, 1991)

Appadurai, Arjun, 'Disjuncture and difference in the global cultural economy', in Featherstone, M. (ed), *Global Culture: Nationalism, Globalization and Modernity* (London, 1990), pp 295-310

Arjomandi, Gholamreza, 'The impacts of direct broadcasting by satellite on the Iranian media sphere'. Paper presented to the ARTICLE 19 conference on 'Satellite Broadcasting in the Middle East and North Africa' (Cairo, February 1999)

ARTICLE 19, *The Egyptian Predicament: Islamists, the State and Censorship* (London, 1997)

—— *Surveillance and Repression: Freedom of Expression in Tunisia* (London, 1998)

—— *Walls of Silence: Media and Censorship in Syria* (London, 1998)

Ayish, Muhammad, 'Arab television goes commercial', *Gazette* 59 (December 1997), pp 473-93

Baker, Raymond, 'Combative cultural politics: film art and political spaces in Egypt', *Alif Journal of Comparative Poetics* 15 (1995), pp 19-32

Baskerville Communications Corporation, *Middle East Television* (Shrub Oak: NY, 1996)

Bellchambers, William, 'Kyoto is an opportunity to revitalise an old and honoured organisation', *Intermedia* 22/4 (August-September 1994), pp 32-5

Bobbio, Norberto, 'Gramsci and the concept of civil society', in Keane, J. (ed), *Civil Society and the State* (London, 1988), pp 73-99

Bogart, Leo et al, 'Media moguls and megalomania', *Index on Censorship* 23 (September/October 1994), pp 14-62

Boyd, Douglas A., 'Saudi Arabia's international media strategy: influence through multinational ownership'. Paper presented at the Annual Meeting of the Association for Education in Journalism and Mass Communication (Baltimore: Maryland, August 1998)

—— *Broadcasting in the Arab World: A Survey of the Electronic Media in the Middle East*, 3rd edn (Ames: Iowa, 1999)

Braman, Sandra, 'Trade and information policy', *Media, Culture & Society* 12/3 (1990), pp 361-85

Brown, Nathan, 'The Supreme Constitutional Court and the meaning of liberal legality in Egypt'. Paper presented at the 29th Annual Meeting of the Middle East Studies Association of North America (Washington: DC, December 1995)

Camilleri, Joseph and Falk, Jim, *The End of Sovereignty?* (Aldershot, 1992)

Campagna, Joel/Committee to Protect Journalists, *Bloodied and Beleaguered: A Multimedia Report on Threats against Palestinian Journalists in the Occupied Territories* (New York, 2000)

Codding Jr, George, *The Future of Satellite Communications* (Boulder: CO, 1990)

Cohen, Robin, *Global Diasporas: An Introduction* (London, 1997)

Collectif 95 Maghreb Egalité, *Les Maghrébines entre violences symboliques et violences physiques* (Rabat, 1999)

Cooper, Robert, *The Post-Modern State and the World Order* (London, 1996)

Cox, Robert and Jacobson, Harold, *The Anatomy of Influence* (New Haven: CT and London, 1973)

Dabous, Sonia, 1994, 'Nasser and the Egyptian press', in Tripp, C. (ed), *Contemporary Egypt: Through Egyptian Eyes* (London, 1993), pp 100–21

—— 'Egypt', in Kamalipour, Yahya R. and Mowlana, Hamid (eds), *Mass Media in the Middle East* (Westport: CT, 1994), pp 60–73

Dajani, Karen Finlon, 'Egypt's Role as a Major Media Producer, Supplier and Distributor to the Arab World: An Historical Descriptive Study', PhD thesis (University of Michigan, Ann Arbor, 1980)

Dajani, Nabil, *Disoriented Media in a Fragmented Society: The Lebanese Experience* (Beirut, 1992)

—— 'The confessional scene in Lebanese TV'. Paper presented at the Carsten Niebuhr Institute workshop on 'Islam on TV' (Copenhagen, December 1999)

Dhaheri, Amina, 'The image of women in Arab media'. Paper presented to a seminar on 'Media Realities and Horizons in the Arab World' at the Ajman University for Science and Technology (UAE, 10 May 2000)

Donelly, Jack, 'International human rights: a regime analysis', *International Organization* 40/3 (Summer 1996), pp 599–642

Doyle, Gillian, 'Towards a pan-European directive? From "concentration and pluralism" to "media ownership"', *Communications Law* 3/1 (1998), pp 11–15

Economist Intelligence Unit, *The EIU Guide to the New GATT* (London, 1994)

—— *Egypt Country Profile 1995–96* (London, 1995)

—— *The EIU Guide to World Trade under the WTO* (London, 1995)

—— *Egypt Country Profile 1998–99* (London, 1998)

—— *Bahrain/Qatar Country Profile 1999–2000* (London, 1999)

—— *Jordan Country Profile 1999–2000* (London, 1999)

Egyptian Radio and Television Union, *External Services of Radio Cairo* (Cairo, 1991)

—— *Yearbook 1996/97* (Cairo, 1997)

El-Emary, Naglaa, 'L'Industrie du feuilleton télévision égyptien à l'ère des télévisions transfrontières', *Revue Tiers Monde* 37/146 (April–June 1996), pp 251–62

El Hachem, Bassam, *Radio Orient* (Paris, 1998)

El Shal, Inshirah, 'Introduction à la télévision égyptienne: quelques repères chronologiques', *Revue Tiers Monde* 37/146 (April–June 1996), pp 249–50

European Commission, *Euro-Mediterranean Partnership: Information Notes* (Brussels, April 1999)

Eutelsat, *Cable and Satellite Penetration Results* (Paris, 1997, 1998 and 1999)

Faqir, Fadia, 'The price of honour: violence against women in Jordan'. Draft paper, March 2000

Ferguson, Marjorie, 'The mythology about globalization', *European Journal of Communication* 7 (1992), pp 69–93

Field, Michael, *The Merchants: The Big Business Families of Arabia* (London, 1984)

Foote, Joe, 'CNE in Egypt: some light at the end of an arduous tunnel', *tbsjournal.com* 1 (August 1998)

Forrester, Veronica, 'The German political foundations', in Stevens, C. and Verloren van Themaat, J. (eds), *Pressure Groups, Policies and Development: The Private Sector and EEC-Third World Policy* (London, 1985), pp 40–60

Foulquier, Jean-Michel, *Arabie Séoudite: La Dictature Protégée* (Paris, 1995)

Frederick, Howard, 'Communication, peace and international law', in Roach, C. (ed), *Communication and Culture in War and Peace* (London, 1993), pp 216–51

Gamble, Andrew, 'The new political economy', *Political Studies* XLIII (September 1995), pp 516–30

Garnham, Nicholas, *Capitalism and Communication* (London, 1990)

Giddens, Anthony, *The Constitution of Society: Outline of the Theory of Structuration* (Cambridge, 1984)

Giugale, Marcelo M. and Mobarak, Hamed (eds), *Private Sector Development in Egypt* (Cairo, 1996)

Golding, Peter, 'Media professionalism in the Third World: the transfer of an ideology', in Curran, J., Gurevitch, M. and Woollacott, J. (eds), *Mass Communication and Society* (London, 1977), pp 291–308

Gross, Leo, 'Some international law aspects of the freedom of information and the right to communicate', in Nordenstreng, K. and Schiller, H. (eds), *National Sovereignty and International Communication* (Norwood: NJ, 1979), pp 195–216

Hajj, Jean Dib, 'NGO networking in the Arab world'. Paper presented to the Third Mediterranean Development Forum (Cairo, March 2000)

Hamelink, Cees, *The Politics of World Communication* (London, 1994)

—— 'The People's Communication Charter', *tbsjournal.com* 2 (Spring 1999)

Hargreaves, Alec G. and Mahdjoub, Dalila, 'Satellite television viewing among ethnic minorities in France', *European Journal of Communication* 12/4 (1997), pp 459–77

Harvey, David, *The Condition of Postmodernity* (Oxford, 1990)

Hasanat, Abdullah, 'Impediments to freedom of expression in Jordan'. Paper presented to a conference on 'Culture and Communication in the Global Information Society' (Amman, November 1998)

Hassan, Bahey El Din, 'The dilemma of the Arab human rights movement'. Paper presented to the 33rd Annual Meeting of the Middle East Studies Association (Washington: DC, November 1999)

Held, David and McGrew, Anthony, 'Globalization and the liberal democratic state', *Government and Opposition* 28/2 (1993), pp 261–85

Herman, Edward S. and McChesney, Robert W., *The Global Media: The New Missionaries of Corporate Capitalism* (London, 1997)

Hicks, Neil, 'Escalating attacks on human rights protection in Egypt', in *Report of the Lawyers' Committee for Human Rights* (New York, September 1995), pp 8–9

Hills, Jill, *The Democracy Gap: The Policies of Information and Communication Technologies in the United States and Europe* (New York, 1991)

Hoare, Quintin and Nowell Smith, Geoffrey (eds and trans), *Selections from the Prison Notebooks of Antonio Gramsci* (London, 1971)

Holden, David and Johns, Richard, *The House of Saud* (London, 1982)

Hoodfar, Homa, 'Women at the intersection of citizenship and the Family Code', in Joseh, S. (ed), *Gender and Citizenship in the Middle East* (New York, 2000), pp 287-313

Human Rights Watch/Middle East, *Lebanon: Restrictions on Broadcasting* (New York, 1997)

Hurrell, Andrew, 'International society and the study of regimes: a reflective approach', in Rittberger, V. (ed), *Regime Theory and International Relations* (Oxford, 1993), pp 49-72

Hurrell, Andrew and Woods, Ngaire, 'Globalisation and inequality', *Millennium: Journal of International Studies* 24/3 (1995), pp 447-70

Innis, H.A., *Empire and Communications* (Oxford, 1950)

International Telecommunication Union, *World Telecommunication Development Report* (Geneva, 1999)

Jemstone Network, *A Practical Handbook on Independent and Investigative Journalism* (Amman, November 1999)

Jerichow, Anders, *The Saudi File: People, Power, Politics* (Richmond, 1998)

Jerusalem Film Institute/Internews, *Proceedings of Conference on Palestinian Broadcasting: Promises and Challenges* (Jerusalem, 1994)

Kakabadse, Mario, 'The WTO and the commodification of cultural products: implications for Asia', *Media Asia* 22/2 (1995), pp 71-7

Keane, John, *The Media and Democracy* (Oxford: Polity Press, 1991)

—— 'Structural transformations of the public sphere', *The Communication Review* 1/1 (1995), pp 1-22

—— 'Global civil society'. Draft paper, August 2000

Kennedy, Susannah, 'Navigating the satellite sky: watching Arabic-language television in Europe'. Paper presented at the ARTICLE 19 conference on 'Satellite Broadcasting in the Middle East and North Africa' (Cairo, February 1999)

Keohane, Robert O., *After Hegemony: Cooperation and Discord in the World Political Economy* (Princeton: NJ, 1984)

Keohane, Robert O. and Nye, Joseph S., *Power and Interdependence*, 2nd edn (Glenview: IL, 1989)

—— 'Power and interdependence in the information age', *Foreign Affairs*, September/October 1998, pp 81-94

Khachani, Mohamed, 'Migration from Arab Maghreb countries to Europe: present situation and prospects', *Forum: Newsletter of the Economic Research Forum in Cairo* 5/1 (1998), pp 23-4

Khouri, Nicole, 'La politique antiterroriste de l'état Egyptien à la télévision en 1994', *Revue Tiers Monde* 37/146 (April-June 1996), pp 263-83

Kienle, Eberhard, 'More than a response to Islamism: the political deliberalization of Egypt in the 1990s', *Middle East Journal* 52/2 (Spring 1998), pp 219-35

Kirby, Andrew, 'State, local state, context and spatiality: a reappraisal of state theory', in Caporaso, J.A. (ed), *The Elusive State: International and Comparative Perspectives* (London, 1989), pp 204-26

Kleinwächter, Wolfgang, 'A new trilateralism in global communication negotiations? How governments, industry and citizens try to create a new "Global Communications Charter"', *Javnost/The Public* 5/4 (1998), pp 74–80

Korany, Bahgat, 'The old/new Middle East', in Guazzone, L. (ed), *The Middle East in Global Change: The Politics and Economics of Interdependence versus Fragmentation* (London, 1997), pp 135–50

Krasner, Stephen D., 'Structural causes and regime consequences: regimes as intervening variables', *International Organization* 36/2 (Spring 1982), pp 185–205

—— *Structural Conflict: The Third World against Global Liberalism* (Berkeley and Los Angeles, 1985)

—— 'Global Communications and National Power', in *World Politics* 43/3 (April 1991), pp 336–66

—— 'Sovereignty, regimes and human rights', in Rittberger, V. (ed), *Regime Theory and International Relations* (Oxford, 1993), pp 139–67

Kuttab, Daoud, 'Palestinian diaries: grassroots TV production in the Occupied Territories', in Dowmunt, T. (ed), *Channels of Resistance: Global Television and Local Empowerment* (London, 1993), pp 138–45

Lorfing, Irene, *Women, Media and Sustainable Development* (Beirut, 1997)

Luther, Sara Fletcher, *The United States and the Direct Broadcast Satellite: The Politics of International Broadcasting in Space* (Oxford, 1988)

MacBride Commission, 'Many voices, one world', in Boyd-Barrett, O. and Braham, P. (eds), *Media, Knowledge and Power* (London, 1987), pp 5–31

McChesney, Robert W., 'Media convergence and globalisation', in Thussu, D. K., *Electronic Empires: Global Media and Local Resistance* (London, 1998)

Madani, Lotfi, 'Les télévisions étrangères par satellite en Algérie: formation des audiences et des usages', *Revue Tiers Monde* 37/146 (April–June 1996), pp 315–30

MED TV, *The International Impact of MED TV* (London, 1996)

Miller, Toby, 'National policy and the traded image', in Drummond, P., Paterson, R. and Willis, J. (eds), *National Identity and Europe: The Television Revolution* (London, 1993), pp 95–109

Moran, Albert, *Copycat TV: Globalisation, Program Formats and Cultural Identity* (Luton, 1998)

Morgan, Roger, 'A European "society of states" – but only states of mind?', *International Affairs* 76/3 (July 2000), pp 559–74

Mosco, Vincent, 'Free trade in communication: building a world business order', in Nordenstreng, K. and Schiller, H. (eds), *Beyond National Sovereignty: International Communication in the 1990s* (Norwood: NJ, 1993), pp 193–209

Mostefaoui, Belkacem, *La Télévision Française au Maghreb* (Paris, 1995)

Murdock, Graham, 'Redrawing the map of the communication industries: concentration and ownership in the era of privatization', in Ferguson, M. (ed), *Public Communication: The New Imperatives* (London, 1990)

Napoli, James J., Amin, Hussein Y. and Boylan, Richard F., *Assessment of the Egyptian Print and Electronic Media*. Report submitted to the United States Agency for International Development, 1995

Napoli, James J., Amin, Hussein Y. and Napoli, Luanne R., 'Privatization of the Egyptian media', *Journal of South Asian and Middle Eastern Studies* XVIII/4 (Summer 1995), pp 39-57

Nelson, Michael, *War of the Black Heavens: The Battles of Western Broadcasting in the Cold War* (Syracuse, 1997)

O'Siochru, Sean, 'Voices 21: a global movement for people's media and communications in the 21st century', *tbsjournal.com* 2 (1999)

OTA (US Congress Office of Technology Assessment), *The 1992 World Administrative Radio Conference: Issues for US International Spectrum Policy – Background Paper* (Washington: DC, 1991)

—— *The 1992 World Administrative Radio Conference: Technology and Policy Implications* (Washington: DC, 1993)

Peixoto, Otavio, 'Grassroots associations, non-governmental organizations, and the growth of civil society in Egypt', *Forum: Newsletter of the Economic Research Forum for the Arab States, Turkey and Iran* 3/1 (1996), pp 14-15

Raboy, Marc, 'Challenges for the global regulation of communication', *Javnost/The Public* 5/4 (1998), pp 64-71

Robertson, Roland, *Globalization: Social Theory and Global Culture* (London, 1992)

Robinson, Piers, 'World politics and media power: problems of research design', *Media, Culture & Society* 22 (2000), pp 227-32

Rosenau, James N., 'The state in an era of cascading politics', in Caporaso, J.A. (ed), *The Elusive State: International and Comparative Perspectives* (London, 1989), pp 17-48

Saad, Reem, 'Shame, reputation and Egypt's lovers: a controversy over the nation's image', *Visual Anthropology*.10 (1997), pp 410-12

Sakr, Naomi, 'Media Concerns in an Emerging State: A Case Study of Developing Palestinian Media Structures in the West Bank and Gaza Strip, 1993-94', MA thesis (Institute of Education, University of London, 1994)

—— 'Frontiers of freedom: diverse responses to satellite television in the Middle East and North Africa', *Javnost/The Public* 6/1 (1999), pp 93-106

—— 'The Making and Implementation of Egyptian Policy towards Satellite Television Broadcasting', PhD thesis (University of Westminster, 1999)

—— 'Satellite television and development in the Middle East', *Middle East Report* 210 (Spring 1999), pp 6-8

—— 'Contested blueprints for Egypt's satellite channels', *Gazette* 63/2-3 (May 2001), pp 149-67

Sakr, Naomi and CMF-MENA, *Women's Rights and the Arab Media* (London, 2000)

Savage, James, *The Politics of International Telecommunications Regulation* (Boulder: CO, 1989)

Schleifer, Abdullah, 'Video Cairo Sat: breaking new ground as usual, but this time on Nilesat', *tbsjournal.com* 3 (Fall 1999)

Scholte, Jan Aart, 'Global capitalism and the state', *International Affairs* 73/3 (1997), pp 427-52

—— 'Review of "The New Realism: Perspectives on Multilateralism and World Order" edited by Robert Cox', *International Affairs* 73/4 (1997), p 771

Sewell, James P., 'UNESCO: pluralism rampant', in Cox, R. and Jacobson, H. (eds), *The Anatomy of Influence* (New Haven: CT and London, 1973), pp 139-74

Sinclair, John, Jacka, Elizabeth and Cunningham, Stuart (eds), *New Patterns in Global Television: Peripheral Vision* (Oxford, 1996)

Sklair, Leslie, *Sociology of the Global System*, 2nd edn (London, 1995)

Sogge, David, 'Northern lights', in Sogge, D. (ed), *Compassion and Calculation: The Business of Private Foreign Aid* (London, 1996), pp 144-78

Sparks, Colin, 'Is there a global public sphere?', in Thussu, D.K. (ed), *Electronic Empires: Global Media and Local Resistance* (London, 1998)

Stanley, Bruce, 'Review of "Civil Society in the Middle East" edited by Augustus Richard Norton, Vol 1', *Middle East Policy* III/4 (April 1995), pp 128-31

—— 'NGO-PNA relations in Palestine'. Paper presented to the annual conference of the British Society for Middle Eastern Studies (Oxford, July 1997)

State Information Service, *Arab Republic of Egypt Yearbook 1994* (Cairo, 1995)

—— *Egypt Yearbook 1995* (Cairo, 1996)

Strange, Susan, 'Cave! Hic dragones: a critique of regime analysis', *International Organization* 36/2 (Spring 1982), pp 479-96

—— *The Retreat of the State: The Diffusion of Power in the World Economy* (Cambridge, 1996)

Sung, Liching, 'WARC-92: setting the agenda for the future', *Telecommunications Policy* 16/8 (1992), pp 624-34

Taishoff, Marika Natasha, *State Responsibility and the Direct Broadcast Satellite* (London, 1987)

Taylor, Philip M., *War and the Media: Propaganda and Persuasion in the Gulf War* (Manchester, 1992)

Thomas, Gareth, Houpis, George, Kupisz, Richard and Cantor, David, 'Allocation of geostationary orbit and frequency resources for Europe', *Telecommunications Policy* 18/9 (1994), pp 715-24

Thomson, John B., 'The Theory of Structuration', in Held, D. and Thompson, J.B. (eds), *Social Theory of Modern Societies: Anthony Giddens and His Critics* (Cambridge, 1989), pp 56-76

Tomlinson, John, *Cultural Imperialism* (London, 1991)

—— 'Internationalism, globalization and cultural imperialism', in Thompson, K. (ed), *Media and Cultural Regulation* (London, 1997), pp 118-63

Tunstall, Jeremy and Palmer, Michael, *Media Moguls* (London, 1991)

Turner, Ted, 'CNN: news, war and government control', in Weisenborn, R. (ed), *Media in the Midst of War* (Cairo, 1992), pp 83-6

UNDP, *Human Development Report 1999* (New York, 1999)

—— *Human Development Report 2000* (New York, 2000)

UNESCO, *Basic Texts in Communication 89-95* (Paris, 1996)

—— *Final Report of the Seminar on Promoting Independent and Pluralistic Arab Media* (Paris, 1996)

Vogler, John, *The Global Commons: A Regime Analysis* (Chichester, 1995)

Volkmer, Ingrid, *News in the Global Sphere* (Luton, 1999)

Wallerstein, Immanuel, *The Capitalist World Economy* (Cambridge, 1979)

Weisenborn Ray E., 'Cool media, the war, and then - CNN', in Weisenborn, R. (ed), *Media in the Midst of War* (Cairo, 1992), pp 3-13

Willetts, Peter, 'Political globalization and the impact of NGOs upon transnational companies', in Mitchell, J. (ed), *Companies in a World of Conflict: NGOs, Sanctions and Corporate Responsibility* (London, 1998), pp 195-226

Winseck, Dwayne, 'Gulf war in the global village: CNN, democracy and the information age', in Wasko, J. and Mosco, V. (eds), *Democratic Communications in the Information Age* (Toronto, 1992), pp 60-74

Winston, Brian, *Media Technology and Society: A History from the Telegraph to the Internet* (New York, 1998)

Yamani, Mai, *Changed Identities: The Challenge of the New Generation in Saudi Arabia* (London, 2000)

—— 'Awakening', *The World Today* 56/12 (December 2000), pp 21-2

Zacker, Mark and Sutton, Brent, *Governing Global Networks* (Cambridge, 1996)

Zaki, Moheb, *Civil Society and Democratization in Egypt, 1981-1994* (Cairo, 1995)

Zenith Media, *Middle East and Africa Market and MediaFact* (London, 1996)

Zimmerman, Ann, 'Kurdish broadcasting in Iraq', *Middle East Report* No 189, 24/4 (July-August 1994), pp 20-1

# Index